Understanding Reading Development

For Mary

Understanding Reading Development

Colin Harrison

SAGE Publications

London ● Thousand Oaks ● New Delhi

SAGE Publications Ltd
6 Bonhill Street
London EC2A 4PU

SAGE Publications Inc
2455 Teller Road
Thousand Oaks, California 91320

SAGE Publications India Pvt Ltd
B-42 Panchsheel Enclave
Post Box 4109
New Delhi 110 017

Library of Congress Control Number available

A catalogue record for this book is available from the
British Library

ISBN 0-7619-4250-5
ISBN 0-7619-4251-3 (pbk)

Typeset by Pantek Arts Ltd, Maidstone, Kent
Printed in Great Britain by Athenaeum Press, Gateshead

Contents

Acknowledgments

The co-authors named in Chapters 3, 5 and 6 each contributed significantly to a key section of the chapter that bears their name. John Perry undertook the latent semantic analysis study reported in Chapter 3, although I reworked the data and reran the LSA analyses before writing that part of the text. Geraldine Kotsis was kind enough to send me a folder of material containing information on 17 DARTs activities that she taught in an inner-city primary school in Glasgow, and upon which I draw in Chapter 5. Alan Dewar and Steve Willshaw were both courageous enough to permit me to team teach with them in secondary English lessons in their schools, and Chapter 6 includes extracts from recordings made during or, in one case, following those lessons. I am and shall remain deeply grateful to these exceptional teachers and to their students for the insights they shared and the opportunities they offered me to reflect on reading development processes in action.

Note: Every effort has been made to contact the publishers of Figure 1.1 for permission to use the photograph. We apologise for any inconvenience or offence caused by the use of this image.

The author

Colin Harrison is Professor of Literacy in Educaton at the University of Nottingham.

After teaching English at secondary level he worked on the Schools Council project 'The Effective Use of Reading', during which time he chaired the Schools Council's Evaluator's Group. His books include *Readability in the Classroom, Interactive Learning and New Technologies* and *The Reading for Real Handbook*. He was a founding editor of the *Journal of Research in Reading* and is past president of the United Kingdom Reading Association, representing UKRA and other European reading associations on the International Reading Association's Family Literacy Commission. He has directed thirty funded research projects, including nine in the field of new technology.

Chapter 1

Reading reading

'What?', 'how?' and 'why?'

This book is for teachers, and its central focus is on the question of how we understand, and how we bring about, reading development. This first chapter also includes a discussion of the nature of reading and of why we read. I would want to argue that such a discussion is a necessary prelude to the later chapters in the book, but also that for understandable reasons, within the teaching profession, such a discussion is overdue. The reasons for this are not due to professional negligence, but rather, I would suggest, to the increasingly pervasive influence of governments of English-speaking countries in determining the curriculum and research agendas for literacy, and while this has been done with the best of intentions, it has had the effect of marginalising discussion of some of these wider issues.

In England, for example, throughout the 1980s and for most of the 1990s under successive Conservative governments, important discussions about what should determine the content of the literacy curriculum – about what should be taught and why – took place, often behind closed doors, in committees whose membership excluded nominees from the professional subject associations such as the National Association for the Teaching of English and the United Kingdom Reading Association.

In the late 1990s and early part of the new millennium, under successive 'New Labour' governments, a new spirit of openness, collegiality and cooperation has come into education in the UK, particularly in England. Ministers, and the advisers close to them, declared themselves to be keen to work in partnership with teachers, headteachers, teacher unions and researchers to advance policy and to enhance good practice, and the appointment of senior academics to positions of responsibility within the (then) Department of Education and Employment and the pronouncements of government advisers on the importance of 'evidence-driven policy' seemed to augur well for the future. But, while it was certainly the case that the government wanted evidence-driven policy and that this was broadly speaking good news for academics who wanted research funding, it also became clear that government was not only setting the research

1

agenda, it had very clear expectations about the role of research. As Geoff Mulgan, the then Head of the Performance and Innovation Unit in the Cabinet Office, put it:

> *Scientific knowledge in all its forms is now much more explicitly part of the governing process and there's a very important reason for that. We have seen a reducing role for ideology; the conviction politics of both the 70's and the 80's has gone into decline and ... knowledge about what works has, to some extent, filled that space ...*
>
> (Mulgan, 2001)

Understandably, a government that values research is likely to have a clear agenda in relation to the key questions that it feels need to be answered and clear notions about the findings that are anticipated. 'What works?' is the generic form of the question currently being put by government to academics on both sides of the Atlantic, and this form of question can lead to distortion and polarisation. As the recent furore about the place of phonics in the US makes plain, when it comes to the teaching of reading, when governments turn to science, science turns to rhetoric.

The point I wish to make here is that under neither Conservatives during the 1980s and 1990s, nor under 'New Labour' in more recent years, has there been an atmosphere such as that which prevailed during the time of the Bullock Report (1975), when government (through the inspectorate of schools), academics and teachers came together to thrash out both the principles that should underpin the curriculum for literacy and literature, and to set out not only an agenda for change in teaching but also a set of principles that might act as theoretical and moral scaffolding for those changes. Under the Conservatives, the 'what' of the curriculum was appropriated by government in the name of freedom from academic cosiness. Under New Labour, the 'how' of the curriculum, which, to be fair, was held under the Conservatives to be sacrosanct, was appropriated by government in the name of standards, and under both governments the 'why' of reading has been seen as either an implicitly irrelevant or implicitly utilitarian question. In this book, I want not only to discuss the 'what' and the 'how' of reading development, but also the 'why?'

In this extended chapter I therefore have three goals, each of which relates to my superordinate goal of not only contributing to our understanding of evidence-based practice, but also of paying some attention to the assumptions and to the theoretical and moral scaffolding that underpin that evidence. First, I want to consider the issue of exactly why it is so important to develop reading. My reasoning here is that we pay little enough attention to such issues even within a literary perspective on why we read, and even less within a psychological or developmental perspective. Second, I want to make some attempt to achieve a synthesis of historical, psychological and literary perspectives on reading development: experts from each of these fields have contributed enormously to our understanding of reading, but it is difficult to find the time to attend to more than one of these perspectives, and even more difficult to identify the correspondences and congruence that might extend and deepen that understanding. Third, I want to suggest some ways in which research in reading, in its many forms, can inform and extend good practice: through identifying findings that already underpin our current practice, through identifying findings that suggest where we might change our current practice, and finally through identifying were we need more evidence than is currently available.

Why is reading so important?

Why is reading so important, and why should teachers devote so much time to supporting children in becoming confident and fluent readers? My starting point in answering this question is not taken from government statements identifying national goals or national strategies in reading; it is a quotation from a letter written by Gustave Flaubert in 1857:

> *Do not read, as children do, to amuse yourself, or like the ambitious, for the purpose of instruction. No, read in order to live.*
>
> (Flaubert, 1857)

I shall revisit this quotation, but at the very beginning of this book I want to emphasise the importance of reading in relation to human development. Teachers can be forgiven for forgetting sometimes the joy and delight that most young children experience as they discover what words can do. Much of this book will be about reading for information, but I want to make no distinction between reading stories and reading for information in relation to the question of what we gain from reading. I want us to remind ourselves that reading not only increases our life skills and extends our knowledge, it goes much deeper – I want to argue that in many respects reading determines how we are able to think, that it has a fundamental effect on the development of the imagination, and thus exerts a powerful influence on the development of emotional and moral as well as verbal intelligence and therefore on the kind of person we are capable of becoming.

Narrative

Many teachers of my generation were influenced by Barbara Hardy's essay on 'Narrative as a primary act of mind', taken from the book *The Cool Web*

(Hardy, 1977), in which she argued that 'inner and outer storytelling' plays a major role in our sleeping and waking lives. She wrote:

> *... For we dream in narrative, daydream in narrative, remember, anticipate, hope, despair, believe, doubt, plan, revise, criticise, construct, gossip, learn, hate, and love by narrative. In order really to live, we make up stories about ourselves and others, about the personal as well as the social past and future.*
>
> (Hardy, 1977, p. 13)

The importance of narrative, she agues, is not simply about enjoyment of stories, or even about understanding ourselves. Narrative is a fundamental tool in the construction of intersubjectivity – the ability to recognise mental states in ourselves, and through imagination and projection to recognise the potential reciprocity of mental states in others – their beliefs, intentions, desires and the like – and it is this (and not simply the existence of language) that makes us distinctive as human beings. Jerome Bruner put this point very powerfully:

> *I want to propose that this deep, primitive form of human cognition [i.e. intersubjectivity] is captured linguistically in the form of narrative.*
>
> (Bruner, 2000, p. 33)

Bruner was arguing here that intersubjectivity, our very ability to relate to other people in characteristically human ways, is fundamentally related to our use of the linguistic form of narrative. This is a profoundly important point, so let's take a moment to reflect on what it looks like in practice.

Many parents take delight in recognising moments of developing intersubjectivity in their children, and fondly wish they had recorded more of them when their children have grown up. One parent who took the trouble to record many such moments was Shelby Anne Wolf, who in collaboration with Shirley Brice Heath wrote a book chronicling the ways in which her two daughters' development as people, not simply in terms of their reading ability or vocabulary, was fundamentally changed and enriched by their interaction with books. As a four-year-old, Shelby's daughter Ashley was with her mother, dropping off the older sister at gym class, when they emerged from the building to be greeted by a brilliantly blue evening sky. The mother exclaimed, 'Look at that sky. It's beautiful.' The following exchange then took place:

> *Ashley gazed up into the darkening sky. 'Yes, it's a blue and nightingale sky.' I grasped her hand and praised her metaphor, 'What a beautiful thing to say!' We continued walking in silence, watching the sky. But when we reached the car, Ashley turned to me and asked, 'What's a nightingale?'*

Shelby Wolf goes on to say that Ashley had read some months before *The Nightingale* by Hans Christian Andersen, which they had borrowed from a library. Ashley had forgotten the definition of 'nightingale', but she remembered the sense of beauty associated with that word.

We aren't born knowing that there is beauty in the world. We learn (or don't learn) about beauty from those around us, and from the cultural discourses within which we live. But the spontaneous, only partly understood, but nevertheless very powerful metaphor that Ashley uses tells us more – that she has already internalised an awareness that a fragment of an association from a story can, in a single word, evoke a complex world of associations, and that these can be shared, and can evoke a different but related set of associations in the mind of another. It is this implicit awareness of other possible worlds, both those held and instantiated in the narrative and those that can be shared with another person, that make up intersubjectivity.

I share her mother's belief that Ashley's capacity for recognising beauty in a brilliantly blue evening sky was intimately related to the exploration of possible worlds through narrative with which she had been engaging almost from birth. We might also remind ourselves that what was so unusual about this moment is not so much that it happened, but rather that it was recorded, and that the mother was able to identify the connection with a story read many months before.

Bruner argued, convincingly in my view, that narrative is fundamental to human development. Reading, therefore, is about much more than gaining a skill: it is about learning to be. And it is precisely because this is such a difficult and sensitive subject to talk about that we avoid talking about it, and this leaves an enormous vacuum. Because reading is so important, that vacuum becomes filled by other discourses, and often these have an emphasis on skills, on employment, on the economy and on reading for practical purposes. In the pages that follow, we shall discuss many of these practical purposes, but I would nevertheless wish to emphasise that it is neither maudlin nor romantic to emphasise from the outset that when we are looking at reading development, although we rarely acknowledge it, we are talking about giving people tools to be human.

Moral purpose

One author who is not afraid to remind us of the strong sense of moral purpose in reading is Philip Pullman, who in an interview about the trilogy *His*

Dark Materials, said, 'I'm trying to write a book about what it means to be human, to grow up, to suffer and learn.' Later in this chapter, I shall argue that we have moral duty to read. After all, if learning to read opens significant additional possibilities in terms of understanding how we might live, then we can argue that we have a moral duty to read, and, therefore as teachers, a moral duty to teach reading.

There will not be a major emphasis on beginning reading in this book, but I want to argue that it is enormously valuable for all teachers to have some understanding of how children learn to read, and of the remarkable potential of early literacy experiences to influence children's development. In a nursery that I visit regularly I heard the following story from the mother of Henry, then a cheerful little boy of 22 months. His language was developing well, which is to say that he was beginning to talk confidently, even though he was sometimes frustrated because he did not yet have the words to explain everything he wanted to say. But the remarkable incident which followed his being bitten by another child showed that Henry could use a book to communicate his feelings, even before he had learned the words to utter them.

One afternoon, when Henry's mum arrived to pick him up from nursery, Henry's key worker took her aside and asked her to sign her section of an accident form. 'Everything's alright,' said the key worker, 'but I have to tell you that I'm afraid Henry was bitten this afternoon by another child. I have had a conversation with the other child and explained how serious it is to bite someone, and have asked him not to do it again.' Naturally, this being a modern nursery, there was no mention of the name of the biter. When Henry's mum went to pick up Henry, there was no sign of anguish, anger or upset, but Henry proudly rolled up his sleeve and revealed a fine set of teeth marks on his forearm. He then became increasingly agitated and clenched his little fists with frustration as he realised he could not tell his mum what had happened. Suddenly, he rushed over to the book corner and fetched a book, ran back to his mum and opened it. The book had a number of pictures of reptiles, and Henry turned the pages determinedly until he found the picture he wanted. It was a photograph of a very large crocodile with its jaws wide open revealing a full set of sharp teeth. Henry pointed to the photograph, then he pointed to the bite on his arm. Then he pointed to his best friend, another little boy, who was sitting across the room, working with great concentration on a drawing. 'Snap! Snap!' said Henry as he pointed to his pal. His mum understood.

What is intriguing about this anecdote are the connections between the infant's intentionality, his communication strategies and his emergent literacy. Henry understood, even before his speech was anything like fully developed, that books, as well as people, can communicate, and he used this understanding to make an announcement that was richer and far more dramatic than would have been possible without access to the book. What exactly was happening here? First, Henry was initiating a literacy event: a child who was not yet two was demonstrating an awareness that a book could be used as a bridge – a third possible world that might be used to link his own mental world to the mental world of his mum. Second, he already understood the potential of metaphor – that one event or object which had a partial set of correspondences with another event or object could be used to stand proxy for that event or object, and could evoke a set of associations in the mind of another. Third, he implicitly understood how powerful a metaphor could be: his little pal, the biter, had not sprung from a jungle river and torn off his arm, but Henry used the evocative image of the crocodile to striking effect and to call up in his mother's mind associations with the atavistic fear of being attacked by a giant reptile. And these things did not just happen: they occurred because Henry inhabited a world surrounded by books – in the kitchen of his home, in his bedroom, at his grandparents' house and in the nursery that he had attended daily since he had been six months old. They happened because since before he had been just a few months old, adults had been sharing books with him, and initiating him into the awareness of possible worlds that are accessed through books, and into the visual and linguistic representations that made up those worlds.

I want to suggest that it is interesting that this example of developing intersubjectivity used an information book: I want to argue that narrative and story are important in distinctive ways in human development, but I also want to assert that information books are important, too. Historians tell us that the first written texts were not stories or poetry but information texts – facts about ownership, law, the permanent recording of important details and events. Stories offer us models of how to live, but information books – even word books, such as the wonderful books of Richard Scarry – give us the power to store, to name, to retrieve, to share, to explore, to wonder at and to bring order to our representations of the world. For information is always about order, and information books are inevitably attempts (often relatively unsuccessful attempts) to represent one set of relationships, located in the real world of objects and events, by another set of relationships, expressed by sets of propositions and images, located and ordered within the framework of a more or less explicitly signalled text structure.

Texts are forever. Their whole *raison d'être* is about permanence, about representing what cannot be truly captured, about the construction of a representation, which, although flawed, has the virtue of immortality. All texts are produced in order to communicate, and with all texts there exists a hermeneutic gap between text and reader, and an inevitably greater gap between writer and reader. And as electronic texts proliferate, and the shared or common elements of different cultures are spread ever more thinly across the planet, these hermeneutic differences between writer and reader may become greater rather than smaller. All the more reason, therefore, for us to explore as fully as we are able the nature of the relationship between author and text, and between text and reader, and the ways in which as teachers or mentors we can guide children towards a more complete and more profound experience understanding of texts and how they might be used.

The need for historical, psychological and literary perspectives on reading

Let us begin by considering an image of reading. Please try to create the following image in your head. The scene is a library. Three people, each of whom seems to be unaware of the existence of the others, are standing, looking at books. One person is holding a book and reading, one person is frozen in the act of taking a book from a shelf, and the third is standing, hands in pockets, looking at the books above him on a shelf (see Figure 1.1).

But when you look at this picture, what I have described so far does not touch upon what is most striking about it, for the scene is one of desolation. This picture was taken in London in 1940, after an air raid, by an unidentified photographer, and what is most astonishing about the picture is the image it presents of readers caught in a state of obliviousness to their surroundings, looking at books as if they were in an antiquarian bookshop or a public library rather than on a bombsite, and lost to the world while they are doing so; we might describe them as *in flagrante lectio*. Of course this photograph is a very gendered image, and only one of hundreds of possible images I might have selected to present the act of reading, but I feel that it is a helpful one to use to represent some aspects of what I want to say about reading and reading processes in this chapter, not least because it poses in a powerful and evocative manner the central questions 'Why do we read, and why is reading so important?'

As teachers, we perhaps take the importance of reading for granted, but in the main part of this chapter, I want to share a personal attempt to problematise and address the assumptions that we make about reading. I want to argue that it is valuable to consider reading from three perspectives – historical, psychological and literary – and that to do so can provide insights that are revealing in the contrasts they yield, but also in some of the parallels and correspondences they display. In reflecting upon and linking together the three perspectives, I also want to suggest some ways in which they lead us towards insights related to the teaching of reading.

I want to describe how these three perspectives lead to the following propositions concerning reading:

1 Writing began because of the need to read for information.
2 We have a moral duty to read.
3 All books are hypertexts.

Figure 1.1 Bombed library: London 1940

4 We need to rethink reading comprehension and reading assessment.

5 All import restrictions aimed at reducing the risk of 'Bovarysme' should be permanently lifted.

Proposition 1: Writing began because of the need to read for information

A study of the history of reading is very rewarding for teachers who are interested in what we call reading for information, an area which is sometimes perceived in schools (and perhaps universities too) as unfashionable, utilitarian and a rather poor relation of the reading of literature. This is because it turns out that reading for information is the oldest form of reading.

The beginning of the history of reading is coterminous with the beginning of writing, which was approximately six thousand years ago, the point at which Sumerian scribes first made written signs on tablets of clay. Some scholars have gone so far as to argue that history itself, at least as a discipline, began at this time, since a society without writing is unable to move beyond a linear sense of time and space, and cannot move beyond myth in its descriptions of itself.

The first uses of reading and writing were essentially legal and commercial. There is evidence that narrative and poetry were flourishing at the time writing began, but since these could be shared and preserved through an oral tradition, there was less of an imperative to record them in written form. There was, however, a need in the worlds of business and law for a permanent record of what was otherwise ephemeral information, in order to assert a law, record a transaction or provide evidence of a debt.

Among the earliest examples of a written text are the Syrian clay tablets shown in Figure 1.2. The tablet on the left has two indentations, and archaeologists tell us that one indentation represents a goat, and the other the number ten. The illustration is taken from Alberto Manguel's fascinating book *A History of Reading* (Manguel, 1996).

In a rare moment of unanimity, scholars have agreed that this text might have meant 'ten goats'. We could have fun with this two-word text today, celebrating its Hemingwayan terseness and immediacy, discussing its animalistic Jungian theme, noting the author's playful invitation to the reader to penetrate the text in order to supply a verb, and so on, but such games should not deflect us from recognising the essential point that the whole reason for the existence of this written text was that its meaning should be fixed and unequivocal, even after the death of its author.

But of course ambiguity is inescapable: the fundamental purposes of writing – to eliminate ambiguity, to overcome the limitations of memory and to fix meaning – in clay, stone, ink, iron oxide or the polymer dye layer of a CD – are ultimately doomed. The first Sumerian and Syrian authors are dead, and we are unable to be sure whether this tablet's meaning was:

Figure 1.2 Syrian clay tablets
(*Source*: Manguel, 1996.)

Here are ten goats.
Here were ten goats.
I owe you ten goats.
You have paid me ten goats.
Pay the bearer on demand the sum of ten goats.

And the possibilities of ambiguity are inexhaustible. Archaeologists are not even completely certain whether the animals on the Syrian tablet were really sheep or goats (a problem of classification which has proved to be a recurring one in the academic world). Of course, to argue that ambiguity is inevitable is not to assert that meaning is a matter of personal whim; if it were, reading and writing could not have developed as they have. The point I would emphasise, however, is that uniformity of agreement about a text's meaning is by no means inevitable, and it is certainly no more inevitable in what we might loosely call 'information texts' than it is in stories or poetry.

The first uses of writing, then, were instrumental, and this means that what our American colleagues call 'content area reading', or reading for information of the kind which is important at school, far from being a minor tributary of reading, represents a main source for the whole river.

But if the first uses of writing were instrumental, there were some importantly different ways in which that instrumentality operated. Writing may have begun simply as an extension of memory, but what began as an extension of an individual's memory soon became a tool for administration and regulation at a societal level, and what started as a personal tool for representing the world became a political tool for regulating the world. One corollary of this is that reading has to be recognised as constituting a social or even a socio-political activity, in which the reader's role is not limited to comprehension but extends to social action. Gaining access to the texts which regulate a society, understanding and using them, and also, when necessary, calling into question their clarity, adequacy and appropriateness, is to engage in political action, and teachers, who develop the skills of literacy, are feared in oppressive and coercive societies, just as they are praised and valued in humane and benevolent societies. The teacher of reading does not have to boycott government tests in order to become a political agent; an act of political agency has already occurred as soon as the teacher shares a book with a student.

I want to touch on two further aspects of the history of reading, and their place in our understanding of what it is to read; these are the alphabet and silent reading. So far as we know, the alphabet developed only once, and all alphabetic languages on earth have evolved from the late cuneiform script of Mesopotamia, which changed from pictographic to phonetic during the period up to 2000 BC. The significance of our language's being alphabetic has been written about extensively, but suffice it to say here that the significance is enormous, since it gives the power of creating a new word to everyone who can write, and the power of being able to read a newly created word to everyone who can read.

This emancipatory power of the alphabet was also important in relation to such technologies as glossaries, indexes, dictionaries and subject lists in books such as encyclopaedias. To be able to make use of tools such as an index or a glossary is not normally taken to be of earthshaking significance, but Ivan Illich (1988) argued that the development of these tools in the Middle Ages was as important as the development of the alphabet two thousand years earlier, since they provided a means of accessing knowledge for non-specialists, something which was hitherto unavailable and which has since become indispensable in an open society. In the next part of the chapter, therefore, I want to look more closely at reading in the Middle Ages.

Proposition 2: We have a moral duty to read

The development of alphabetic writing was of enormous importance, but interestingly, Illich (1993) has recently suggested that the flowering of what we are pleased to call western civilisation came about, not because of the alphabetic nature of post-Sumerian languages, nor from the invention of moveable type, but rather from the growth of silent reading. Illich's arguments tend to resemble Gothic cathedrals, soaring into the stratosphere, buttressed by delicate traceries of logic which lead us upward, wondering how we ever got so far from where we began, unwilling to share the author's confidence that we are safe in our precipitous location, but unable find any other route back to terra firma. *In the Vineyard of the Text* is a wonderful book though. It is a commentary on what Illich argues is the first book on the art of reading, St Hugh's *Didascalion*, which was written about 1128.

Illich suggests that St Hugh brought about a revolution in reading, since the *Didascalion* distinguishes for the first time two main types of reading: oral reading which was a liturgical act related to prayer and spiritual development, and silent reading which was a search for knowledge. Illich calls the first monastic reading and the second scholastic reading, and he charts the beginnings of western thought from the beginnings of scholastic reading. In terms of chronology, this argument seems be a strong one: within a hundred years of the appearance of the *Didascalion*, the alphabetised tools of scholarship (such as the glossary and index) came to be widely used, scholarship in Europe began to become secularised and to be accessible in languages other than Latin, and the universities of Bologna, Paris, Oxford and Cambridge had been established.

There are other respects in which St Hugh's book not only has relevance for us as teachers of reading, but also seems remarkably modern. Hugh proposed one of the first accounts of the reading process; he offered an interesting model of comprehension and memory; finally, he offered an account of motivation and intentionality, discussing why we should read. In the course of the book he proposed what we would today regard as the very modern argument that the art of reading can only be understood if it is linked to an understanding of memory.

Hugh's model of the reading process explained how understanding came from reading, and had a sort of reverse optics: the central purpose of monastic reading was the search for wisdom, or more specifically for light. But light was not external to the reader: the act of reading brought light back into the world from which sin had banned it. The reader made a metaphorical pilgrimage through the text, bringing to the text and to the world the light of understanding. I'm happy to leave to our colleagues in the Department of Psychology the challenge of getting a doctoral student to establish conditions of falsifiability for this model of the reading process.

In Hugh's account, study skills and memory work were very much a part of the spiritual discipline of reading: a central aim of reading was to construct a treasure chest (*arca*) in the reader's heart in which knowledge was to be stored, and a number of accounts have survived describing how monks were instructed to train their memories to store and retrieve facts by visualising whole galleries or cathedrals in which knowledge was stored in a three-dimensional array, with one fact or sentence stored at each location. Augustine wrote that his friend Simplicius had memorised the whole of Virgil using this technique and could recite any part of it – forwards or backwards. (One might add that history does not report that Simplicius had more than the one friend.) At this point, however, and before we unjustly suggest that St Hugh's methods may account for the origins of dyslexia, we should remind ourselves that these topological approaches to memorisation were necessary because other techniques had not been invented, and that although the Latin language was phonetic, it took hundreds of years for its alphabetisation to be made use of for study purposes.

Nevertheless, the point remains that the first book on the art of reading focused both on reading aloud for liturgical purposes and on silent reading for study. It is also important to note that it did so in a way that was not divorced from the affective and spiritual part of the reader's response. For Hugh, both monastic and scholastic reading represented a moral rather than a technical activity, and he stated clearly that monks had a moral duty to read, and he argued that everyone, be they powerful or weak, more or less able, became blameworthy if they refused to advance in learning. Hugh also emphasised that the monk had a duty beyond the cloister walls: the old Benedictine tradition had emphasised personal humility and virtue; Hugh's call was for the reader to be a teacher, one who teaches through their life, through their wisdom and by example. And through the methods of reading and study that he proposed, monks were for the first time encouraged to engage in scholarship which took their study skills and their wisdom into the community. St Hugh did not go so far as to propose universal education, but it was his outward-facing approach to the dissemination of knowledge and wisdom that enabled the idea to gain currency in the century which followed.

Proposition 3: All books are hypertexts

How does the reading process operate? I would want to argue that there is currently much less disagreement on this point among scholars than is commonly thought. This is because it is widely accepted that, since the early 1980s, better eye-movement monitoring equipment and faster computers have enabled us to answer many of the pressing questions about what the eye tells the brain. So I share the view of those who suggest that there is now broad unanimity in descriptions of how we read.

What is less clear, however, is whether we need new accounts of the reading process in relation to computer texts. Dozens of commentators, though perhaps none more eloquent than Rand Spiro (1992, 1994), have noted that reading habits seem to be changing as we face a future that will be dominated by computer screens and data storage devices that appear to redefine the reading process and to demand new skills. The reading skills and study skills that have developed over the past eight hundred years, runs the argument, are already passé; new skills are needed to deal with the demands of flickering type fonts and unknown or unfamiliar data structures. Hypertexts are replacing books, and a new generation of readers, whose minds have been rotted by what our American colleagues call 'eye candy', will be doubly disabled: having not been brought up to read, they will be illiterate; having too little understanding of how to cope with electronic texts, they will be unable to handle the twenty-first-century demand of becoming e-literate – electronically literate.

Well, that's how the argument runs, and I want to oppose it. I want to suggest that while the term 'hypertext' is new, and while it is unquestionably the case that new methods of storing data in electronic form have been developed and will continue to develop, there is no case for sustaining the apocalyptic view that young readers are having their cognitive teeth rotted by 'eye candy', nor is it the case that new types of reading skill are going to be needed in order to cope with electronic texts. And the point is not simply a socio-cultural one; these issues are fundamental to our understanding of what it is to develop reading, and to develop reading comprehension, and I want to build my case on two research studies carried out in the School of Education at the University of Nottingham.

First, on the matter of whether or not a new generation of readers is growing up unable to read and unable to concentrate on a visual stimulus (unless it is a computer graphic which mutates, kills, explodes or scores a goal), many teachers will by now be aware of the recent national replication, by Martin Coles, Val Fraser and Chris Hall, of Frank Whitehead's 1970s survey of children's reading interests (Hall and Coles, 1999). The project reported clear evidence that children's reading habits have remained remarkably stable over the past 20 years. There are of course plenty of children today who read few or no books and who watch a great deal of television. The main difference in the two populations, however, is not that there are more non-readers today, but rather that 20 years ago, non-readers watched less television. Today, plenty of non-readers choose to play computer games, but Hall and Coles made the point that they found no causal relationship between higher levels of computer usage and lower levels of book reading. This view of stable reading standards has been confirmed by Greg Brooks's recent review of national reading survey data in the UK over the past 50 years, which argues that there is no evidence of any decline in reading standards since the 1950s.

Second, we should note that, again in the 1970s, the *Effective Use of Reading* project (Lunzer and Gardner, 1979) found that children's reading in school was already fragmentary, that many children found school textbooks too difficult and many teachers found school textbooks too expensive, with the result that there was something of an avoidance of print. The classroom observation data collected by the project team in 1974 and 1975 reported that most reading in secondary school took place in bursts of less than 15 seconds in a minute.

In other words, the need for children to develop the skill of learning effectively from brief bursts of reading is not new, nor is it a function of the television age or the CD-ROM; it is simply one way in which we use printed texts.

The third part of my argument relates to the nature of printed texts, particularly school texts. During the 1970s and early 1980s, many research groups, including those of Richard Anderson at the University of Illinois and the Schools Council teams at the University of Nottingham, studied how children learned from schools texts. What we found, and what our US colleagues found, was that school texts were often 'inconsiderate' in that they were unhelpful to readers, either because they did not give the reader signposts to the structure of the argument of the text or because they did not have a clear or coherent structure in the first place.

The Nottingham teams developed and evaluated classroom strategies for helping children to explore and identify the macrostructures which lay under the surface of texts, the rationale being that to do this would enable readers to learn much more effectively from texts than would otherwise be the case. These strategies were called DARTs – Directed Activities Related to Texts – and there were about thirty of them, of which deletion, sequencing and prediction were three, all of which were developed in collaboration with teachers in classrooms (Lunzer and Gardner, 1984). All the DARTs activities involved the reader in an active interrogation of the text, exploring its surface features, but going deeper and exploring the strata underneath. Small group work was a central part of the pedagogy of DARTs, since it was our belief that a reader could learn the processes and strategies of reading by seeing those processes modelled by one of his or her peers. But consider what was happening here: readers were taking texts apart, discovering that the deep structure of the text was not linear, deciding what that deep structure was and then working out how best to navigate around it. To do this is precisely what is required in exploring a hypertext.

A hypertext is an *n*-dimensional rather than a linear text. The term is generally applied to electronic texts, but it is also applied to certain types of printed text, for example a programmed novel, in which the reader makes strategic choices and follows a non-linear pathway through the book (Kill the king? – go to page 349. Watch a play? – go to page 85. Procrastinate? – stay on this page but watch your back, and so on). A hypertext on a computer is made up of two sorts of object: information (often this is text, but it could be graphics or a video clip) and links to other information. The challenge for the reader is therefore threefold: to construct meaning from the text, to navigate to another chunk of text, and finally to integrate information from what is found in the new location with what is already known.

What I would want to argue is that there is nothing fundamentally new in all this; it seems new because the medium is new and the surface features of the text are unfamiliar: new text fonts, unfamiliar text framing tools and new hardware devices. But in some respects, the task of the reader in front of a computer screen is easier than that of a person reading a book: at least a computer interface declares its novelty and offers socially acceptable permission to succeed or fail (if I succeed, it's because I'm good with technology; if I fail, then I remind myself that those who succeed with technology are nerds, and at least I'm not a nerd). By contrast, I'm suggesting that most information books are hypertexts, that their deep structure is *n*-dimensional and that the reader's role is to navigate within that non-linear space, but the reader's job is often very difficult because the signposting of that structure is poor or the structure is weak.

Of course there are some aspects of electronic texts which are new and different: the potential speed of access to information over the World Wide Web, for example, is new: a web browser conducts a free-text Boolean search of 3,000 million websites in under a second. But I would still argue that these challenges are essentially quantitatively rather than qualitatively different; they don't require a new model of the reading process. I would go further and suggest that if we can support children to use DARTs or similar approaches successfully, they will be well equipped not only to read books, but also to make effective use of the power of electronic media.

Proposition 4: We need to rethink reading comprehension and reading assessment

Let us turn now to consider some parallels between what has happened over the past twenty years in the psychology of reading and within the field of English literature. I want to note that there are interesting parallels between the emphasis on active approaches to the processing of text which come from psychology, and accounts of reading and the role of the reader which come from contemporary literary theory, and that the DARTs activities which I mentioned above, which were derived from a psychological perspective on reading development, could have equally been derived from literary theory.

In a chapter in my book on reading assessment, Mary Bailey, Alan Dewar and I (Harrison, Bailey and Dewar, 1998) quoted Terry Eagleton's comment that in recent years there has been a marked shift of attention in literary theory away from the author (the focus of nineteenth-century criticism) and the text (the focus of structuralist criticism in the early and middle years of the twentieth century), towards the most underprivileged of the trio, the reader. Wolfgang Iser, in developing his reception theory, argued that the text is unfinished without the reader's contribution to making meaning: it is the reader who, in partnership with the author, brings to it his or her own experience and understanding, and resolves the conflicts and indeterminacies which the author leaves unresolved. This is exactly what happens in DARTs activities: the reader, in collaboration with his or her peers, is engaged in the process of constructing meaning, and is encouraged to adopt a constructively critical disposition towards the author.

This reassessment of the concept of meaning, of the role of the reader and of the authority in text, raises profound questions about the nature of reading assessment, particularly in its traditional forms, and it is these questions which have led me to the bold formulation that there is no such thing as reading comprehension, at least not as we have often been inclined to understand it – as a steady state of knowledge formed in the reader's mind following the reading of a text. Like other teachers, I have given children reading comprehension exercises, tried to develop their reading comprehension, and have used the phrase to refer to what readers understand from what they have read, but I think that it is important, too, to remind ourselves that reading comprehension processes are elusive, evanescent, and in many respects inaccessible.

I would go further, and suggest that a sort of uncertainty principle operates, such that it is not possible to investigate someone's reading comprehension without affecting the nature of their response. It is in this sense that I want to suggest that there is no such 'thing' as reading comprehension. Certainly readers comprehend, but the product of reading comprehension is not stable, and if you ask someone a question about their understanding, the answer you get will be the product of a new inter-action between the text, the reader's response to it and your question. As Walter Kintsch put it, 'asking questions as a method for the assessment of knowledge is fraught with problems' (Kintsch, 1998, p. 296). He went fur-ther, suggesting that it is 'an unnatural act when a teacher asks a student for something that the teacher knows better than the student.'

I want to suggest that, most of the time at least, we haven't yet dared to or haven't had the imagination to consider the implications for assessing response to reading, or measuring reading comprehension, of the postmod-ern positions we adopt as teachers. There's a chasm between the liberal positions of our pedagogy and the coercive positions of our assessment mechanisms and the assumptions which underpin them, and at the very least it is important to recognise this, and to set ourselves the agenda of bridging the chasm.

Later on in this book I shall argue that we can derive some principles for reading assessment based on an analysis of postmodernism and literary theory. Here is a summary of those principles which I have called principles of Responsive Assessment:

- assessment should be potentially useful for both teacher and student;
- the subjectivity of both teacher and student should be valued, not regarded as a problem;
- the content of what is regarded as evidence of reading achievement should be negotiated;
- the reading activity under discussion should be based on an authentic task;
- evidence of the reader's response should be sought and given status;
- the reader's role as a maker of meaning should be given status.

I have suggested elsewhere (Harrison, 1996) that the National Curriculum in England and Wales currently presents an ultimately damaging model of assessment, and that if teachers were permitted to move towards a portfolio assessment system within which evidence of reading activity was collected according to these principles of Responsive Assessment, then most of the problems associated with National Curriculum assess-ment would evaporate. I have worked with a group of primary and secondary teachers in Nottinghamshire over the past six years who have been talking about and trying out in the classroom some new approaches to reading assessment. We have also been in touch electronically with some teachers in Michigan who have been investigating new approaches in their classrooms, and we set up an e-mail network to share ideas. Some of this work will be discussed later in this book. I shall not suggest that our tentative steps provide a full model for future national assessment, but I do believe that unless approaches that link curriculum and assessment are developed and piloted by teachers in classrooms our national assessment practices in England will remain coercive and damaging.

Proposition 5: All import restrictions aimed at reducing the risk of 'Bovarysme' should be permanently lifted

St Hugh's approach to reading was to emphasise two roles of the reader, the first predicated on the reader's duty to God and the second on the call to scholarship. I have suggested that these roles approximate to our contemporary notions of reading for personal or spiritual development and reading for research or information. The emphasis of many literary critics has been on a third area, focusing on what has been called the joy of text, and I am going to suggest that this third purpose for reading, which we might call reading for enjoyment, is worthy of separate consideration.

Psychologists have studied motivation and interest level as important variables of reader response since the 1920s, but contemporary literary critics have also given close attention to the matter of how readers enjoy texts, and have done so in ways that put an interesting emphasis on the discourse of pleasure. Some literary critics have so embraced metaphors of eroticism in relation to the act of reading that desire, textual foreplay and ultimately jouissance are so important that a reader who does not feel passionate about reading begins to have anxieties about literary impotence.

For those undertheorised and possibly insecure individuals whose sheltered lives have led them to be unaware of precisely what jouissance entails, I am happy to say that I have worked out my own definition: jouissance is that delectable feeling of release from unbearable physical tension that occurs when after what seems an eternity of expectation, and with lungs bursting and mind in turmoil, one finally encounters a main clause in one of Proust's three-page sentences. Lest I be accused here of both wandering off the point and of taking this chapter into an unacceptably tasteless cul-de-sac, let me say at once in my defence that my irreverent humour is entirely in harmony with the spirit of playfulness which suffuses contemporary literary theory, in which eroticism has become a branch of philosophy.

One delightful book which builds the most amusing and elegant bridge between contemporary critical theory and the teaching of reading in school and which deals brilliantly with the issue of the joy of reading is Daniel Pennac's *Reads Like a Novel* (1992). I want to spend a moment talking about this book, because I think it says much that captures precisely why many people who love books choose to become teachers. Pennac was a literature teacher at a *lycée* in Paris, but in his book he presents an instantly and internationally recognisable set of students, who are not the sort who are going to go on to the top universities, who have changed from being children who drank up stories as naturally and thirstily as they once drank milk into adolescents who can't bear to read, and who now believe that they do not like reading.

So what does the teacher do? (And here we recall St Hugh's imperative that the monk has not only a moral duty to read, but to read aloud.) He reads to his students. He reads aloud, fending off their scepticism and their injured protestations that they are too old to be read to with an offer of a vote on the matter after ten minutes. And it works – not only do the students enjoy listening to their teacher reading, they can't wait the interminable time it would take for him to read the whole thing to them and they ask to borrow the book so that they can take it home to read.

Pennac makes three points about why this method works. The first is that the teacher was not so much teaching as playing the role of a guide whose job is to start people off on a pilgrimage. The second is that it was vital that the teacher did not present himself as an interpreter, analyst or critic, but simply as a reader. The third is that the teacher did not require the reader to demonstrate that he or she had understood the book, and it was this emancipation that permitted the act of reading to become pleasurable.

Towards the end of the book, Pennac issues what one reviewer called 'a magnificent call to the barricades', a list of ten rights of readers, which he feels should be inviolable:

The Reader's Rights
1   The right not to read
2   The right to skip pages
3   The right not to finish a book
4   The right to reread
5   The right to read anything
6   The right to 'Bovarysme' (a textually transmissible disease)
7   The right to read anywhere
8   The right to browse
9   The right to read out loud
10   The right to remain silent.

I agree with Pennac about all ten, but I want to comment on numbers 5 and 6 – 'The right to read anything' and 'The right to 'Bovarysme' (a textually transmissible disease)'. From within an elitist institution, the *lycée*, Pennac produces an eminently calm and sane defence of reading for enjoyment, for what he terms 'the instant satisfaction of our feelings in literature'. The argument here is that the teacher cannot ultimately be successful in attempting to put over a connoisseurship model of reading; instead, all he or she can do is to present opportunities to read, and support the reader in coming to make their own choices. Readers need to decide for themselves how to view a character, for example the overwrought and desperate Madame Bovary. The teacher can try, but he or she cannot do the job for the reader. But equally, the reader can and must be trusted. To quote Pennac:

> *... Another way of putting this is to say that just because some girl collects Mills and Boon romances, it doesn't mean that she is going to end up swallowing ladlefuls of arsenic.*

Pennac's point is illustrated in an English school context in a reading interview reported in a chapter written by Mary Bailey, Chris Foster and me in another book on reading assessment (Harrison, Bailey and Foster, 1998). In that chapter we argue that a reading interview can be a much more useful source of information about a reader's achievement than any test result. A student, anonymised in the chapter as 'Emma', was a voracious 13-year-old reader, and in our chapter we try to make the point that her wide and eclectic reading, which includes twenty books a month, has not rotted her brain. Instead, Emma gives plenty of evidence that she has enjoyed projecting herself into the fantasy of the romances, but also has an ironic distance on the texts she reads:

Teacher: ... would you say that ... reading books helps you to think about your life in any way?
Emma: Yes and no, because sometimes it, in a book, if, like the Sweet Valley High books, there's one person in the Sweet Valley High that I'd like to be like. But the thing is, if I was like her then my school work would go down and I wouldn't really be very good at home. You know, I'd be always making excuses, but like, it does help me some ways 'cause like it's like if she does something in one situation it makes me think about what I'd do in that situation ...
Teacher: So does that mean that you don't have to do it because you can just imagine it?
Emma: You don't have to; the thing is it like puts ideas into your head.
Teacher: Mm.
Emma: Some of the books, um, they're very unrealistic. You know, it's things that wouldn't happen.

It may be difficult to connect Emma's remarks with National Curriculum levels of attainment, but there is certainly evidence of her personal response, a clear sense that she is able to distance herself from the text and is aware that the text offers not only an area of imaginative projection into other worlds, but also one which helps her to place herself in the real world.

I want to make one final point about Bovarysme. Pennac's use of the term slightly collapses two issues: the reader's right to read anything, and the reader's right to Bovarysme, and to be trusted to form their own judgments. I share Pennac's view that it is good to encourage readers to read what they want to read, on the principle that their taste will improve over time. But Bovarysme is not simply about the right to read for enjoyment; it is about the reader's right not to be preached at. When Madame Bovary was published, it led to a court case and caused as much of a furore as *Ulysses*, *Lady Chatterley's Lover* and *Last Exit to Brooklyn* all put together. This was not because Flaubert had written a book which spoke frankly about adultery (the Parisian book trade would have collapsed had this been a problem), but because the book did not present a moral: the author refused to editorialise, and presented Emma Bovary's emotional immaturity and desperate search for love and selfhood without comment.

Pennac's plea for Bovarysme is a thus very profound one for teachers, because it is so difficult for us not to editorialise – we regard it as part of the job, and part of our moral responsibility.

More on moral purpose

I began this chapter by putting emphasis on the importance of reading for information, but this is not where I want to end: in moving towards a conclusion, I want to dwell a little further on the moral responsibilities of teachers of reading, and I want to suggest that introducing children to stories and poetry ranks first among those responsibilities. Teachers have many responsibilities: to their students, to parents, to their employers, and ultimately, in a democracy, to the government. Since the Second World War, governments in the UK have put a great emphasis on improving literacy levels, and have tended to argue, or at least assert, that it is important for teachers to raise literacy levels because greater literacy will lead to higher employment, high economic and industrial output and wealth creation. This view has been challenged, however, by commentators such as Michael Apple, who argue that transnational industrial and financial forces, over which governments have little influence, are much more powerful determinants of a nation's economic well-being. Governments of the right and of the left have also asserted that improved literacy will lead to a reduction in crime. The rationale for this is again economic: people with poor literacy levels find it difficult to get jobs, and those without jobs turn to crime; if their literacy levels improved, runs the argument, potential criminals would find employment and the economy would improve.

My own view is that this argument too is specious, but I do want to suggest, not that literacy reduces crime, but that reading has the potential to reduce crime, though not because improved literacy aids the economy. The author Michelle Morgan, who works with adults in prisons, helping them to learn to read and write, reports that many violent criminals and murderers have a close to total inability to empathise, to imagine themselves into the head and world of another person and to construct a sense of the feelings of another. As a result, they seem hardly able to think of those whom they have injured or killed as real people. She points out, very compellingly in my view, that while it would be facile to suggest that books can rectify any amount of psychological damage, it is nevertheless the case that what we get from stories and poetry, namely an engagement on a deep and personal level with the lives and feelings of others, can be nothing less than vital – that is, necessary to living.

Flaubert wrote the letter from which I quoted earlier to Mademoiselle Leroyer de Chantepie, about three years after *Madame Bovary* was published. He said to her:

> *Do not read, as children do, to amuse yourself, or like the ambitious, for the purpose of instruction. No, read in order to live.*
>
> (Letters; June 1857)

Flaubert's correspondent was a person whom he never met, a minor author twenty years his senior who suffered from a similarly disabling depressive illness to his own. They corresponded for ten years, initially with long letters about the relationship between life and art and the unhappiness in their own lives. The letter from which this quotation is taken is encouraging and uplifting; its tone gave way, over a decade, to one of stiff politeness and thinly disguised irritation, as Flaubert came to realise that his words had not been effectual. In many respects, one feels that the real addressee of these letters was Flaubert himself, and that the lengthy accounts of how to deal with misery through immersing oneself in literature were part of the process every reader must go through to locate the text of their own lives in relation to the world of the book.

So I would argue that Flaubert's injunction is, at the deepest level, appropriate, and that reading is about far more than enjoyment or information; it is about learning how to live, and I want to go on to suggest that books have the potential to engage us in a deeper exploration of alternative worlds than is possible with other media such as film or TV, for the simple reason that reading a book takes up all of our attention, and engages with all of our faculties, and does so for a sustained period. The depth and permanence of this experience are perhaps related to the way in which books require that the reader construct, word by word and sentence by sentence, the meanings, images, associations, sensations, characters, plot and indeed the world which the author presents. Literary accounts of the death of the author emphasise how great is the reader's responsibility here, but contemporary psychological accounts of the reading process are also instructive in suggesting, for example, that readers fixate and process a far higher proportion of words than used to be the case, and that up to four times a second the reader not only decodes a word but also updates his or her comprehension monitoring processes, integrating the new word into an updated model of the emerging text. We know that there is a direct relationship between depth of processing and the amount of time something is remembered. Little wonder, then, that the images, phrases and associations which bounce around in our brain after we have been reading a book sometimes echo in our heads for decades.

Proust talked in a very lyrical and incisive way about these feelings in his wonderful essay *On Reading*. He described, for example, the feeling of resentment towards the author and personal loss that we feel when we come to the end of a book. He wrote:

> *Was there no more to the book than this, then? These beings to whom one had given more of one's attention and affection than those in real life, not always daring to admit to what extent one loved them ...*
>
> *One would have so much wanted the book to continue, or, if that was impossible, to learn other facts about all these characters, to learn something of their lives now, to employ our own life on things not altogether alien to the love they had inspired in us.*
>
> (Marcel Proust, *On Reading*, 1905)

It seems pretentious to suggest that the job of a teacher of reading is to help people to learn how to live. So we rarely admit it and tolerate the more socially acceptable formulations of governments and curriculum agencies. But I would suggest that it is the possibility of this kind of learning that we have in mind when we read, or when we recommend or lend a book to our students. We are offering them the opportunity to imagine what we have been led to imagine, hopeful, and on a good day confident, that their lives will be the richer for it.

Why do we read, and why is reading so important?

Let us now return to the image of reading from earlier in this chapter, the three men in the bombed library, and the questions 'Why do we read, and why is reading so important?' I want to suggest that we can reconsider, or reread, this image, in the light of my discussion of the three central purposes for reading. Let me share with you what I have come to see in this photograph as I thought about how we read reading.

Look again at the three readers: one immersed in a book, one selecting a volume and one engaged in contemplation. Might we not interpret them as representing the three purposes of reading? The young man, with the open book, carried away on the wings of imagination, representing the answer 'joy' (or delight, or enjoyment); the second, seeking out a tome to research, representing the quest for information or knowledge; the third, engaged in an act of contemplation, representing the attempt through reflection on reading to learn how to live.

And from this point it is only a small step to bring together historical, literary and psychological perspectives, and to read the photograph as a picture of every reader's mind: a cathedral-library organised and filled with representations of knowledge and ideas, with the three readers representing the mind's desire for pleasure, the quest for knowledge and the hope of understanding, and with the mess, the rubble in the centre, representing the emotions, the partial knowledge and the incomplete understandings of our inner and outer lives, over which we strive to gain control, using our reading selves as our agents and allies.

Read in this way, the photograph of the bombed library can provide us with an image of reading which is one of optimism rather than desolation, representing at least the possibility of the triumph of order over chaos, of realism over romanticism, and of hope over despair.

It is my hope that this image, and the three interlinked perspectives on reading – historical, psychological and literary – that it encompasses, will carry us forward into a deeper consideration of reading development than would otherwise be possible.

Chapter 2

What does research tell us about the reading process and the early stages of reading development?

In Chapter 1 I argued that learning to read is pointless unless a reader comes to value, enjoy and in some sense possess the books and stories that they read. In a book I edited with Martin Coles (Harrison and Coles, 1992/2002), I quoted the work of Margaret Meek (1988) and Liz Waterland (1985), who believe that it is crucial to help children to encounter 'real books', since such children, in Meek's words, 'learn many lessons that are hidden for ever from those who move directly from the reading scheme to the worksheet.' I tried to suggest that it is important to place meaning, enjoyment and the stimulation of the imagination at the heart of reading. This book is about reading development, and I want to suggest that as well as stressing the importance of enjoying good books, it is also important for us to understand the nature of reading development, and therefore to give some serious attention to research – both because it is valuable for all teachers to have an understanding of reading processes and because research has much to tell us about how to teach reading. However, interpreting reading research can itself be a challenge.

Understanding why are there so many battles over reading research

Psychologists are in broad agreement about how adults read, but there have continued to be fierce debates about how best to teach reading, and these debates seem to become especially acrimonious if there is any likelihood of influencing government policy in the literacy field.

Research into reading no longer exists (if it ever did) only in the laboratory. It has become public property, aided by anxious governments and a media machine that becomes particularly active when it sniffs the possibility of internecine strife. Professor Usha Goswami, one of the most significant researchers into early reading in the UK, and currently leading the Centre for Neuroscience in Education at the University of Cambridge, went off on maternity leave from University College London in 1998 with her career on a high. Her work on the importance of rhyme and analogy in early reading (Goswami and Bryant, 1990) had caught the wave of interest in phonological development, and she was regarded as one of the most able and sought-after authors and speakers on the subject of how children's phonological skills develop and mature.

She returned from maternity leave after two years to a painful new reality: she was being vilified as not only misguided but also as directly responsible for children failing to learn to read. The reason? Her work was being interpreted as a call for 'analytic phonics' (a term Goswami had never used to describe her own position), and this was attacked as implying a 'work it out for yourself' approach, as opposed to what was held to be the more direct instruction of 'synthetic phonics', an approach described by one commentator as the 'Holy Grail' of early reading instruction (Burkard, 1999).

Burkard's paper had been published by the Centre for Policy Studies (CPS), a right-wing think tank set up in the 1970s by Margaret Thatcher. The CPS has the goal of influencing public policy through its publications, and through 'a range of informal contacts with politicians, civil servants and the press, in Britain and abroad' (CPS, 2002). The Centre's core principles include 'the value of free markets, the importance of individual choice and responsibility, and the concepts of duty, family, respect for the law, national independence, individualism and liberty' (CPS, 2002). These concerns have a remarkable commonality of purpose with similar groups in the USA, and Burkard's pamphlet was given a good deal of publicity, since it argued that:

- one in three children couldn't read properly;
- the national literacy strategy (in England) wouldn't work;
- there was an urgent need to curb the influence of the 'wrong kind of phonics' ('analytic phonics'), which was responsible for poor reading standards, and to introduce the right kind of phonics ('synthetic phonics').

My point here is not to review the evidence related to Burkard's claim (Goswami did this very successfully herself, in an article cited below and published in the *Journal of Research in Reading*: Goswami, 1999), but rather to discuss the issue of how reading research comes to find itself so controversial. And the answer is a somewhat frustrating one for teachers (or indeed for government officials and other policy makers). The answer is that – unfortunately – the concepts of 'truth', 'knowledge', 'evidence' and even 'science' itself are problematic, in the sense that they are all contested, and when it comes to research into reading pedagogy, the discourse tools of rhetoric sometimes seem to be more dominant than the language of science.

Since around the year 2000, peace has broken out in the UK in relation to the 'reading wars' and the place of phonics in early reading instruction. Perhaps the main reason for this is that the teaching of phonics is now pretty-well mandatory in English state schools, and the issues for debate are mostly around classroom implementation rather than grand theory. But at the time of writing, this is far from the case in the USA, where the phrase 'scientifically based research' is being enshrined in legislation related to the pedagogy of reading. The term is used no fewer than 111 times in the 'No Child Left Behind Act of 2001', according to a US government information service (EDinfo, 2002). This repetition is a clear example of a point I made in Chapter 1: when governments turn to science, science turns to rhetoric. The phenomenon was amply illustrated in a seminar run in February 2002 by the US government to publicise the Act, at which 'leading experts in the fields of education and science' addressed the issue of how taking a 'scientific' approach leads inexorably towards clarity in reading pedagogy. Valerie Reyna, representing the US Office of Education, was given the unenviable task of explaining to the American public the inescapable logic of the government's position. This distinguished researcher was given the title 'What Is Scientifically Based Evidence? What Is Its Logic?', and had 20 minutes in which to encapsulate four hundred years of scientific method, and to explain why a positivist position was the only 'logical' one (Reyna, 2002a). With characteristically democratic generosity of intent, the US government put the transcript of the whole seminar up on the web (US Department of Education, 2002), and if you read this transcript, two things immediately become clear: first, the argument that logic leads us inexorably to a positivist methodological position turns out to be a fragile one; second, for a researcher who is telling us that 'logic' should lead us to accept her argument, Reyna leans very strongly on the tools of rhetoric and persuasion.

We shall pass over the early part of Reyna's argument, which is weak mainly because of the shortage of time and the somewhat incoherent nature of some of what she said (most of us would squirm if we had to endure being held to account for the grammatical and propositional coherence of our spoken discourse in a lecture), and concentrate on her main tenet – which was to do with the importance of making educational decisions based on strong evidence, particularly evidence based on control groups and clinical trials of approaches and materials. Reyna stated:

Clinical trials in fact are the only way to really be sure about what works in medicine ... This is the only design that allows you to do that, to make a causal inference. Everything else is subject to a whole bunch of other possible interpretations.

(Reyna, 2002a)

This is indeed a very strong positivist position. Reyna is arguing that only with the level of rigour of a medical model of methodology can we make confident assumptions about causality in research. And she goes on to suggest that 'logic' leads us to apply the same set of principles to educational research in general and reading research in particular.

But even if one is broadly sympathetic to her methodological position (and in fact I am), to the questions 'does this argument work?' and 'does this argument work independently of the bolstering effects of rhetoric?' my answer has to be 'no'. To begin with, the argument that scientific knowledge and confident attribution of causality can proceed only from the methodology of clinical trials and randomised control groups is suspect. Reyna argues that 'scientific research' is 'the only defensible foundation for educational practice', and that the alternatives are 'tradition', 'superstition' and 'anecdote' (Reyna, 2002b). But on her own admission, clinical trials were only introduced in the 1940s, and it would be astonishing to suggest that no causal links had been confidently established in medicine before that time. As she develops her argument, Reyna also makes some interesting rhetorical moves.

Reyna argues that only by using clinical trials and a randomised control group can you 'make inferences about what works', and that the rules for making inferences '... are exactly the same for educational practice as they are would be for medical practice. Same rules, exactly the same logic, whether you are talking about a treatment for cancer or whether you're talking about an intervention to help children learn'.

She puts up an overhead slide containing the phrase *brain surgery*, then continues:

> *The reason I have the word 'brain surgery' up there is that I think, you know, when we talk about medicine and things like brain surgery and cancer, it is very, very important to get it right ... when we teach students, we really are engaging in a kind of brain surgery. We are effecting them* [sic] *one way or the other. Sometimes what we do helps, sometimes what we do, in fact, inadvertently, harms.*
>
> (Reyna, 2002a)

This is a very powerful argument, but it is not so much about logic as about rhetoric. The alternative to 'scientific research', according to Reyna, is not professional wisdom based on decades of skilled practice but 'tradition', 'superstition' and 'anecdote', and she has already reminded us that it was practising these principles that killed the first president of the USA: 'The ... example, of course, is the classic one of when they used to bleed people. People would get sick. You know, I think it was when George Washington was bled that contributed to his death.' So the rhetorical part of Reyna's argument is rather more powerful than the scientific part: she is suggesting that those who deny the appropriateness of the 'scientific research' approach are declaring an allegiance to the same dangerous principles that killed a president. Furthermore, they are advocating a laissez-faire approach to brain surgery and cures for cancer. There is even a strong suggestion that these non-'scientific' teachers are taking the scalpel in their own hands and carving chunks out of children's brains. No wonder she is worried.

But hang on a minute. How easy is it to test the adequacy of a reading scheme using a randomised clinical trial design? It costs millions of dollars to write and publish a reading scheme, and while it is certainly possible to give identical-looking drug capsules, one of which is a placebo, to two patients, it is not quite so easy to give two children in adjacent desks one version each of two different reading schemes, one of which is the new improved scheme and the other of which is the nasty dangerous product written by those non-'scientific' monsters with whom we have all been interacting at reading conferences for the past twenty years. We must not forget that it is important too that the teacher needs to be unaware which child is receiving which programme, otherwise the teacher's intervention could interact with the programme to produce unintended consequences.

It must be clear by now that I would wish to suggest that there are a number of major problems in Reyna's argument, problems that make it unsustainable. Most of these relate to the generalisability of clinical models of research methodology to classroom contexts. I am completely happy to give cognitive scientists the respect they deserve, but we need also to consider the difference between the lab and the classroom, and the difference between evaluating the effects of a literacy development programme compared with isolating the effects on the human body of a targeted drug. Research methods need to be appropriate for a research context, and most researchers acknowledge this. Towards the end of her paper, Reyna noted with dismay that in the year 2000, out of 84 programme evaluations and studies planned by the Department of Education for the fiscal year 2000, just one involved a randomised field trial. She implied that this situation would be likely to change, as the Department sought to implement more 'evidence-based education'. Well, on the basis of what was presented at the 'scientific research' seminar, I'm afraid my prediction is that even with more 'scientific' research being funded, controversy over reading pedagogy will not diminish.

So where does this leave us? Am I saying that there is no truth in research? Well the answer is yes – and no. As both a teacher and as a researcher I do have many strongly held beliefs about how reading works and how good teaching helps to produce good readers, but I would still want to say, just as strongly, that every research project, every researcher and everyone who makes use of the results of research operates within a personal and professional belief system, and that the implication of this is that what we call 'evidence' or 'knowledge' or reify with the name 'science' is in fact a fluid and continuously evolving epistemological surface in which the knowledge and belief systems of individuals exist in a state of socially and rhetorically contextualised tension. It is good news for researchers when governments seek to develop 'evidence-driven policy', since the opposite is generally think-tank-driven policy which can marginalise research totally. But finding incontrovertible 'evidence' is not as straightforward as governments would wish it to be, and this is incredibly frustrating for decision makers who, understandably enough, want clear answers for the millions they spend on research.

I have argued in a paper on compellingness in reading research that there are a great many unacknowledged assumptions operating whenever anyone engages in or evaluates research, and that in deciding what we believe we often look not so much at what was found or the quality of the methodology as who wrote the paper (Harrison and Gough, 1996). Theorists would also say that any research paper in reading is likely to include acknowledged or unacknowledged assumptions in at least four areas – ontological, epistemological, methodological and causal – and to look at these, even briefly, is to lay bare some of the reasons why researchers and governments often seem to be on a collision course over interpreting research into the teaching of reading.

To ground the four sets of assumptions in a specific case, let's look again at both the surface features and the assumptions behind Valerie Reyna's argument. Figure 2.1 shows the surface features of her main argument. The argument proceeds on a path well trodden by governments on both sides of the Atlantic: reading standards are low, and since the job of educators is to teach reading, the education system is to blame. But if reading pedagogy is a complex matter, it is hardly fair to blame teachers for ignorance in this area; so teacher educators should be held responsible, and if they have failed in the task thus far, one can hardly have confidence in this group to deliver improvement. An alternative is needed that can offer rigour in both methodology, research conclusions and in suggesting potentially successful pedagogy. And what better than a medical model – one that offers the promise of a much more 'scientific', clinical approach, where researchers use designs whose aim is to eliminate false positives and 'Hawthorne effects' by careful 'double-blind' designs and placebo groups. And, as Reyna says, the clinical approach is 'the only way to really be sure what works'.

If we look more closely at Reyna's argument, however, we see that it contains a great many unacknowledged assumptions, and that these make the acceptance of her argument problematic. First, as I have tried

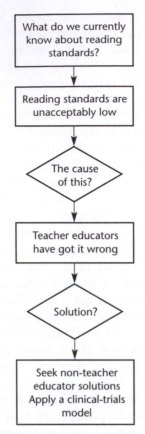

Figure 2.1 The logic of reading research – a representation of Reyna's argument (assumptions not shown)

to show in Figure 2.2 below, any researcher operates within a series of personal and professional belief systems. Even scientists do not all share the same set of beliefs about the nature of existence and of truth (the ontological belief system), and the status of research findings in relation to changing what we feel we know and perceive to be the case (the epistemological belief system). And researchers themselves sometimes have serious disagreements over methodology and over how causal attribution is determined. I have shown these belief systems in dotted lines in the figure to emphasise that they are often unacknowledged, but I want to argue both that they have to be present (i.e. there is no knowledge independent of a belief system), and that at the societal level the dominant belief system is not that which is the most logical, but rather that which gets the most votes. Most educational research involves highly complex environments, such as classrooms, where it is incredibly difficult to control the administration and mediation of pedagogical approaches in the way medical researchers can control the clinical trials of a new drug, and it is hopelessly difficult to even attempt to replicate the type of 'double-blind' design using placebo drugs that can be used in medicine. So if 'the only way to really be sure what works' is through a medical model of clinical drug trials, the world of education is in big trouble. But education is not medicine. In fact, in the areas where medical research does begin to have some similarity with educational research, for example in the field of epidemiology, we see exactly the same sort of unresolved conflict that occurs in education. In the UK, for example, there have recently been powerfully expressed arguments about the dangers of possible side effects of the MMR vaccine that have not been resolved by simply asking scientists to tell us what research has found. Scientists themselves have been in serious professional disagreement about how to interpret the evidence in this complex and challenging field, in which research data, rhetoric, the beliefs of individuals and the authority and status of the particular scientist have all played a part in the construction of our understanding of 'what works'.

Researchers who do not share Reyna's view of the pathology of reading failure are not necessarily less 'scientific' than she is. It is interesting that those who claim that reading standards are in serious decline and that 'science' is the key to arresting that decline are sometimes the least attentive to research into reading standards. In the UK, a meta-analysis of research into reading standards over the past 50 years conducted by the National Foundation for Educational Research (Brooks, 1997) concluded that standards had remained more or less constant (a conclusion presumably not accepted by Burkard in his 1999 paper, who would perhaps regard such an analysis as part of a collusive conspiracy to deny the 'reality' of falling standards). The path down the right-hand side of Figure 2.2 does not therefore represent a 'non-scientific' route; if anything, given my caveats concerning the applicability of the clinical trials model, it may well represent a more coherent and arguably a more 'logical' 'scientific' route which could be at least as stoutly defended as that chosen by Reyna. But, on my own analysis, I can't say that Reyna is 'wrong'; I can only say that I disagree with her, and that my claims, and hers, as to how things are, are problematic in that they are contested. It is for this reason that I've shown both sets of statements in dotted lines. And the dotted lines only disappear when there is a consensus that they should disappear.

The fact that I have a socially contextualised theory of truth does not stop me from conducting research or from reporting it. Nor does it prevent me from writing reviews of research or from changing my beliefs when I encounter new research. But it does lead me to try to be very careful about using the word 'truth' in research, and to be very cautious around the use of rhetorical tools such as 'in fact ...' Equally, it would be silly to assert a claim to methodological (even worse, moral) high ground simply because I

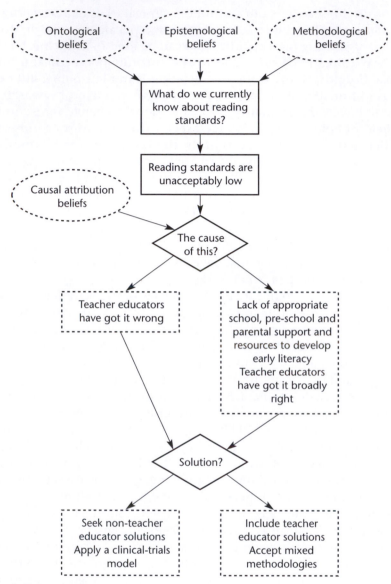

Figure 2.2 The logic of reading research – a representation of Reyna's argument (assumptions shown with contested or problematic areas enclosed in dotted lines)

happen to use a different set of lenses than some others to try to reach some understanding of reading research. Ultimately, what matters is whether the set of conceptual tools I am proposing is useful. In this book I am attempting to offer a research-based appraisal of how we read, and of how we can work as teachers to help others to improve as readers. In doing so, I would want to say that an analysis based on an acceptance of the fact that different researchers live in different worlds in terms of their ontological, epistemological, methodological and causal beliefs has helped me to understand some of the conflicts that occur in our field.

Understanding the reading process: the importance of rapid, automatic, context-free word recognition

Ken and Yetta Goodman, by their example and by their writings, enabled many of us to begin to become more knowledgeable about the reading process, and offered legitimacy to many of our own observations of how children read and of how they learn to read. For young children, meaning is paramount, and a book often seems to be not so much a text in which every word needs to be read, but rather a map in which any route is permissible in the journey towards making meaning. However, Goodman's account of the reading process in fluent readers is now felt to be somewhat inaccurate. Goodman (1970) wrote that reading is 'a selective process. It involves partial use of available minimal language cues selected from perceptual input on the basis of the reader's expectations.' On Goodman's view, then, a reader's sampling of the text is 'minimal', but the reader makes maximum use of contextual information in the quest for meaning. Frank Smith's account was very similar to this. He wrote, 'fluent reading does not normally require the identification of individual words' (1971, p. 105).

In contrast to this view, however, the evidence currently available suggests that for fluent readers the visual processing of text is both fairly complete and very fast, and that, most of the time, engaging in hypothesis-testing behaviour seems to play a minimal role in the process of word recognition. This is not to suggest that reading is now thought of as a wholly 'bottom-up' process (that is, one in which reading is solely based upon a letter-by-letter analysis of the words on the page, without any input from information stored in memory). The currently accepted view of reading among psychologists is that an *interactive* model of reading best fits the available data, with the reading process largely following a 'bottom-up' model, but with input from 'top-down' processes being used when necessary (Rayner and Pollatsek, 1989). Evidence for the current view comes primarily from eye-movement data, much of which has become available since 1975, the time since which more powerful computers, coupled with new infrared and low-powered laser technology, have permitted much more accurate recording of eye movements than had hitherto been possible (Rayner, 1983; Just and Carpenter, 1985; Rayner and Pollatsek, 1989). These new and more accurate procedures permit experimenters to know to within a single letter where a reader is fixating (fixing his or her gaze) during reading. We now know that, in normal reading, adults, far from only minimally sampling the graphic information in a text, fixate nearly all words (over 80 per cent of content words, and over 40 per cent of function words, such as *of* or *the*), and almost never skip over more than two words. Fixations on words generally last from a fifth to a quarter of a second (200–250 milliseconds) and, what is more important, it is now thought that a reader accesses the meaning of a word which is being fixated *before* moving to the next fixation. The current view, therefore, is that for fluent readers in normal reading, rapid, automatic, context-free word recognition is what occurs most of the time, with fixation duration largely related to the relative word frequency of different words. This model does not deny the use of context as an aid to comprehension, nor is phonemic decoding ruled out, but these are both assumed to be aids to word recognition that are mostly unnecessary for fluent readers. It is in this respect that reading is now regarded as an *interactive-compensatory* process.

Understanding the 'interactive-compensatory' nature of the reading process

In a celebrated paper, Keith Stanovich (1980) put forward the view that reading should be viewed as an 'interactive-compensatory' process. He suggested that the proportion of time given by any reader to word recognition and to comprehension was not fixed; it was variable, according to the needs of the reader. Stanovich argued that good readers recognised words rapidly because their word recognition was automatic. It was poor readers, by contrast, who needed to make the greatest use of context in order to facilitate word recognition, and they did so at the expense of needing to devote extra time to this part of the process. By 'automatic', researchers mean that the rapid word recognition of a fluent reader is not under conscious control. It therefore takes up very little processing capacity, and this is very important, since this frees up processing resources for comprehension. A fluent reader, on the interactive-compensatory model, uses very little processing capacity for word recognition, and is thus able to devote additional mental resources to interpretation. The process is compensatory in that, when necessary, readers compensate by devoting additional resources to the word recognition part of the process.

What are the implications of all this? The obvious implication is that accurate, rapid word recognition is really important in fluent reading. It would, however, be unfortunate if such a realisation made some teachers discourage guessing in beginning reading, and revert to a Victorian insistence on accurate, error-free word-attack drills. This would be counterproductive, and the reason is to do with the difference between *being* a fluent reader and *learning to become* a fluent reader. While a child is learning to read, the 'compensatory' part of the reading process is vital. When children are building up confidence, and gradually extending their lexicon of rapidly recognised words, they need to use all the tools available, including intelligent guesswork. Rapid word recognition is important in that it is ultimately one of the facets of good fluent reading. But it is not how we begin, nor is it a goal in its own right. The *purpose* of reading is to gain meaning, not simply to recognise words rapidly. For this reason, it is important to consider the pedagogical implications of our current view of the reading process.

Why we need neither 10,000 flash-cards in a big tin box nor 'death by phonics'

To some teachers, the realisation that one of the features that distinguishes good readers from poor readers is their ability to use automatic, context-free whole-word recognition would seem to have one inevitable implication – that we should go back to teaching children by a 'whole-word' approach. So just to be clear: I do not think that look and say should be revived, and that teachers should now each have a large tin box containing 10,000 words to be used for daily whole-word recognition practice. Having a large vocabulary of rapidly recognised words is the *result* of being a good reader, not the *cause* of being a good reader, and practising with flash-cards would not necessarily achieve anything except boredom and random guessing for many children. To make the point even more firmly, I would now encourage teachers to accept that what we call 'sight words' (because they are recognised on sight, apparently as wholes) are not processed as 'wholes' at all, but are processed using the same letter-by-letter analysis that takes place in normal fluent reading; it's just that the processing occurs very rapidly (in perhaps a twentieth of a second), and is therefore not apparent to the teacher. What a teacher calls a 'sight word' is also often an exception word in terms of letter-sound relationship (for example *come*, which is not pronounced as in *home* or *tome*), and a child does need to learn to recognise and pronounce such exception words.

In the past, whole-word approaches generally stressed some useful aspects of pedagogy – they encouraged children to use picture and context cues, and they often put an emphasis on enjoyment. These approaches are reasonable ones to include as part of the teaching of reading. I cannot imagine any basis, however, on which a decontextualised study of dozens (or hundreds) of flash-cards could be beneficial. If anything, I would sympathise more with the use of flash-cards, on a limited basis, not to teach whole-word recognition but to teach phonics, with, for example, differences between letters and letter groups in individual words being compared. For this very specific purpose, a limited amount of 'decontextualised' analysis of certain words is defensible. It is worth adding, however, that any 'decontextualised' teaching will be pointless unless it is offered to children in a way that enables them to make connections with what they know and understand already.

Understanding the importance of learning to behave like a reader

The most fundamental aspect of learning to read is not about skills; it is about learning to behave like a reader. Successful readers pick up books, curl up with them on a bean bag, worry or get excited about what is going to happen to the characters in a story, and later talk spontaneously about what they have been reading to their parents or their friends. Reading a book on one's own is an intensely personal matter, but books are cultural artefacts, and while they may be read in private they exist and are read in a social and cultural context.

As children, many of us became so keen on books that we read under the bedclothes by torchlight, risking the anger or concern of our parents and admonitions that we would ruin our sight. Why does this happen? One answer, as we have seen in Chapter 1, is that we must have learned that books can give some very special pleasure. Frank Whitehead (1975) argued that readers have to give more of themselves to a book they are reading than is the case if they are watching television or a film, and that this extra engagement is repaid in our becoming more absorbed and, ultimately, in our getting closer to the characters about whom we are reading. When Margaret Meek (1988) embarked on her project to teach 'unteachable' children to read, one of her first goals was to enable the young people to obtain some of this sense of enjoyment, of mystery, of commitment to the book they were reading, and to feel that they were doing the things that fluent readers did.

But as well as having experience of a social context in which books are valued, beginning readers need to have at least four other kinds of knowledge: knowledge of how the world works, knowledge of how language works, knowledge of how stories work and knowledge of how a book works, and we shall look at these more closely in a moment. Catherine Snow and her co-authors (Snow, Burns and Griffin, 1998), in the US government-sponsored report *Preventing Reading Difficulties in Young Children*, offered their own account of what is necessary for a child to learn to read, based on a careful analysis of hundreds of research articles. Their formulation helpfully reminds us that reading is about much more than knowledge, and these five areas for development, of which knowledge is one – decoding, fluency, background knowledge, comprehension monitoring and motivation – highlight the complexity of the child's role in becoming a reader:

> Adequate progress in learning to read English (or any alphabetic language) beyond the initial level depends on:
>
> ▶ having a working understanding of how sounds are represented alphabetically,
>
> ▶ sufficient practice in reading to achieve fluency with different kinds of texts,
>
> ▶ sufficient background knowledge and vocabulary to render written texts meaningful and interesting,
>
> ▶ control over procedures for monitoring comprehension and repairing misunderstandings, and
>
> ▶ continued interest and motivation to read for a variety of purposes.
>
> (Snow, Burns and Griffin, 1998, executive summary)

These five areas are all enormously important, and introduce themes to which we shall return many times during the remainder of this book.

Understanding beginning reading: phonology, analogy, pedagogy

In this section, we shall briefly review the four types of knowledge that a child needs to have in order to learn to read, and then look in more detail at the issues of phonology, analogy and pedagogy.

The first kind of knowledge that a child needs to have in order to understand a text is knowledge of the world. We are able to generate hypotheses about what's happening in a text because we know things about the world and how things happen in it. World knowledge, cultural knowledge and knowledge of social conventions are necessary to understand a book. The second type of knowledge needed by a reader is of how our language works. A child needs not only a vocabulary but also an understanding of how the language fits together, and a familiarity with many different syntactic structures. The language knowledge needed here is not the declarative knowledge of formal linguistic description, of course. What the child needs is a familiarity with the forms an author uses, so that he or she can recognise and comprehend what is happening in a story or information book.

Knowledge of how texts work is also very important in early reading. Half the fun for children comes from their being able to anticipate what might happen and from finding that their guess is confirmed or, better still, finding that what follows is a surprise, albeit an unexpected but satisfying one. This can only happen if the author and the reader share a common 'grammar' of story structure in which certain events are predictable. A story which begins:

> *Once upon a time, a little princess with two long braids of golden hair lived in a castle with her father, the King, and her mother, the Queen. She had no brothers or sisters, but often played happily by herself, in the gardens of the castle. Her favourite toy was a golden ball that glittered as she tossed it in the air.*
>
> *(The Frog Prince)*

is probably going to be a fairy story or a tall story, we would guess, since the phrase 'once upon a time' usually signals the opening of a fairy story. The little princess is likely to encounter some problem or obstacle before the story ends, probably happily, and perhaps one obstacle will involve the temporary loss of the golden ball. Children's understanding of narrative structure (often very detailed as a result of their watching television) can be very sophisticated. It certainly is one type of knowledge that a reader needs to have, and which nearly all children bring to the classroom when they start school (even if their familiarity with books is low), and upon which the teacher can draw.

The fourth type of knowledge that children need to have in order to begin to read concerns the conventions of print and familiarity with how a book is put together. Marie Clay's *Concepts of Print* test (Clay, 1979) covers many of these conventions, running from understanding how a book is held and which way up illustrations should be to much more complex things such as being able to point out speech marks, words and capital letters. One important point should be made here. Knowledge of the concepts of print is quite a good correlate of early reading competence, but we should beware the causal fallacy – children who are already familiar with books do well at this test, but it would be inappropriate for a teacher to teach these concepts independently of reading good books for enjoyment. Children who have had books read to them are those who become familiar with the concepts of print.

It is important for beginning readers to have these four types of knowledge, but let me emphasise once again that we should not wait for a child to acquire them before embarking upon developing that child's literacy. Children gain and develop all four types of knowledge in many social situations, from watching television to going to the shops, but teachers can also develop this knowledge systematically. A teacher who uses a book such as the wonderful *The Lighthouse Keeper's Lunch* (Armitage and Armitage, 1989) will be doing this. *The Lighthouse Keeper's Lunch*, while being a delight to read just as a story, can incidentally develop (among other things) children's understanding of science, problem-solving, justice, geography and food. The book also makes fascinating use of quaint vocabulary and has a story structure that echoes many of Aesop's fables, dealing as it does with the problem of outwitting greedy seagulls. As teachers, one of our most important goals is to help children to become skilled readers, and developing their book-related knowledge is an important part of this. However, unless we also have the goal of helping children to become enthusiastic and self-motivated readers, we may find our efforts ineffectual. Being more aware of the components of knowledge that make up reading can make us more effective teachers, so long as we are aware of the dangers of a utilitarian approach, and provided we work to avoid teaching the components in a fragmented and incoherent way.

It is now generally accepted that children need to be able to develop both an automatic (i.e. an unattended) and a phonological approach to recognising words. Automatic, rapid, context-free word-recognition is one of the hallmarks of fluent reading, but a phonological approach to word recognition is necessary for words which are not yet well enough known to be recognised automatically. Children also need to be able to make use of context and all the other types of knowledge they can make available (remember: the fluent reader still makes use of context but is not dependent upon it for word recognition). So what's the problem? The problem is that 'phonics' and real reading have not been good bedfellows. Real reading is not about decoding. It is about teaching children to learn to be readers. Liz Waterland argued in 1985 that conventional practice in schools concentrated on the wrong things, and her argument would find favour with teachers in England who believe that there is currently an unhealthy overemphasis on phonics in the National Strategy for literacy. She referred to those who were 'obsessed with teaching decoding' (1985, p. 15), and if her tone seems harsh, we should remember that she was not so much challenging the approach of other professionals as describing her own practice in earlier years.

Very few teachers would disagree with the suggestion that it is valuable for beginning readers to acquire the ability to work out how to recognise words they have not met before. The issue, however, is how this ability is acquired, and this leads us to a conundrum: how is it that some of the poorest readers in our schools are the ones who have had years of the teaching of 'phonics'? This problem puzzled me for years, and yet the answer is simple and comes in two parts. One answer is that the reader may have been taught phonics in a poor or ineffectual way, but the second answer is that no child can profit from the teaching of phonics unless they have *phonemic awareness*. It is very important for us to understand that phonemic awareness is totally different from 'phonics'. Phonemes are the small units of sound which go to make up a word; phonemic awareness is the ability to hear sounds in our head and to categorise them, and is not directly about print. 'Phonics' is about the relationship between sounds and print. Phonemic awareness is what you have if you can play 'I spy'. It is what you have if you can say which of these three words (said aloud) is the odd one out because it does not rhyme: 'fish, dish, *book*'. Unless you have phonemic awareness, therefore, it is impossible to gain much from instruction in 'phonics'.

We know that children who read early have had a variety of educational and cultural experiences that have supported their early literacy development, and that parents who read to their children pass on and develop the different types of knowledge necessary for reading. In recent years, however, we have also come to understand much more about the importance of phonemic awareness, for it is now thought that this is a vital part of the learning-to-read process. Evidence for this comes from a number of sources, but the best known researchers in the field are Lynette Bradley, Usha Goswami and Peter Bryant. Since the early 1980s, these researchers have been developing three arguments through a series of projects. The first is that there is a strong correlational link between knowing nursery rhymes and acquiring phonemic awareness; the second is that there is a strong correlation between acquiring phonemic awareness and learning to read; the third is that these connections are causal ones. As we have already noted, establishing causal connections is very difficult, but Bryant and his co-workers believe that in their longitudinal studies of more than twenty schools they have established such a connection.

The good news is that these research findings offer tremendous endorsement for the things parents and teachers already do, and indicate the importance of time spent on nursery rhymes, action rhymes and word games as crucial elements in developing literacy. The book by Goswami and Bryant (1990) referred to earlier gives a detailed account of their argument, but the position is also well summarised in a journal article. It is worth quoting from the abstract to this article, since it puts their argument in a nutshell:

Nursery rhymes are an almost universal part of young English-speaking children's lives. We have already established that there are strong links between children's early knowledge of nursery rhymes at 3;3 and their developing phonological skills over the next year and a quarter. Since such skills are known to be related to children's success in learning to read this result suggests the hypothesis that acquaintance with nursery rhymes might also affect children's reading. We now report longitudinal data from a group of 64 children from the age of 3;4 to 6;3 which support this hypothesis. There is a strong relation between early knowledge of nursery rhymes and success in reading and spelling over the next three years even after differences in social background, I.Q. and the children's phonological skills at the start of the project are taken into account.

(Bryant et al., 1989)

The causal connection is established through a multiple regression procedure whereby the effects of a number of variables that are correlated with subsequent success in reading and spelling, such as social background, IQ and initial phonological skill, are removed, and at the final stage one is left with a relationship between the two key factors – in this case, nursery rhyme knowledge at age 3 and reading and spelling at age 6. What Bryant and his co-workers found was that children's knowledge of nursery rhymes did indeed predict success in reading and spelling two to three years later and, more importantly, that this connection was not the result of differences in the children's intelligence or social background, or even in their initial phonological knowledge, because all these variables were controlled. What Bryant argued was that familiarity with nursery rhymes was what enabled children to become familiar with rhymes, which in turn led to their acquiring phonological awareness, which in turn helped them to succeed in reading.

The next question to consider is precisely *why* phonemic awareness is so important, and to answer it we return to one of Frank Smith's sayings, that we learn to read by reading. What exactly did Frank Smith mean? How is it that simply by reading we come to read more successfully? The answer to this question takes us to our final theoretical concept – the use of analogies in reading. What I want to suggest is that as children practise their reading not only do they develop their knowledge of the world and widen their knowledge of language, text types and print conventions, they also use analogies to increase gradually the store of words they can recognise easily and rapidly. This is why reading new books and rereading old favourites are both so important. What are the stages in which this happens?

Initially, as most parents know, children begin by 'reading' books they know off by heart. This is indeed reading, though at an elementary level; children can match the words on the page to the words of a story they know and enjoy. A word is 'read' without any phonemic segmentation, and words are matched by rote association with those in the story. In the first year of formal schooling, if they have not done so before, children begin to be able to 'read' in this way. At the same time, they become more familiar with printed words in a wide range of contexts: as labels, on posters, on displays and in new books. The teacher reads books to and with the children, encourages the learning of letters and sounds through games, stories and poems, and begins to develop early writing activities. But at this first stage a child's reading is very context-dependent. A child can read a book he or she knows, but can't recognise words from it in isolation. Equally, a child can say that a road sign says 'STOP' or that a wrapper says 'Mars', but he or she would not recognise the word if the case of the letters were altered and the word encountered in an unfamiliar context.

Then comes the second stage, which is in some ways the most exciting for the child, the teacher and the parents. Following models of active meaning-making which the teacher and others have provided, children begin to do three things at once: they begin to use context to make predictions about what is happening in a story, they begin to use semantic and syntactic cues to help make predictions about individual words, and they also begin to make rudimentary analogies in order to help in word recognition. This is when independence in reading begins, and when the encouragement of intelligent guessing is enormously helpful to the beginning reader, for there must be guessing at this stage. What will make the guessing most valuable will be feedback, discussion and encouragement. Wild guessing can lead to frustration, but if there is a supportive dialogue between the beginning reader and a fluent reader, the beginner can learn from the model of the fluent reader how meaning is built up and how guessing can best be used.

The use of analogies is crude at this stage; a child may be able to guess a word using the initial letter as a clue, but little more. The analogy may be no more sophisticated than 'the word *cat* starts with a c, so perhaps this new word which begins with c is going to begin with the same sound'. Nevertheless, one can appreciate the crucial part played by phonemic awareness in making analogies even at this early stage. However, children can only make this type of simple analogy if they have three things – letter knowledge, letter-sound correspondence knowledge and the ability to hear the sound of the first phoneme in a word so that they can transfer it to another context.

I said earlier that in order to benefit from the teaching of phonics, a child needs to have phonemic awareness, but I also emphasised that the teaching of letter–sound relationships needs to be done well, so that a reader can operate independently and benefit from his or her natural ability to generate analogies and thus to recognise new words. This does not need a two-year programme of worksheets in which learning the letters of the alphabet becomes more important than becoming familiar with Wibbly Pig, Farmer Duck or the Owl Babies. Phonemic awareness is crucial for generating analogies, but I would also stress that there is an increasing consensus among experts – including real books advocates – that children will only generate analogies successfully if they also have a basic understanding of letter–sound relationships, i.e. (a) they know the letters of the alphabet and how they are commonly pronounced, and (b) they know how to represent as letters the sounds they hear a word make in their head.

The use of the term 'stages' may appear to suggest that children's reading development progresses in a fixed and regular pattern. Of course it does not. Children accelerate and regress within a stage, depending on the book they are reading and their mood. But in general this is how progression takes place, and it takes most children a year or more to move to the third stage, in which more complex analogies are made. It is in this third stage that children make tremendous progress in word recognition, using the knowledge that a word can probably be decoded by analogy with other known words. Early analogies are based on rhymes and initial letters, but later children are able to work out how to recognise a word which they have not seen before based upon other sound or spelling patterns, such as recognising *wink* from the analogous word *tank*. Equally, a word with a complex spelling pattern such as *fight* may be recognised by analogy with the word *light*. Over a period of perhaps two years, children use their ability to make analogies, together with other sources of information in the text, to assist in word recognition. They gradually increase the number of words they can recognise rapidly, without the need for recourse to the slower processes of using context or decoding by analogy, until they reach the final stage, which is that of the independent reader. For most children, this stage is reached between the ages of 8 and 10. The independent reader can not only analyse words into phonemes when necessary, but he or she can also use 'higher-order' rules to decode difficult words such as *cipher*, in which the *c* is soft because it precedes the letter *i*.

In order for children to become fluent readers it is not enough to be intelligent, to have supportive teaching, to know your letters and to have phonological awareness. In order to become fluent readers, children have to read, and they have to read widely. It is very valuable for children to reread favourite books for enjoyment, but also because initially it is unlikely that every word will have been transferred to their rapid word-recognition store. Analogies can only be made by generalising from well-known and retrievable words, so rereading old favourites may have extra value in reinforcing that reservoir of words from which analogies can be made. But to become a fluent reader, a child needs to generate thousands of analogies, and clearly this cannot be done on the basis of just a few books. Here, then, is support from research for the most deeply held belief of 'real reading' teachers – that children learn to read by reading. Put the other way, you can't learn to read *without* reading — there isn't a short-cut. A child who reaches this second stage but who chooses not to read will be likely to remain at that stage and *become* a poor reader, even if he or she did not start out with any reading problem.

The final point to make in this section is the importance of offering children good books which are valuable in their own right, but which also develop phonological awareness. There are dozens of such books, and in this chapter I shall mention only two. *The Cat in the Hat* and *Each Peach Pear Plum. The Cat in the Hat* is a wonderful example of a book that teaches through fun. It is subversive, dramatic, humorous and simple to read, and children go back to it time and again, often for years, enjoying the cat's scrapes and adventures. It is easy to read because 'Dr Seuss' wrote the book in simple, uncluttered rhymes, with repetition and rhyming never obtrusively dominating the story. In a different way, Janet and Allan Ahlberg's *Each Peach Pear Plum* uses repetition and rhyme in a beautifully controlled manner to lead the reader on a journey in which a gallery of characters eventually meet together when Baby Bunting is rescued and plum pie is enjoyed by everyone. This story is perfect in structure and wonderfully illustrated. Its use of rhyme and repetition is incidental to the story, but was no accident. The story includes rhymes and themes with which many children are familiar from well before they began to learn to read, but this is why so many very young children love the book – it is precisely because of this familiarity that they can read it easily.

Many reading scheme books give special attention to offering repetition and a sequenced development of phonemes and letter clusters in order that children are faced with a gentle slope of learning. This is entirely reasonable, but what the teacher must decide is whether the book is valuable in its own right, too. There are some delightful books in some reading schemes, and equally there are some awful 'real books'. The important point for the teacher to bear in mind is that, by one route or another, a child will need to read extensively in order to become fluent.

What then needs to be in place in order for a child to learn to read? I attempted (Harrison, 1999) to summarise my answer to this question in Table 2.1, together with some implications, as I see them, for what the teacher should do in his or her classroom. The aim in including this table is to demonstrate that the research literature, in this case a major government-sponsored US review of the research into early reading instruction (Snow et al., 1998a/b), fully supports the approach I am advocating in this chapter, and that there is no theoretical impediment to our arguing for an approach based on good literature, so long as it includes all the appropriate skill development.

Table 2.1 What needs to be in place for the teaching of phonics to be effective?*

Effective teaching of letter–sound relationships can only occur if	Pedagogical implications
• The teaching of phonics takes place within a programme which forges coherent links between the learning of letter–sound relationships and the fundamental purposes of **reading for meaning** and for personal gratification or development	• Make phonics fun • Link phonics to texts which are both worthwhile and fun (e.g. *The Cat in the Hat*) • Link phonics to texts which have significance for the readers (e.g. texts they have composed themselves)
• The learning of phonics occurs in parallel with the reader's becoming aware of the nature of books and the **concepts of print**	• Introduce the reading of stories and sharing of big books both before and alongside the teaching of phonics
• The teaching of phonics takes place within a programme that forges coherent links between the development of **reading, writing and spelling**	• Plan the teaching of reading, writing and spelling in a single, coherent programme, and continuously reinforce the relationship between these for the learner
• The learner already has, or is in the process of acquiring, **phonological awareness**	• Develop, and continue to develop, phonological awareness from the earliest stages of infancy, in the family, and with the emphasis on enjoyment rather than formal attention to the phonemes of English
• The learner has, or is in the process of acquiring, **letter knowledge** – the ability to recognise and discriminate between the letters of the alphabet, both upper and lower case	• Encourage children's exposure to informal print-related activities during pre-school years; don't worry too much about possible confusions between case, but try to emphasise lower case and letter sounds in preference to upper case and letter names

Table 2.1 Continued

● Effective reading instruction must also include: – extensive **practice** in reading – exposure to a **variety** of worthwhile texts – continuing to develop the reader's **oral language** and **world knowledge**	● Beginning readers should be offered: – opportunities to reread enjoyable, familiar texts – opportunities to read interesting, worthwhile, unfamiliar texts, including non-fiction and picture books – talk and dramatic play activities

* All points included in this table are derived from Snow et al. (1998a/b, Chapter 6).

It should be clear now why we do not need 'death by phonics'. Instead, teachers' priorities should be on introducing phonemic awareness, through word games, poems, 'rapping' and nursery rhymes. Teachers should also ensure that included on their bookshelves are books that develop phonemic awareness. Next, they should ensure that children have opportunities to move through the four stages of reading described earlier in this section by developing their confidence, extending their enjoyment of books and widening the number of rapidly recognised words through using a wide range of reading material. Finally, while all these things are happening, most children will benefit from explicit teaching of letter–sound relationships.

I have included one further table in this chapter. Table 2.2 offers some suggestions, also derived from research but this time using a more eclectic perspective, on how the teaching of letter–sound relationships might be approached (see Harrison, 1999, for a fuller rationale for the suggestions). This table puts more emphasis on phonics and touches areas which are not developed in this chapter, such as the reading–writing–spelling connections, which are also enormously important and in which a real books approach can make learning both enjoyable and effective. Again, the intention is not to burden the teacher or the child with a decontextualised 'skills' approach, but to recognise that there are some aspects of learning to read which involve skills, and that our teaching is more effective if we are aware of these and how and why they might best be developed.

Table 2.2 How to teach phonics effectively

Effective teaching of letter–sound relationships	Pedagogical implications
● Build on a reader's **phonological awareness**	● Develop, or continue to develop, this through verbal play, rhyming activities, clapping or tapping games
● Develop **letter knowledge**	● Develop familiarity with letters and letter sounds

Table 2.2 Continued

• **Teach spelling** at the same time as you teach reading	• Help children to recognise a letter's sound wherever they encounter it
• **Don't worry** about children using invented spelling	• Encourage children's writing of letters
• **Praise** and gently try to emphasise correct spelling from the outset	• Encourage the child's spelling aloud of such words
• Teach familiarity with the names of **letters of the alphabet after** – not before – teaching letter sounds	• Discuss 'temporary' spellings
• Do not assume that **environmental print** will of itself induce understanding – it will enhance learning only as a supplement to other more direct instructional methods	• Use plastic letters, letter blocks or letter cards to help children who are just beginning to learn to write
	• Be systematic: make sure that children get help in learning to recognise all basic sounds
• Develop **segmentation ability**	• Offer teacher-given models of segmenting words into onset and rime in order to sound them out
• Help children to segment words into **onset and rime** parts (develop the ability to segment independently of the ability to understand or recognise rhymes)	• Make use of what we have learned about the staged development of children's ability to use analogies
• Help children to segment words into **syllables**	• Focus on initial letters and letter groups first
	• Offer teacher-given models of how to segment words into syllables in order to pronounce, recognise and spell them
• **Link** the teaching of reading and writing	• Teach common spelling conventions; reinforce these in both reading and writing contexts
	• Make use of words grouped by spelling patterns

How should teachers support children in becoming good readers?

The young fluent readers who were the subject of Margaret Clark's celebrated book were avid readers (1976, p. 50). Their parents found it difficult to tell researchers what type of reading their child preferred because they 'devoured anything in print that was available'. These children became in many important respects independent readers before the age of 7. Every one of the children identified in Clark's study had had the good fortune to have been in the presence of at least one '… interested adult with time to spare to interact in a stimulating, encouraging environment'. Time is always the teacher's enemy, but allies in the form of other adults and older children can assist in offering that 'stimulating, encouraging environment'. In his book on adolescent reading, Frank Whitehead (1975) considered the factors that were associated with avid reading. He found that one factor was more important than any other – and that was the teacher. In Whitehead's study, in every case of a school in which children read many more books than the average, a teacher (and sometimes it was just one in a whole school) was identified as an important provider of encouragement, enthusiasm and resources. A teacher's enthusiasm and encouragement are the greatest gifts they can share with the children they teach, for without them any amount of resources and knowledge may be potentially profitless. But knowledge and resources are important, too, and this book attempts to disseminate knowledge as well as to identify some useful pedagogical resources.

Chapter 3

Understanding understanding: how we learn from texts

Colin Harrison and John Perry

Introduction

At a recent conference on the National Literacy Strategy in England, when one of us gave a position paper on reading comprehension (Harrison, 2001), the starting point was definition. This was because, although people rarely disagree about what it is to read, definitions of comprehension turn out to be rather more problematic. One might assume that we know about reading comprehension: it's the part of reading that's beyond word recognition, it's about understanding what you read, and it develops gradually and 'naturally' as a reader becomes more fluent, more experienced and more confident. Doesn't it? Well – no. We want to suggest that in many respects reading comprehension does not develop 'naturally', that it can be helpful to consider separately the development of reading fluency and the development of reading comprehension, and that broadly speaking, current research suggests that reading comprehension is harder to get at, harder to develop and even more complex than most of us had realised.

What do we know about comprehension?

If we want to begin at the beginning, it's usually wise to begin with definitions and the dictionary. But in the case of comprehension, we hit a difficulty. Definitions of the word *comprehension* are sometimes vague and mostly problematic, one way or another. The *Oxford English Dictionary* has

Comprehension: *the action of comprehending; the action or fact of comprehending with the mind; understanding. The ability to understand a passage of text and answer questions on it, as at school or psychological exercise.*

The first part of this definition is circular, and even the reference to a synonym, *understanding*, does not carry us very far forward. The second part of the definition is tautological: *comprehension* is what a comprehension test tests. Similarly, *Chambers's* dictionary defines *comprehension* as the 'power of the mind to understand', and then later defines *to understand* as 'to comprehend'. *Webster's Collegiate Dictionary* gives 'the act or action of grasping with the intellect: understanding', and then works hard to avoid circularity in its definitions of *understand*, putting an emphasis on the very different ways the verb is used in context, but finally noting that the words *comprehension* and *understanding* are often used interchangeably.

The International Reading Association's *Dictionary of Reading* (1982, subsequently revised), does take us further, and gives:

> the process of getting meaning of a communication, as in a personal letter, speech, sign language; the knowledge or understanding that is the result of such a process.

This is a fuller definition, and while it gives more exemplars, it also turns primarily on our interpretation of the word *understanding*. The IRA Dictionary does, however, give much fuller definitions of *reading*: definitions which are complex, and which include not only comprehension, but also notions of *behavioural adaptation* in the light of what is read. The IRA Dictionary defines *reading comprehension* just as fully, and its multiple definitions include:

- *understanding what is read*
- *understanding in relation to a presumed hierarchy of comprehension processes*
- *interpreting*
- *evaluating*
- *reacting in a creative, intuitive way.*

The IRA Dictionary definition of reading comprehension also quotes two definitions from authoritative sources, both from researchers who have conducted classical studies in the field:

- 'Comprehension involves the recovery and interpretation of the abstract deep structural relations underlying sentences' *(Bransford and Johnson).*
- 'Comprehension is a process of integrating new sentences with antecedent information in extrasentential structures' *(P. Thorndyke).*

We can discern two strands within these approaches to definition:

- definitions that talk about the *products* of reading;
- definitions that attempt to get at the *processes* of reading.

It is not easy to get at the processes that underpin reading comprehension, but it is much easier to get at the products, or at least some of them, and so it is understandable that some definitions should define comprehension in relation to experimental data, since such definitions are at least based on evidence rather than conjecture. However, in this chapter we want to argue that in order to develop comprehension we need to have a deeper understanding of what it is about, and to do this we have to consider the theories, and the processes that attempt to test and verify the theories.

Both of the IRA *Dictionary of Reading* definitions, in compressed and elegant ways, say helpful and illuminating things about the processes. Bransford and Johnson's definition emphasises the fact that comprehension is not simply about vocabulary, and it's not just about surface meaning. It's about getting under the surface and gaining some understanding of the relationships between the structural elements – whether these are words, concepts or propositions. Thorndyke's definition takes the theme of processing and integrating chunks of information two stages further. It first emphasises the importance within comprehension of the reader's integrating new information with that which has gone before (we could characterise this as creating internal cohesion); at the same time, the reader is also relating new information encountered in a text to their own model of the world, and these are the extrasentential structures to which Thorndyke's definition refers (we could characterise this as creating external cohesion). Taken together, these two definitions go a long way towards clarifying for us how challenging, complex and distinctively individual are the processes of comprehension.

These definitions also introduce some key themes in our consideration of the nature of comprehension, which, we want to argue, will help us to understand how we can support the development of comprehension. The themes are as follows:

▶ the elusiveness of reading comprehension;
▶ the importance of memory in understanding comprehension;
▶ 'top-down' models of comprehension: story grammars, scripts and schemas;
▶ propositional models of text processing;
▶ semantic models of text understanding.

The elusiveness of reading comprehension

In Chapter 1 of this book it was suggested, partly just to see how far the argument could be sustained, that there is no such thing as reading comprehension. This was meant in the sense that we can no longer simply consider texts as 'understood' or 'not understood'. Understanding is context and task-related, as well as text-related, and because of this, comprehension itself has to be considered context-specific as well as text-specific. In comprehension, a kind of Uncertainty Principle operates. In quantum mechanics the concept of uncertainty, or indeterminacy, relates to the fact that at the sub-atomic level, it is not possible to measure simultaneously both the position and the momentum of an electron (put more simply, you can know where an electron is, or you can know how fast it is going, but you cannot know both at once). Indeed, the more accurately you measure the one, the less confident you can be about the accuracy of measurement of the other. In reading comprehension, the principle of indeterminacy operates in the following manner: there is such a thing as a person's understanding of a text, but the more you probe it, the more the probing itself changes a person's state of understanding and reflection and brings about a new and different state of understanding. This uncertainty, or indeterminacy, is an aspect of reading comprehension to which we shall return in the chapter on the assessment of reading.

The importance of memory in understanding comprehension

We want to suggest that it is not really possible to engage in even a surface analysis of the nature of reading comprehension without paying at least some attention to the nature of memory and of memory processes. This is because we cannot consider the nature of learning from or remembering texts without having some sort of notion of representation – of how the information in texts is recognised, chunked, stored and recalled, and to look at these processes is to look at human memory.

Theories of memory have often been controversial within the field of psychology: different models of memory come from very different theoretical and empirical traditions and are, if not incompatible, at least tested and validated using completely different types of experiment. Some of the most readily understandable and intuitively attractive theories of text comprehension (schema theory and script theory, for example) are 'top-down' models of how the brain functions, which are reasonably effective in accounting for what the brain does at the macrostructure level, but much less effective at modelling at the synapse level. By contrast, some of the least immediately comprehensible theories of text comprehension, Walter Kintsch's Construction-Integration model (Kintsch, 1998) and Tom Landauer's Latent Semantic Analysis, for example (Landauer, 2002), are 'bottom-up', in that they use mathematical models of human information processing in an attempt to simulate possible cognitive processes at the microstructure as well as the macrostructure level, dealing with text as a set of propositions (in the case of Kintsch) or semantic vectors (in the case of

Landauer). In our view, both types of models are important, and we shall therefore talk about both and, since the approaches of Kintsch and Landauer are more recent and far less well known than the 'top-down' theories, we shall devote more space to these.

Let's just review some of the relatively uncontested theories of memory, and look at the building blocks from which all these models of text comprehension are constructed. Most psychologists believe that there are three fundamental types of memory: a sensory information store, a short-term memory (STM) store and a long-term memory (LTM) store. A fourth term, long-term working memory (LTWM), is used by Kintsch to describe the material that is put into long-term storage but not fully assimilated and transformed, but this is still essentially a subset of LTM.

Sensory information (from the eyes or ears or from touch, etc.) comes to the brain and is either ignored or sent into short-term memory. It is crucial that the brain either ignores or overwrites most of the information held in the sensory information store very rapidly in order to free up the brain for further processing. This part of the memory system is regarded as a sort of pre-amplifier: it doesn't do deep cognitive processing, but rather it makes an executive decision about whether or not to give attention to the input. When children (or indeed adults) drive their nearest and dearest crazy by appearing not to have heard something that was said clearly, within two feet of them (did we mention that the television was on, by the way?), this is probably a problem with the pre-amp (it got turned down, at least until half-time!).

Think, for example, about how much information at the edge of the visual field is ignored, until a person notices an unusual or unexpected movement towards the edge of the field, at which point conscious attention is immediately given to the new source of input (a spider creeping along the wall above your computer monitor, a student's arm making a throwing rather than a writing movement, a flashing red light up ahead). Once incoming information is marked for attention, it is transferred into STM. And short-term means short: most estimates of how long a chunk of information remains in STM are between 15 and 30 seconds. This is about the length of time most of us can remember an unfamiliar phone number. After that time, the information is either transferred, lost or misremembered. In terms of text processing, STM is assumed to be the scratch-pad on which we begin to process information at the sentence level, to do basic grammar and coherence checks, and to make some sort of decision about what is to be transferred into LTM. So basically, when we talk about reading comprehension, we are talking about the information that is stored in LTM.

Again, there is more than one account of long-term memory, but there is a broad consensus among psychologists that it is helpful to distinguish between two main types of storage in LTM, declarative and procedural, and within declarative memory, two main sub-types, semantic and episodic. As Figure 3.1 shows, this is a fairly simple model of memory, but it is very powerful, in that it will enable us to pinpoint and understand some of the factors that readers bring to the comprehension of text, and some of the challenges that texts bring to the reader. Broadly speaking, declarative knowledge is knowledge of words and facts, knowledge that is capable of being brought into the open. Procedural knowledge is internalised, and although it is organised, it may not be easily accessed or explained. One may know how to skim a stone over a pond: that is procedural knowledge. The declarative knowledge associated with that task involves applied mathematics and an understanding of parabolic momentum (the path of the stone) and angular momentum (the spin on the stone), expressed in a more or less technical manner. Declarative knowledge is generally broken down into two parts – semantic and episodic. As is shown in Figure 3.1, semantic memory is our memory for words, and a good deal of experimentation has been carried out in this area. It broadly supports the notion that semantic memory is organised in a series of linked hierarchical networks that can be represented within a kind of tree or root structure. Experiments based on speed of response to questions of classification ('Is a pear a fruit?', 'Is a nut a fruit?') have contributed to our understanding of semantic memory. Episodic memory is our memory for events. It's what enables us to answer such questions as 'Where did you spend last Christmas?' or 'Where did I park my car when I came to work this morning?'

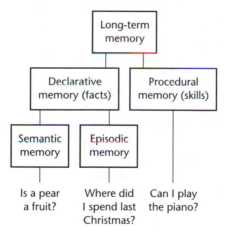

Figure 3.1 The structure of long-term memory

Of course, our brain does not neatly separate out its knowledge into these compartments: a child trying to understand a text that talks about 'acid rain' will be bringing to the text procedural knowledge of how people and things behave in the rain, episodic memories of rainy days and possibly declarative knowledge that would enable him or her to offer some kind of definition of the words 'acid' and 'rain' based on semantic associations and recall of other texts. Nevertheless, this broad account of the main types of memory is widely accepted, primarily because there is so much experimental evidence to support it.

'Top-down' models of comprehension: story grammars, scripts and schemas

'Top-down' approaches to memory start by trying to describe with our memories rather than with the architecture and neural networks of the brain. A good place to start in considering 'top-down' models of understanding is with stories, because one thing most adults and most children can do is to recognise, understand and recall a story. Many, perhaps most, children in the world get to hear stories, because stories are such a fundamental part of so many cultures. As we recalled in Chapter 1, narrative has been called a 'primary act of mind' (Hardy, 1977). Not all children in westernised countries get to hear many stories, but even if they see only a few books, most children in western cultures know about stories through their experience with television. They recognise the start of a story, and they know where they are in a story; they know when the problem in a story is about to be resolved, and they hate to be told 'Sorry – you can't see the end of this right now – it's time to go to school/to have dinner/to go to bed'. They know when an ending is unsatisfactory, because for example the main plot has concluded, but a sub-plot has been left unresolved. Seminal work on our comprehension and recall of stories in the 1970s (for example, Mandler and Johnson, 1977; Rumelhart, 1975; Thorndyke, 1977) suggested that we construct a cognitive template for understanding and storing stories, and we do this using elements of a story grammar that has a similar function to that of phrase-structure grammar that is generally applied to sentences.

We can take a first look at story grammar through considering the case of professional storytellers. A number of remarkable insights into how we store and recall stories are brought together in Ulrich Neisser's edited collection *Memory Observed* (Neisser, 1982). The papers in this book report on how memory works in natural contexts, such as courtrooms and village social gatherings. A particularly interesting case reported in the book is that of the oral poets of the former Yugoslavia, all of whom knew and could perform between thirty and a hundred epic poems, some of which were several thousand lines long. Data collected in the 1930s (Lord, 1982) reported that not only did these poets have remarkable memories, but also that they claimed to be able to learn a new epic poem from another performer on just one hearing:

[Interviewer:] *Is that possible ...?*

[Oral poet:] *It's possible ... I know from my own experience. When I was together with my brothers ... I would hear a singer sing a song ... and after an hour I would sing his whole song. I can't write. I would give every word and not make a mistake on a single one.*

(Lord, 1982, p. 250)

The interviewer asks the poet how he learned the epic poem that he had performed the previous evening:

I heard him one night in my coffee house. I wasn't busy. I had a waiter and he waited on my guests, and I sat down beside the singer and in one night I picked up that song. I went home, and the next night I sang it myself ... The same song, word for word, and line for line. I didn't add a single line, and I didn't make a single mistake ...

(Lord, 1982, p. 250)

How is such a feat of memory possible? The answer clearly has to do with how the poem is structured. Lord argues that the poet chunks, stores and recalls the information that makes up the epic, and must have schemata that operate at both the phrase and at the paragraph level, and indeed we learn from the data presented that both at the phrase level and at the paragraph level there is a good deal of formulaic composition. The main themes of an epic at the paragraph level are plot events that occur in many different songs: a council of war, the arming of a warrior or the return of the hero in disguise, for example. Then, at the phrase or sentence level, the poet may have a dozen or so formulaic ways of describing events such as the break of day ('When the dawn had put forth its wings,' or 'When the sun had warmed the earth,' for example), and he draws upon his repertoire of phrases and larger text elements to compose the epic anew for each rendition.

Was the poet lying when he said that he never changed a line in the poem in his renditions? Lord argues that he was not, but rather that the rules we apply to written texts (i.e. that in performance they are performed exactly as originally written) just do not apply to the performance of epic poetry in Yugoslavia, where it is perfectly acceptable for the poet to create a performer-initiated cadenza that is based on variations on the main theme, though carried out within the bounds of certain textual, stylistic and literacy conventions.

So the oral poets do not repeat verbatim exactly what was said. Despite the poet's claim that he repeats word for word the song of another, the poets in reality vary the formulaic details of the song each time they sing it, and as performers, approximate more to virtuoso jazz players rather than opera singers when they perform. Within this tradition of constant recreation, however, there is a significant stability of theme and detail. Lord (1982, p. 252) reported that he had the good fortune to tape-record the same song from one oral poet, with the recordings separated by 17 years, and although it was not word for word, Lord reported that the second rendition was '... remarkably close to the earlier version.'

Story grammars go a long way towards explaining how we are able to understand, remember and then retell stories. Most story grammars are hierarchical, and one way or another contain the major elements of: characters and a setting, a set of events that occur within a structure which is recursive (including an initiating event (usually a problem), a reaction to the initiating event and a response) and a resolution. The best known approach, that of Mandler and Johnson (1977), has been found particularly valuable because it can accommodate complex as well as simple story structures. Figure 3.2

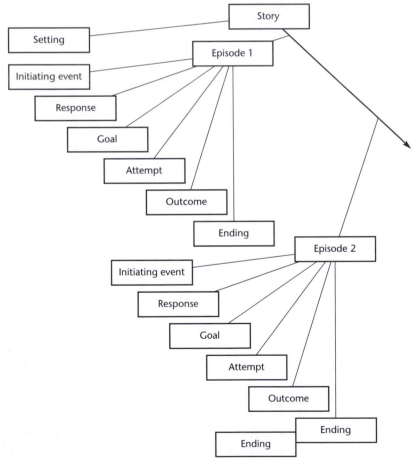

Figure 3.2 Story grammar (after Mandler and Johnson 1977)

shows one version of Mandler and Johnson's story grammar, and the way in which episodes have a similar deep structure and a recursive form that repeats or could even be nested within a single element of an episode. This story grammar also puts a strong emphasis on the goal-directed nature of action in a narrative, with the goal–attempt–outcome sequence at the heart of the structure. This is a very attractive model, since it takes account not only of the relational elements that made up the structure of a story, but also of its broader psychological direction, with problem-solving and the over-coming of barriers or hurdles or journey towards an ultimate goal as the conclusion. Such a structure can deal with narratives from the simple – *Wibbly Pig is Upset* (Inkpen, 1995a), for example – to the complex – *The Brothers Karamazov* (Dostoyevsky, 1880/1958), for example.

Story grammars offer psychologists useful insights into how people understand and store stories, and how they apply fix-up strategies when they are asked to recall a story. The pioneering Cambridge psychologist, Sir Frederic Bartlett (1931), used a Native American story 'The War of the Ghosts' to explore how English people recalled a story, which appears mys-tifyingly elliptical and confusing to anyone unfamiliar with the Native American culture. Here is the story:

One night two young men from Egulac went down to the river to hunt seals and while they were there it became foggy and calm. Then they heard war-cries, and they thought: 'Maybe this is a war-party'. They escaped to the shore, and hid behind a log. Now canoes came up, and they heard the noise of paddles, and saw one canoe coming up to them. There were five men in the canoe, and they said:

'What do you think? We wish to take you along. We are going up the river to make war on the people.'

One of the young men said, 'I have no arrows.'

'Arrows are in the canoe,' they said.

'I will not go along. I might be killed. My relatives do not know where I have gone. But you,' he said, turning to the other, 'may go with them.'

So one of the young men went, but the other returned home.

And the warriors went on up the river to a town on the other side of Kalama. The people came down to the water and they began to fight, and many were killed. But presently the young man heard one of the warriors say, 'Quick, let us go home: that Indian has been hit.' Now he thought: 'Oh, they are ghosts.' He did not feel sick, but they said he had been shot.

So the canoes went back to Egulac and the young man went ashore to his house and made a fire. And he told everybody and said: 'Behold I accompanied the ghosts, and we went to fight. Many of our fellows were killed, and many of those who attacked us were killed. They said I was hit, and I did not feel sick.'

He told it all, and then he became quiet. When the sun rose he fell down. Something black came out of his mouth. His face became contorted. The people jumped up and cried.

He was dead.

(From Bartlett, 1931)

Many students who took Psychology 101 will recall the puzzling challenge of trying to recall and write down this story. And having heard the whole story does not help you to understand the ending! It is incredibly confusing. The reader is left with so many unanswered questions. There seem to be dozens of unspecific pronouns (who is 'he'?, who are 'they'?, and who is the 'I'? What was the black stuff? The story is called 'War of the Ghosts': was everyone a ghost, or was just one person (the one who didn't realise that he had in fact been killed) a ghost?

Bartlett argued that remembering demonstrated an 'effort after meaning' that emphasised the human tendency to make sense of unintelligible or unclear material. He saw memory as an 'active reconstruction of past events', and in this sense would have been entirely happy with the approach to authenticity of the Yugoslavian oral poets – memory does not simply recreate, it creates. But it also tell us much about how we store texts, and in the case of the 'War of the Ghosts' it tells us about story grammar, or at least the set of schemata onto which we map our nascent understanding.

What Bartlett found was that when people tried to recall 'War of the Ghosts', they reshaped the story to map it more fully onto their internalised notion of a story. The result of this was that some details were recalled extremely well. But other details were altered and squeezed to fit in with their pre-existing schema, altered in the direction of the cultural expectations of the reader. And some information couldn't be mapped onto the reader's framework, and this information tended to be recalled very poorly. It is for this work that Bartlett has been portrayed by some as the father of cognitive psychology, some forty years before the term was ever used.

But if story grammars can help us understand how people recall stories in the direction of their cultural expectations, they can also give us tools for considering the stories themselves, and the extent to which they conform to, or deviate from, archetypal patterns, and why. Such considerations have much to teach us in relation to why some stories are remembered and others forgotten, why some move us, while others leave us untouched. The Wibbly Pig story to which we referred above, for example, is simple and elegant, a gentle story of an anthropomorphised pig who is upset for a reason that every western child can understand – he loses his scoop of ice cream when it drops off a cone. Wibbly Pig is the Character, and the seaside is the Setting. Clearly, the loss of the ice cream is an Initiating Event; the Response is immediate – and tearful; the Goal, just as clearly, is to obtain another ice cream; and the Outcome is a happy one – he gets his ice cream. The whole story takes place in six double-page spreads in a book that is small and that also makes good use of white space, so there is little room for recursion or even for an explicit Attempt and a separate Ending (the Outcome is the Ending). But nevertheless all the key story grammar elements are present.

We could contrast this book with a superficially almost identical book by the same author, *Wibbly Pig Likes Bananas* (Inkpen, 1995b). This book, too, has charming illustrations and a delightful protagonist. But it has no plot. The first page reads: *Wibbly Pig likes bananas. What do you like?* There is no setting, or if the kitchen is the implied setting, it is not sustained on the next page, which reads *Wibbly Pig likes the wibbly balloon. Which one do you like?* (Inkpen, 1995b). There is no forward movement in the text, at least in the sense that there is no problem, no goal and therefore no resolution. The publisher of *Wibbly Pig Likes Bananas* will not have been surprised by this difference, of course. No doubt the goal in publishing the book was to encourage parent–child discussion rather than to present a story, but my point still stands – character, setting and episodic structure are what tend to make a text memorable.

The concepts of story grammar also offer a useful basis for comparing two famous Dr Seuss books, *The Cat in the Hat* (Dr Seuss, 1957) and *Green Eggs and Ham* (Dr Seuss, 1962). *The Cat in the Hat* has a much more complex and recognisable story structure than *Green Eggs and Ham*. Both books have characters and plot episodes, but in *The Cat in the Hat*, these are complex, often embedded, and evolving: the initial goal is simply to avoid boredom, but this goal is supplemented by three further sets of goals: dealing with the anarchic behaviour of the Cat in the Hat, curtailing the indoor kite-flying of Thing One and Thing Two, and then tidying up the house in order to avoid the mother's anger. By contrast, *Green Eggs and Ham* has a much more limited plot: the main characters, Sam-I-am , and the 'I' who is repeatedly offered a plate of green eggs and ham, exist is a series of settings that are both sketchy and completely arbitrary in terms of the plot, but which are organised in pairs of rhymes (in a house or with a mouse; in a box or with a fox). Additional settings involve other places that do not rhyme with each other, but which permit the introduction of additional new phonetically regular words (in a car, in a tree, on a train, etc.). However, the eleven episodes of offer and rejection in *Green Eggs and Ham* do not vary significantly, and the final reversal (green eggs and ham are good after all) feels unsatisfactory to many readers, partly because it is simply an excuse for the author to repeat all the words introduced in the earlier part of the book. Both stories have a resolution (the Cat in the Hat rides in on his magical tidying vehicle and saves the day; the 'I' discovers that he likes green eggs and ham), but *The Cat in the Hat* has both an outcome and an ending, with the resolution followed by the coda of the moral dilemma posed to the reader of whether or not to tell the mother all that has happened. I'm suggesting then that story grammars provide at least a partial basis for accounting for how the brain deals with a narrative and a useful tool for describing and evaluating the elements that an author includes in a story.

But story grammars can account for only a part of how we are able to learn from texts. First, there are many text types that are not in story form; second, there is a great deal of learning that is not organised in story form. Another important category of mental representation in relation to the understanding of texts is the concept of a *script*. Scripts are action sequences that enable us to live our lives without having to think every day about how to put one foot in front of the other. We have a script for getting up, one for having breakfast, and another script for going to school or to work. We have a script for what happens at a children's birthday party, and another for what to do in a restaurant. If the script disappears, we are unable to live. There are outwardly perfectly normal people in psychiatric hospitals whose script for getting the day started keeps getting lost, and the challenge of deciding which sock to put on first (which gets to us all sometimes) is for them so difficult that they are unable to dress themselves. Clearly scripts would seem to belong to episodic memory rather than semantic memory, but they are very important in text comprehension, since they enable us to make inferences, often from very limited information, about what is happening and what is likely to happen next in a text.

The archetypal script that is discussed in psychology classes is the restaurant script. This script naturally varies slightly between different people, but there is a high degree of accord between experimental subjects about the most common actions or events that occur. In this much-replicated experiment, all participants mention a menu, for example, all refer to ordering food, and all mention paying the bill. They also group actions in similar ways. It has been found that even three-year-olds have scripts that they can talk about, for eating dinner and other common activities. In the context of the present chapter the importance of scripts is in relation to the issue of how much non-print knowledge is essential for text comprehension. It is because nearly all children have extensive script knowledge that even if they have poor print awareness, they may be good at comprehension, while computers are broadly speaking poor at comprehension. The 'world knowledge' of scripts that a reader brings to a text is not declarative knowledge (Lima is the capital of Peru) but rather knowledge from a number of areas of memory – which range across all the areas of procedural memory, episodic memory and semantic memory.

For a more general account of how we organise and understand the world, it is also important that we give some attention to schema theory (for a fuller account of how schema theory relates to text learning a good starting point is the paper by Armbruster, 1996). Schemas (the Greek plural form 'schemata' is used less widely these days) are mental representations – templates, if you like – that permit us to store, recognise and remember information. Having a schema for a chair is what enables us to recognise as a chair an object that has the attributes of a chair, but which is different to any chair that we have ever seen before. We also have schemas that enable us to recognise the people we know, a set of schemas for places that enable us to wake up and recognise that we are on a train going to London rather than at home in bed. And importantly, in relation to our concerns in this chapter, we have schemas that enable us to recognise text types, and to process and recall texts. The analogy often used to explain schemas is that of a template with a number of slots, and provided a reasonable number of these are filled, the brain makes a working assumption that the presence of the recognised object is confirmed.

It is worth commenting on how good the brain is at utilising schemas and at recognising things for what they are, often on the basis of very partial information. Computers – even with the astonishing parallel processing power now available – are still way behind humans at recognising an object that is rotated, or presented so that we only see it from a very shallow angle (think too about our ability to recognise for who they are our family and friends in photographs that we have not seen previously, and to see as people we do not know the hundreds of people we pass in a shopping centre, many of whom have a general similarity to people we do know).

The concept of text schemas was given a very prominent place in the 1980s by the research group that led a number of enquiries into learning from school texts, and particularly learning from information texts. The work of Richard Anderson and his associates on schema theory (much of which was summarised by Schallert, 1982), based in the US national research centre on reading, led to a much greater awareness of the fact that (a) text schemas could enable us to understand why textbooks were so difficult for learners (the texts were often 'inconsiderate') and (b) an understanding of text schemas could help us plan better teaching and learning.

Text schemas operate in a similar manner to genres, in that the presence of a schema may be signalled at the phrase level, but operates at the whole text or macrostructure level. The other insight that came from schema theorists is that information texts are not simply a single genre (non-chronological as opposed to chronological, for example). Schema-theoretic approaches focused on a range of text types, some of which were narrative (for example detective stories or romance novels), and some of which were non-narrative (for example lectures, news articles, research articles, sports reports and house sales information).

One of the best known experiments on the importance of schema activation was that carried out by Bransford and Johnson (1972). The task was a simple one – to recall as much as possible from a stimulus passage, and participants were either given, or not given, a title. The text was written in a rather unspecific way, as you can see:

> *The procedure is actually quite simple. First you arrange things into different groups. Of course, one pile may be sufficient depending on how much there is to do. If you have to go somewhere else due to lack of facilities, that is the next step; otherwise you are pretty well set. It is important not to overdo things. That is, it is better to do too few things at once than too many. In the short run this may not seem important, but complications can easily arise. A mistake can be expensive as well. At first the whole procedure will seem complicated. Soon, however, it will become just another facet of life. It is difficult to foresee any end to the necessity for this task in the immediate future, but then one never can tell. After the procedure is completed, one arranges the materials into different groups again. Then they can be put into their appropriate places. Eventually they will be used once more, and the whole cycle will then have to be repeated. However, that is part of life.*

Recalling this text in detail is extremely difficult, especially if the reader is not able to activate a schema while reading it. In the experiment, however, participants who were told in advance that this text was about washing clothes recalled far more of the text than those who were given no title. Knowledge, and even more importantly activation, of the appropriate schema enabled them to link the rather ambiguously expressed details to the schema, and then to store and recall those details. This experiment gives triumphant support for those teachers who teach by the maxim: 'tell 'em what you are going to tell 'em; tell 'em what you have to tell 'em; tell 'em what you just told them'. Put the other way, we could say that research into schema activation encourages us to activate the schemas of our learners before, not after, we introduce new material. We shall return to this theme in the next chapter, when we come to discuss the importance of activating prior knowledge.

Schema-based studies have provided other insights into how we process and understand texts. The celebrated study of Pichert and Anderson (1977), which reported participants' recall of the description of the inside of a house, established that activating one schema rather than another has a significant influence on what gets highlighted and what gets remembered from a test. Readers were given one of two sets of instructions, one inviting the reader to read the text from the point of view of a potential burglar, and the other inviting the reader to read the text from the point of view of a potential purchaser. Participants recalled more information that was relevant to their particular schema, which suggested strongly that schemas have an executive effect in determining storage and recall. Another interesting finding was that in a subsequent task, participants were able to recall previously unrecalled propositions from the second perspective. This finding suggests that under certain circumstances we are able to revive information by using a different schema. In any event, it seems clear that schemas help us to organise learning and have a significant impact on how much we are able to recall. In Chapters 5, 6 and 7 we shall look at the application of DARTs activities to texts, and it is worth mentioning that these approaches are very much in harmony with a schema theoretic approach. The Effective Use of Reading team (Lunzer and Gardner, 1979) worked with Richard Anderson during the time that DARTs were being piloted, and there were reciprocal visits between the leaders of the two research centres.

Propositional models of text processing

Research into learning from texts that adopts a macrostructure approach, such as we see in schema theory or in scripts, is good at both describing how texts work and at highlighting a number of aspects of how learners learn. But these approaches tend to fall apart when they are applied to real-time models of information processing. For a start, we don't operate just one schema at a time. We can have several schemas active at once, just as a computer user can have several programs running at the same time, and this can make it impossibly difficult to predict how the memory is functioning. Next, schema theory would predict that we should drop inconsistent or unexpected information, data that didn't fit in with the schema, but that isn't what happens. Quite often, unexpected or irrelevant information is that which is best remembered.

There are also problems from a computational point of view. Once artificial intelligence (AI) models were applied to test the adequacy of scripts, they proved too inflexible to serve the purpose for which they were designed (Schank, 1982). AI researchers found that they couldn't model learning and transfer of learning using scripts, because either the scripts had to be fully elaborated and fixed (which they clearly were not) or they had to accommodate an endless proliferation of subscripts in order to mimic both the temporal flexibility and the contextual variability of how scripts were used and understood in the real world.

AI approaches needed to begin with processing units that were much smaller than the macrostructure elements of scripts and schemas, and produce a model that began at the propositional level with small units, but had the potential to combine these in powerful ways in order to reflect how the brain deals with large and complex texts. The model we shall look at that attempts this is the construction-integration (CI) model of Walter Kintsch. His model combines a construction process in which a text base is constructed from the linguistic input as well as the comprehender's knowledge base with an integration phase in which this text base is integrated into a coherent whole (Kintsch, 1988, p. 164). In simple terms the construction-integration model says that a person learns by integrating new concepts into the existing complex of the mind, thus creating new mental structures. Initially the construction phase can be very inefficient, and during it the learner makes false starts, errors and misjudgments, but the integration phase is much more efficient and in this phase new concepts are integrated into the mind such that the new knowledge makes most sense in relation to existing knowledge. The CI model sees all knowledge as being related to a greater or lesser degree, and it is a testament to the power of the brain that it can usually make links between quite diverse concepts at astonishing speed. It is also the case that on this analysis the structure of the mind is permanently unstable and reordering itself, because we are constantly experiencing things and we are always open to the potential of new knowledge.

The CI model was originally described by Walter Kintsch in his paper for the *Psychological Review*, 'The role of knowledge in discourse comprehension: a construction-integration model' (Kintsch, 1988). The CI model is described as related to but an improvement on earlier models of text comprehension processes, as developed by Fletcher (1985), Kintsch and Greeno (1985) and Dellarosa (1986). Kintsch recognised that although each of these models had strengths, their weaknesses were too significant to make them viable. Kintsch showed how each of these models worked in a top-down manner, seeking to impose hard rules on comprehension. However, there were simply too many situations for comprehension, which meant that the rules had to be almost infinitely flexible, and this flexibility meant that the rules needed to be adapted to individual contexts in ways that were ultimately unworkable. As an alternative, Kintsch sought a flexible, inherently soft approach to the problem of comprehension, which allowed for the multiplicity of situations which need to be comprehended on a daily basis. This was the construction-integration model of text comprehension.

Kintsch argued that knowledge needed to be represented by 'an associative net, the nodes of which are concepts or propositions' (Kintsch, 1988, p. 165). He went on to show how comprehension is sloppy, inefficient but ultimately effective. Using various examples, including the word 'bank', the sentence 'Lucy persuaded Mary to bake a cake', and longer, more ambiguous words and phrases, Kintsch demonstrated how the mind identifies every word, and begins with the possibility of any of the meanings of each word available from the comprehender's knowledge base. In this manner, potential meaning is constructed. The mind goes on to then analyse these potential meanings of each word and sentence, known as the text base, in terms of the other lexical units involved in the sentence or text. The mind needs to do this in order to discard all the unwanted units of meaning which are not appropriate for the sentence in hand. This is the integration process, which will 'exclude these unwanted elements from the text representation' (Kintsch, 1988, p.168). Kintsch acknowledged that this was inefficient:

> *Of course, such a process will inevitably activate a lot of material that is irrelevant for any given context and, indeed, inconsistent with it. However, the price that has to be paid for promiscuity is not very high: the resulting text base is a connectionist net in which further spreading activation processes rapidly take care of inconsistencies and irrelevancies.*
>
> (Kintsch, 1988, p. 180)

In essence, a Darwinian, 'survival of the fittest' semantic battle for dominance develops, whereby the most appropriate meaning is established and other, less successful meanings are discarded. Subsequently, Kintsch developed and applied the model in *Comprehension: A Paradigm for Cognition* (Kintsch, 1998). Essentially, Kintsch's project was to describe how people learn from text, which is perhaps the principal means of transmission of knowledge in traditional educational settings. In the introduction to *Comprehension: A Paradigm for Cognition*, Kintsch discusses his use of the word 'comprehension'. He uses 'comprehension' and 'understanding' as 'synonyms' (Kintsch, 1998, p. 2), and he contrasts the verbs 'to understand' and 'to perceive',

> *In ordinary usage,* perceive *is used for simple or isolated instances of perception, especially when no specific action is involved.* Understand *is used when the relationship between some object and its context is at issue or when action is required.*
>
> (Kintsch, 1998, p. 2)

In essence, perception is seen as primarily activating visual and semantic memories, while understanding involves making new connections between nodes in semantic memory. An example of perception would be interpreting 'The sky is blue', while an example of understanding would be interpreting 'The sky is blue because of the effects of the earth's atmosphere on the light from the sun'. The first example involves making an observation which is unchallenged and automatic, while the second example involves more direct knowledge of the effects of nature.

Both perception and understanding are described as processes of constraint satisfaction, i.e. the process by which particular criteria or parameters are met by an individual's cognitive activity. The key difference is that perception is automatic, while understanding, or comprehension, involves consciously structuring and ordering thought processes to successfully complete a problem. This process can be 'quite chaotic in its early stages' (Kintsch, 1998, p. 94), but it settles down when the mind has discarded the elements of an idea which do not fit, accepted the elements which do fit and placed them as part of the existing structure of the mind. Thus comprehension works in a 'bottom-up manner that is followed by a constraint satisfaction process in the form of a spreading activation mechanism and that yields the coherence and order that we experience' (Kintsch, 1998, p. 94).

Comprehension in two stages: the textbase and the situation model

Kintsch's model suggests that the comprehension of texts takes place in two stages. The first is the process of identifying the lexical and grammatical information in the text; the second is the process of integrating this knowledge into the current mental state, and updating one's mental model of the world as a result. The basic information derived from the text Kintsch calls the textbase. The more complex evolving mental model of the world Kintsch calls the situation model. The principal idea of the textbase is that it is constructed simply of the words and their interrelationship with the other words on the page. The textbase has various components, including the propositional structure and the surface structure of a text. The situation model, by contrast, is closer to the end-product of comprehension: 'A situation model is ... a construction that integrates the textbase and relevant aspects of the comprehender's knowledge' (Kintsch, 1998, p. 107). There are similarities between this contrasting pair of concepts, 'knowledge telling' and 'knowledge transforming', as described by Bereiter and Scardamalia in relation to composition studies (Bereiter and Scardamalia, 1987). One could say that when a reader has developed his or her understanding of a text from the textbase to the situation model, then real learning has occurred and a significant stage of the CI model has been completed.

Propositional analysis

Kintsch attempts to prove this theory through the use of propositional analysis of texts. The method of a propositional analysis involves the breaking down of a text into its most basic elements of meaning, propositions. A proposition is the phrase Kintsch uses to describe 'a predicate-argument schema' (Kintsch, 1998, p. 37) which is inferred as a 'basic unit of language' (ibid.). A somewhat more simple way of describing propositions was offered by Sue Palmer (2000) in the UK government's *Grammatical Knowledge for Teachers* website, where propositions were described as composed of a 'chunk of nouniness' and a 'chunk of verbiness'. However, propositions have varying levels of complexity, with atomic propositions at the most basic level. These consist of 'a relational term, the predicate, and one or more arguments'. More complex propositions are 'compounds composed of several atomic propositions that are subordinated to a core propositional meaning' (Kintsch, 1998, p. 38).

As we shall see, propositional analysis is complicated and unwieldy. It is not only much less intuitively attractive than schema theory or other accounts of text processing that make use of natural language, it makes the analysis of complex texts extraordinarily difficult. But Kintsch argues that if propositional analysis offers not only a principled theory for how the brain constructs meaning from text, but also seems to fit in with what we know about how the brain might build knowledge systems from nodes and associative networks, then we have to try to cope with the complexity and to develop testable models of how such a system might work. Kintsch puts the point this way: 'Propositions are designed to capture those semantic relations that are most salient in text comprehension, whereas natural language serves many purposes other than representation that is based on meaning' (Kintsch, 1998, p. 69). We might add to this the fact that the breaking down of a text into propositions allows for a statistical, and in that sense an objective and potentially computational, analysis of the semantic relationships both within and between different texts.

If propositional analysis offers us the best model currently available of how the brain builds up understanding of texts, then it is worth spending a little time trying to see not only what a propositionalised text looks like, but also what happens when we use such an analysis to look at how readers store and recall material from a science text. This is what we shall attempt in the next section of the chapter. John Perry, co-author of this chapter, who at the time of writing was a part-time doctoral student in the University of Nottingham as well as full-time Head of English in a comprehensive school in Cornwall, carried out the fieldwork in this case study of propositional analysis in action.

Kintsch provides a very thorough and useful guide to propositionalising texts (Kintsch, 1998, p. 54), to which we would refer the reader for a more detailed account of how to analyse texts into propositions. Suffice it to say that we attempted to follow Kintsch's guide as closely as possible when propositionalising the texts that are described in the next section.

A case study of learning from a science text

The three children who worked with us were from Year 7 (in England this is equivalent to sixth grade in the US), and the text on which they were asked to work was a section from a Y8 science textbook, *Spotlight Science 8* (Johnson, Adamson and Williams, 1994, p. 102). We wanted to use an example of a traditional textbook, since these remain the main reading resource in most secondary school classrooms. There are some problems with regarding textbooks as the principal texts within schools, but we share the view of Wade and Moje that 'a class set of a single textbook [remains] the main source of reading material in most content classrooms' (Wade and Moje, 2000, p. 612). A science textbook was chosen because learning could be more easily gauged and we knew it was a subject that was enjoyed by the children who agreed to participate. In order to reduce prior knowledge effects, a textbook from the following year's science curriculum was chosen. In the event it became clear that the children had previously studied some of the subject matter, not at secondary school, but in primary school, and we shall return to this theme when discussing their levels of prior knowledge later in this chapter. Because they had studied some of the subject matter before and were all interested in science, it could also be argued that the participants were on the cusp of being 'experts' as described by Kintsch, Patel and Ericsson (1999, p. 188). This will become significant later when we go on to discuss the role of long-term working memory (LTWM), a concept which Kintsch considers separately from LTM.

The topic of the source text used in this case study was photosynthesis – how energy is transferred from the sun through plant matter to animals and humans. The textbook is relatively modern and uses colour and illustrations extensively, but we decided to give the readers a rewritten version without the illustrations in order to maximise the opportunity to focus on learning from the propositional content of the passage. However, although we dispensed with colour and illustrations, we chose to keep titles and subheadings because these were integral to the print information of the original text. The revised version, as presented to the students, is reproduced in Figure 3.3.

The three students, David, Amy and Naomi, were all of above average intelligence and had reading age scores at least three years above their chronological age of eleven. All three were popular and articulate children and came from similar backgrounds. The area in which they lived, near the south-west tip of England, is one of the most socio-economically deprived

Energy from the Sun

Making food

Green plants can capture energy in sunlight. The green chemical in their leaves in called **chlorophyll**. It **absorbs** the Sun's energy and uses it to make food. It also makes oxygen for us to breathe. This process is called **photo-synthesis**.

Because plants make food, they are called producers. Animals eat this food – they are consumers. For example, energy could transfer from the Sun to vegetables to humans. This is called a **food-energy chain**.

Biofuel

Plants and animal materials are called **biomass**. As well as being food, biomass can give us energy in other ways:

- Wood is fuel. It can be burnt to give energy for heating.
- In Brazil they grow sugar cane, and they use the sugar to make alcohol. The alcohol is then used in cars, instead of petrol.
- Rotting plants and animal manure can make a gas called methane. This is like the gas you use in a Bunsen burner. If the plants rot in a closed tank, called a **digester**, this gas can be piped away. This is often used in China and India.

Figure 3.3 Source text: energy from the sun. Adapted from *Spotlight Science 8* (Johnson, Adamson and Williams, 1994, p. 102). Emboldened emphasis retained from the source text

areas in the country. The main industry was formerly tin mining, but with the closure of all mines in the county, unemployment rates have risen to one in five males. Nevertheless, the school is generally perceived as a lively place in which to work, with many enthusiastic students of all academic abilities.

The goal of this small study was to explore the students' recall using a propositional analysis to map the relationship between the source text and their verbally recalled representations of the text. The first response was to be an immediate oral recall task, administered to each participant individually and recorded on an audio tape recorder. These responses were then transcribed and broken down into propositions for analysis. In order to familiarise the students with having their responses tape-recorded, the students had previously been asked to provide a tape-recorded verbal protocol on the Towers of Hanoi problem (Ericsson and Simon, 1993, p. 333).

The study took place over a series of lunchtimes in a quiet office adjoining a classroom. The students were asked to read the source text twice. Then each was asked to recall '… everything you can remember from the sheet.' They had also been asked not to discuss the source text with each other. Five weeks later, David, Amy and Naomi were asked to repeat the process, without again seeing the source text. The aim of this was to determine the extent to which the text had become embedded in the subjects' LTM.

Following the propositional analysis of the source text and of each of the subjects' protocols, the amount of overlap was measured by simply determining which propositions in the subjects' responses matched the propositions in the source text. Inevitably an amount of leeway was allowed for, as it was unlikely that the subjects' responses would exactly match the source text. David, for example, began his recall in the following way:

> *OK, um, green plants can absorb energy from the sun and that's called, um, chlorophyll or something*

A propositional analysis of the relevant content of his recall yielded the following:

1. ABSORB [GREEN-PLANTS[ENERGY-FROM-SUN]]

           CALLED [CHLOROPHYLL]

It was matched against propositions 2, 3 and 4 from the source text:

1. MAKING [FOOD]
2. CAPTURE [ENERGY-IN-SUNLIGHT [GREEN-PLANTS]]
3. CALLED [GREEN-CHEMICAL [CHLOROPHYLL]], IN [LEAVES]
4. ABSORBS [C^1[SUN'S ENERGY]], USES-TO-MAKE [FOOD]

We were naturally not anticipating complete semantic overlap, but instead looked for substantial of overlap of propositions representing concepts common to the two texts. The analysis of the source text showed that there were 19 propositions in total, the majority of which were complex propositions. The text followed a path of increasing semantic complexity as it progressed from discussing the process of energy transfer to illustrating the process with examples. To put it another way, the text progressed from theory to application.

In the immediate recall task, subjects' answers varied in length from four propositions long to seven propositions. The three students felt that they were struggling to remember the details of the source text, but in fact virtually everything they said could be related directly to the source text through propositional analysis. In the immediate recall task David produced the smallest number of propositions, four, although they were all complex propositions, and these overlapped with more than four propositions from the source. Despite using only four propositions, the amount of propositional overlap between his text and the source text equated to 32 per cent. Amy performed more effectively with seven propositions, most of which were complex propositions. With Amy's text and the source text there was a 53 per cent overlap of matching propositions. Naomi did not fare quite as well as Amy with an overlap of 41 per cent.

However, it is not appropriate to draw too many conclusions from such raw figures. There are two main problems with such data. The first problem (even if our somewhat subjective procedures for identifying propositional overlap are regarded as unproblematic), as identified by Kintsch, is that the verbal reports based on immediate recall do not necessarily show deep learning of concepts. Immediate recall may simply be based on the reproduction from LTWM and from text-level processing alone. Kintsch discusses the difference between text memory and learning from text thus:

> *I define learning from text as the ability to use the information acquired from the text productively in novel environments ... Mere text memory, on the other hand, may remain inert knowledge – reproducible given the right retrieval cues but not an active component of the reader's knowledge base.*
>
> (Kintsch, 1998, p. 290)

To express the idea in a slightly different form, the difference between text memory and learning from text is the difference between the textbase and the situation model, as described earlier in this chapter. Unfortunately, the extent to which the students moved from a textbase to a situation model is difficult to determine in such a modest case study example.

The second problem in estimating the distance travelled from textbase towards a situation model of the text is related to the subjects' prior knowledge about the information covered by the source text. Their prior knowledge was gauged simply by asking the students after they had completed the recall task what they knew about the subject beforehand. All three reported that they had encountered a basic definition of photosynthesis, but were unfamiliar with the rest of the text. The propositional overlap was recalculated, this time discounting from both source text and verbal recalls any propositions that dealt with photosynthesis. The new figures are shown in the middle column of Table 3.1.

Table 3.1 Percentage of propositional content recalled by David

Name	Immediate recall %	Immediate recall, prior knowledge subtracted %	Delayed recall, prior knowledge subtracted %
David	32	21	14
Naomi	42	36	29
Amy	53	50	50

However, the figures that we have discussed so far can strictly be described as relating to text recall, rather than true learning, since the recalls were gathered within ten minutes of the subjects reading the source text. In order to provide a stronger indicator of learning the students were asked again to recall the source text some four weeks later. There are problems with this approach. It could be argued that simply retesting the subjects after a few weeks does not necessarily measure true learning, but rather 'mere text memory' (Kintsch, 1998, p. 290) which has successfully been assimilated into the subject's long-term memory. In order to gauge true learning, each subject would have to prove their ability to apply the concepts covered by the original source text in a new environment. Kintsch discusses this problem at length, and he is clear about the need for 'empirical methods to assess learning separately from memory' (Kintsch, 1998, p. 295). However, he is also clear about the difficulties of such an enterprise,

> ... because learning and memory cannot be separated even in the theory (textbase and situation model are not two separate structures, but the text-driven and knowledge-driven components of a single structure) ... measurement procedures are not precisely separable into textbase and situation model measures, either.
>
> (Kintsch, 1998, p. 295)

Kintsch develops his response to the problem by discussing various attempts to determine learning from text, including the traditional method of most teachers, asking questions. Yet interestingly for us as educators, this is dismissed as a very unreliable guide to the measurement of learning from text, '...because we do not have a detailed theory of question answering' (Kintsch, 1998, p. 296). An approach which Kintsch suggests is to argue that if learning from text occurs, each subject's knowledge organisation should have changed in accordance with the text organisation. It is a measurement of this type, using propositional analyses, which perhaps offers some basis for exploring embedded learning, and an analysis of delayed recall might be more useful in this respect. The percentage recall of propositions in the delayed recall task is given in the third column of Table 3.1.

From the third column of Table 3.1 the extent of deep learning for each participant becomes clearer. David's immediate recall score was lower than that of both Naomi and Amy, and his delayed recall recovered only 14 per cent of the propositional content of the source text after prior knowledge had been taken into account. Naomi's text recall also decreased over the month, but what is interesting is the extent of Amy's text recall. Although on both occasions her propositional recall was lower when prior knowledge was accounted for, as would be expected, her ability to recall text did not decrease over the month between testing occasions. This suggests that the text had become embedded in LTM and points towards significant learning.

Another piece of evidence that points towards real learning is related to her specific semantic transformations of the words of the text. As the following extract makes clear, Amy's utterances are not simply based on verbatim recall, but rather are rephrasings that cover the same propositional content as the original protocol:

Teacher: *What can you remember about the text we read last month?*

Amy: *Um ... there was something called biomass and fuel can be made from wood and there was a thing called a digester and it used plants or something and they rotted down and it made methane gas which powered something and it was used in India or China or somewhere like that ...*

We have tried to suggest in this section that propositional analysis, though clearly impractical in most classroom contexts, nevertheless offers some important insights into aspects of text processing, comprehension and learning. In brief, propositional analysis is attractive because it offers a basis for looking at text processing that is in harmony with what we currently believe about how the brain functions. It starts with a bottom-up 'small units' approach, based on (a) a semantic memory process that is initially sloppy and provisional but that rapidly becomes powerful and efficient in integrating and predicting information, and (b) the processing of atomic propositions that can easily be nested and embedded in levels of increasing complexity, and built up into macro-level models of text structure.

However, as we have acknowledged, propositional analysis is slow, subjective and very poor at dealing with larger texts. In the final section of this chapter, therefore, we shall take a look at one of the most exciting computer-based approaches to looking at learning from text, latent semantic analysis (LSA). Latent semantic analysis is fast, objective and very good at dealing with large texts. It is also complex mathematically and problematic for a variety of reasons. But we want to suggest that it is far too important to ignore in the context of discussing how we learn from text.

Latent semantic analysis

LSA has been developed by several researchers, some of whom have worked very closely with Kintsch at the University of Colorado, notably

Thomas Landauer, Susan Dumais and Peter Foltz (Landauer and Dumais, 1997; Foltz, Kintsch and Landauer, 1998). Essentially, it is a computerised method of analysing whole texts in a manner that is believed to have a good deal in common with the way in which the brain works. Kintsch described the brain as having an architecture that uses

> ... *simple, bottom-up rules to construct a preliminary but incoherent propositional network, followed by a spreading activation process that integrates this network into a coherent mental representation.*
>
> (Kintsch, 1998, p. 6)

The Colorado team have constructed a computer program that in many important respects attempts to replicate this process. LSA uses a statistical technique that builds a model of meaning by constructing an *n*-dimensional semantic map from any source text that can then be compared with a much larger semantic map built up from an analysis of millions of words of text. The semantic map generated by LSA is a complex one: *n* can be in the range 300–1,000 dimensions, and the map holds information on the distance between all the words as they co-occur, or tend not to co-occur, in a text. The words *dog*, *cat* and *pet* do not mean the same thing, but they tend to occur together, or at least to co-occur more frequently than *dog*, *idea* and *spa*, and this co-occurrence, so the theory goes, is indicative of semantic relatedness: meaning is defined very simply – in terms of semantic relatedness:

> *LSA provides a fully automatic method for comparing units of textual information to each other to determine their semantic relatedness. These units of text are compared to each other using a derived measure of their similarity of meaning. This measure is based on a powerful mathematical analysis of direct and indirect relations among words and passages in a large training corpus. Semantic relatedness should correspond to a measure of coherence because it captures the extent to which two text units are discussing semantically related information.*
>
> (Foltz, Kintsch and Landauer, 1998, p. 286)

The implications of such a computer-based system of analysis are massive, for two reasons. First, Landauer suggests that LSA might provide a basis for modelling all human knowledge acquisition; second, LSA provides an automated basis for comparing readers' representations of a source text with the source text itself – in other words, it gives us an on-line method for estimating a reader's comprehension.

Landauer describes LSA as:

> *... a possible theory about all human knowledge acquisition, ... a homologue of an important underlying mechanism of human cognition in general. In particular, the model employs a means of induction-dimension matching that greatly amplifies its learning ability, allowing it to correctly infer indirect similarity relations only implicit in the temporal correlations of experience. It exhibits human-like generalization that is based on learning and that does not rely on primitive perceptual or conceptual relations or representations.*
>
> (Landuaer and Dumais, 1997, Overview)

Thus it is claimed that LSA operates in the same way as the human mind, and this is where the 'latent' comes in: the *n*-dimensional map of semantic relations that is built up is generative and has the potential to create new associations that were not input directly. Just as a conceptual map of a town held in the head of a person who has just moved in is based on bits of initially unrelated information that the brain pieces together but which are integrated into a larger map that permits that person to set off confidently on a journey that he or she has never made before, so the mappings generated by LSM permit associations to be built up from the training corpus that are different from and go beyond the mappings input from any single input text.

The advantage of LSA for the present study is that it provides a useful scale against which the propositional analyses of both the source text and the participants' responses can be measured. Using the University of Colorado's website dedicated to LSA, which enables visitors to the site to input text and carry out an LSA analysis, it is possible to predict what learning might occur from a particular text and to compare the semantic relatedness of two or more texts. This very generous research opportunity is of course also a highly dangerous one: LSA does not measure comprehension – it measures a correlate of comprehension, namely the semantic relatedness of source and secondary text (for example a text-book extract and a student's summary of that text).

One particularly useful aspect of LSA is that it can show the closeness of the relationship between two texts in a very simple way: by a cosine score. The totality of the semantic interrelatedness in Text A can be reduced to a single vector, an arrow in semantic hyperspace as it were, that can be understood in coordinate geometry terms as representing a unique location determined by all the words that are present and more or less closely related to the other words in the passage. If the source text and secondary text are very closely related, the vector generated by each passage will be similar, and the cosine, representing the angle between the two vectors, will be high (with a theoretical maximum of 1.0, generally this means it will approach 0.9); if the texts are poorly related or unrelated, the cosine will be low (perhaps 0.15) and will approach 0 if they are in different languages.

Research papers published by the LSA group provide plenty of evidence of the efficacy of what might be seen by some as a rather 'black-box' approach to semantic analysis of text. Experimental studies have shown, for example, that LSA is technically a more reliable instrument for judging the adequacy of summaries of a text written by students than are many teachers (Landauer and Dumais, 1997). The team also produced an 'Intelligent Essay Assessor' (1999), and has shown that when students write a multi-paragraph summary of a long text, the cosine scores of individual paragraphs can be used by students to learn more about the adequacy of their summary-writing abilities. For example, if a set of six paragraphs has a run of cosine scores that goes 0.6, 0.2, 0.6, 0.6, 0.6, 0.6, it may well be the case that the second paragraph is either redundant or is perhaps a less coherent representation of the source text (Landauer and Kintsch, 1999).

It is much to their credit that the LSA team have given plenty of health warnings about the possible misuses of LSA data. Just as it can be dangerous to misuse computer-generated data on the readability of text (for example by denying a highly motivated reader access to a text they want to read on the grounds that it is rated by a readability formula as 'too difficult'), so it can be very unwise to assume that a high LSA cosine score inevitably means that a reader has understood a text. Clearly a close to verbatim transcription of a source text would produce a cosine score approaching 1.0 but might not necessarily imply understanding. Far more encouraging might be a lower cosine, but one generated by a reader who had transformed the text and integrated it coherently into their own knowledge system. The extent to which LSA can be fooled is acknowledged with disarming frankness by the research team, who point out that LSA looks at semantic proximity data but not grammar or word order. In other words, if you input as the secondary text the source text typed in reverse order, starting with the final word of the passage, LSA would generate exactly the same vector based on semantic proximities as the source text, and would give a cosine score of 1.0.

LSA offers a number of different approaches to describing semantic relatedness. 'Near Neighbours', for example demonstrates the semantic relatedness of words in a source and can suggest a cosine value that equates to what it might be reasonable to expect a first-year undergraduate to understand. For example, the program predicted an understanding with a cosine score of 0.42 for the word 'photosynthesis', but a higher cosine score of 0.51 for the word 'energy'.

In the present case study we generated cosine scores using the 'Document-to-Document Matrix Comparison' method, which allows a user to compare a number of texts with each other and computes scores reflecting the degree of semantic relatedness between all the texts. In the case of our participants, this analysis was based on protocols generated on the delayed recall task, and in order to focus on new knowledge, propositions dealing with photosynthesis were deleted from both source and protocol texts. To prepare the texts for computer analysis, we also deleted hesitations (there were initially a lot of occurrences of 'um' in the transcripts), and did some minor editing (LSA knew about *photosynthesis*, for example, but not about *photo-synthesis*, the hyphenated form of the word used in the source text). Just to see what would happen, we also took one of the protocols, that of Naomi, and reversed all the words in the text. Figure 3.4 shows the texts that we submitted to LSA for analysis.

Source text
Because plants make food, they are called producers. Animals eat this food – they are consumers. For example, energy could transfer from the Sun to vegetables to humans. This is called a food energy chain. Plants and animal materials are called biomass. As well as being food, biomass can give us energy in other forms. Wood is fuel. It can be burnt to give energy for heating. In Brazil they grow sugar cane, and then use the sugar to make alcohol. The alcohol is then used in cars, instead of petrol. Rotting plants and animal manure can make a gas called methane. This is like the gas you use in a Bunsen burner. If the plants rot in a closed tank, called a digester, the gas can be piped away. This is often in China and India.

David's delayed recall protocol
Plant and animal materials are called biomass and animal manure it makes a gas called methane and this is used in Bunsen burners because when it rots in enclosed areas the gas can be piped away.

Naomi's delayed recall protocol
I remember the plant and animal materials is called biomass; wood is burned to make fuel because fire burns. In Brazil they use sugar and make it into alcohol to fuel their cars

Naomi's delayed recall protocol (text reversed)
cars their fuel to alcohol into it make and sugar use they Brazil In burns fire because fuel make to burned is wood biomass called is materials animal and plant the remember I

Amy's delayed recall protocol
Plants also produce oxygen plants are the producers because, the animals are consumers because they eat the plants. Animals and plants are like a biomass and if you rot plants and things down it produces methane gas and if you put that into a digester then it will suck the gas away and it's used in places like China and India and the plants and the consumers and stuff are a food energy chain I think. Just biomass really, and that wood is a fuel but can be burned to make heat energy.

Figure 3.4 Texts submitted to LSA for analysis

As can be seen from Table 3.2, what we found tied in remarkably well with our own subjective judgments of recall accuracy and coherence. Compared with the source text, the participants generated the following cosine scores: David, 0.48, Naomi, 0.54 and Amy, 0.82. Clearly these scores are indicative only of the nature of the three participants' understanding, but we would want to suggest that they do indeed reflect what we felt was suggested by the recall protocols, namely that David's poor recall was indicative of limited depth of processing (even though there was some verbatim recall), that Naomi's recall suggested at least some of the material had been stored in LTWM and that Amy's protocol offered at least some indications of deep processing and knowledge transformation in LTM. Finally, as predicted, Naomi's score was precisely the same when her text was entered with the words in the reverse order.

Table 3.2 Cosine scores of LSA document-to-document matrix comparison of texts (photosynthesis propositions deleted from source text and recall protocols)

Document	Source text	David's delayed recall score	Naomi's delayed recall score	Naomi's score with text reversed	Amy's delayed recall score
Source text	1.00	0.48	0.54	0.54	0.82
David's delayed recall score	0.48	1.00	0.45	0.45	0.42
Naomi's delayed recall score	0.54	0.45	1.00	1.00	0.37
Naomi's score with text reversed	0.54	0.45	1.00	1.00	0.37
Amy's delayed recall score	0.82	0.42	0.37	0.37	1.00

Our conclusions therefore from these two excursions into propositional analysis and latent semantic analysis have to be cautiously optimistic. Propositional analysis is both tedious and difficult to do, but it is attractive for a number of reasons: it works how we think the brain works – starting with small units, starting with provisionality, and building up into larger units with exponentially increasing accuracy and coherence. All of this is highly relevant to our central theme in this chapter, namely how we think humans learn from texts.

Latent semantic analysis, by contrast, is dangerous precisely because it is neither tedious nor difficult to do (though the mathematics behind it is complex), and while its ease of use is an attraction, this needs to be set alongside the problem that many of those who might explore its use have little understanding of how the semantic vectors are calculated and of how fragile the whole edifice becomes if a whole range of constraints are not met (for example, if key words in a source text are not in the training corpus or not present often enough).

But there are also plenty of good reasons for paying LSM some serious attention. First, the theoretical architecture that underpins LSM has many similarities with how we think the brain might work. Its model of meaning is based purely on semantic networks, and while this will be far too close for comfort to connectionist models of cognition for many psychologists, such models do at least begin to explore the problem space of human learning in ways that can be tested at the neurone level and then generalised to other areas of functioning. Second, LSA learns: it can now pass tests of vocabulary knowledge aimed at English as a second or additional language learners, and what it 'knows' about word meaning in English is more than simply the data that was entered to build the training corpus. Third, and most importantly, it can help us understand how people learn from texts: provided it is used thoughtfully, LSA is a very powerful tool that can enable us to understand more about how people process information and integrate it with previous knowledge.

There is still plenty that LSA does not do: not only is it negligent of word order, it understands little of morphology, grammar and pragmatics, and although vocabulary is important we know from readability research that grammatical complexity contributes around 15 per cent of the variance in studies of what makes texts difficult (vocabulary contributes around 40 per cent), and that the contribution of grammar is independent of the contribution of vocabluary. But despite these caveats we would argue that LSA should continue to be regarded as one of the most exciting areas of current research into how we learn from texts: its ease of use and its proven utility in a wide range of areas of comprehension and cognition mean that it can only continue to gain attention in the field of reading and reading development. And it is to the field of reading development that we now turn in Chapter 4.

Developing reading comprehension – what we have learned from research

Introduction

There is no problem in locating research studies into reading development that go beyond the initial stages. The greater challenge is that of deciding which studies have been the important ones in terms of both the rigour of the research and the significance of the findings for practice. Because supporting the development of readers is so important, a number of researchers and research groups have attempted reviews of the field, and naturally enough these reviews have produced some helpful overlap in relation to agreement on key findings, but there have also been some significant differences that reflect the methodological preferences and ideology of the researchers. In writing this chapter I have drawn upon my own research into reading comprehension over the past 25 years, but I have also attempted a synthesis working from key research studies and important reviews of research. Some of these reviews of research have a bibliography that is composed of several hundred references (in some cases, the references section is more than twice the length of the review), and rather than include in this chapter many pages of references that might be irrelevant for most readers, I have aimed to cite the key studies, and for scholars who want to dig deeper to provide a reference (ideally an Internet reference to a government or university website) leading to a fuller bibliography.

In this chapter we shall give detailed attention to the conclusions of the US National Reading Panel (NRP) in relation to the research base underpinning reading instruction beyond the initial stages (NRP, 2000a). The Panel was composed of a group of eminent researchers that had been charged by the US Congress to assess the extent of our 'research-based knowledge' in relation to the teaching of reading. Because its recommendations included the teaching of initial reading, and because it took a robust line that excluded some studies, just about everything related to the Panel's work, from its criteria for selecting 'scientific' studies to its 'findings and determinations', was regarded by many academics as highly problematic. Nevertheless, in this chapter we shall devote space to reporting some of the Panel's key findings, both because of the thoroughness of the research review process and because of the importance of what was concluded. We shall also review the key conclusions and recommendations of other important US studies into comprehension and reading development.

Reviews of the research underpinning reading instruction have not been confined to the US. In the UK, as in the US, there have been government-sponsored reviews of the research underpinning literacy instruction. In the mid-1990s the then Scottish Office Education Department commissioned a review of research on the teaching of reading, a version of which was widely distributed to schools as part of the *Interchange* programme (Harrison, 1996). In England, the government commissioned a review of research underpinning the National Literacy Strategy (Beard, 1999) which was widely read and cited, and which has been reproduced in a revised form on government websites and in journal articles (Beard, 2000).

More recently, the team responsible for the National Literacy Strategy in England commissioned an update of Beard's review (*The National Literacy Strategy: Roots and Research*, Harrison, 2002a) that was circulated to literacy coordinators and secondary schools in England and also published electronically (Harrison, 2002b). This review took account of the NRP report, and also that of Catherine Snow and her co-workers (Snow, Burns and Griffin, 1998a), whose review of research into preventing reading difficulties in young children had in many respects paved the way for the NRP report two years later. The *Roots and Research* review attempted to break new ground by considering socio-cognitive as well as cognitive research that should inform the teaching of reading beyond the initial stages, and it is important to take such a perspective because, as I shall argue in Chapter 5 and the later chapters of this book, 'joined-up thinking' that takes account of multiple perspectives is essential in order to achieve a coherent strategy for literacy development that can be effective at the systemic as well as at the local level.

The need for multiple perspectives

As I argued in the *Roots and Research* review, understanding how literacy develops is a complex issue, and even though governments understandably seek unequivocal answers with which to steer policy, research findings not only fail to provide simple answers, they also suggest that the questions need to be more subtle than those implied by the 'either-or' argument structure so beloved by the media. Speaking, listening, reading and writing are among the most complex cognitive processes managed by the human brain, and in the real world they occur in complex social and technological contexts that involve rapid and multiple interactions between people, texts and environments. An important implication in this context comes from the research in cognitive psychology of Rand Spiro et al. (1994), who showed that if we are to increase our knowledge in a complex domain, we need to have strategies which include living with complexity and tolerating some ambiguity, at least in the short or medium term. Spiro's research showed that learning in complex domains was much more likely to occur when the learner:

- sought to avoid oversimplification;
- valued multiple representations;
- valued case studies;
- defined meaning as use;
- preferred flexible schemata;
- sought interconnectedness;
- valued human support systems to help deal with complexity.

The problem in a complex domain, therefore, and particularly in one which is not fully defined, is that you cannot advance knowledge if you oversimplify, if you don't value case studies and if you don't connect up the elements. Or to put it the other way round: if you want to have the 'joined-up thinking' which seems to be so fashionable today, you need to pay the price of accepting that there may not be simple answers to complex questions.

Another important challenge that faces us in drawing the implications for practice from research is that we do not yet have a unified theory of language learning. In this chapter, our goal is to consider the research on reading comprehension and its implications for teaching, but we need to acknowledge that if reading development actually involves not only reading, but is also tied up with writing, spelling, speaking and listening, literacy across the curriculum and the teaching of those with special educational needs, then we have a problem. The problem is that there has been fragmentation in these fields, which has resulted in the development of mutually exclusive theoretical and experimental frameworks that make it almost impossible to construct a unified theory of language learning against which to test the empirical data.

In a powerfully argued position paper, Linda Flower (1994) has anatomised the problem of methodological fragmentation in the field of literacy. In a distinguished career in the field of writing, Flower has moved increasingly towards a position that seeks to integrate social with cognitive research perspectives. As Flower puts it:

> *A literate act ... is an attempt to create meaning, and in doing so, it reflects – is itself shaped by – literate, social, and cultural practices ... At the same time, literacy is also a personal, intentional action, an attempt to understand, express, explore, communicate, or influence.*
>
> (Flower, 1994, p. 9)

Flower argues that what is needed is a theory that integrates cognitive and social psychological perspectives. And integrating the more global perspectives of purposes, goals and possible reader responses, suggests Flower, is not to pander to the currently fashionable penchant for sociological analysis, it is crucial to understanding what expert writers do that novice writers do not. Novice readers and writers tend to concentrate on surface content and formal text features, while experts attempt to interpret a text by transforming it into a meaningful, integrated social transaction. To take only a cognitive perspective, and to focus on teaching basic skills, therefore, and to ignore the wider rhetorical and social purposes of text is to deny to the novice models of how to behave like an expert.

It is not a trivial matter to build an integrated theory that links cognitive and social research perspectives. Traditionally, research into cognitive processes is high status, for the sound reason that its findings are, in principle, rigorous and replicable, and are held to be generalisable to other contexts. By contrast, the case studies generated from sociological perspectives may have immediacy and compellingness, but they are assumed to lack generalisability and therefore are often regarded by policy makers as less valuable than experimental research findings.

Some of the more important goals of education – for example that students should develop in authentic learning contexts metacognitive awareness, strategic thinking and reflective learning capabilities – are immensely difficult to research, since they have their roots in the socio-cognitive domain and involve cognitive processes that are difficult to capture and learning goals which may not even be achieved before pupils leave formal education.

These goals are capable of being researched, but such research is likely to privilege case study, vignette and ethnography rather than traditional empirical techniques. Traditional research methods find it close to impossible to capture and make generalisations about the heuristic and context-bound literacy acts in which individuals struggle to clarify goals, deal with partial understanding, then go on to transform knowledge, juggle rhetorical constraints and bring to bear a lifetime of cultural, social and linguistic practices as they compose a text. As Flower acknowledged, even attempting an integration of these cognitive and socio-psychological perspectives is problematic: 'Complexity and dialectic are hard to sell' (1994, p. 32). Nevertheless, on Flower 's own argument it is essential that we make the attempt to create a multidimensional image of learning, using both traditional perspectives which apply classical research designs and socio-cultural perspectives which recognise that literacy acts occur within social and political contexts and within subtle intentional and authority frameworks. There may be pragmatic reasons for valuing simplicity in reporting educational research, but there are ethical reasons for attempting to represent its complexity.

The need to work on vocabulary development

The National Reading Panel devoted the first 8,000 words of its chapter reviewing research into the teaching of comprehension to the issue of vocabulary instruction (NRP, 2000, Chapter 4-1), and there is a sound research rationale for such a decision. In the early factor-analytical studies of reading comprehension, F.B. Davis (Davis, 1942) found that reading ability, as measured by comprehension tests, factored into two groups of skills, the first around word knowledge and the second around inference and verbal reasoning. A similar result was found by the *Effective Use of Reading* team in the UK in the 1970s (Lunzer and Gardner, 1979). Lunzer's team set out to identify a number of reading comprehension subskills in order to support what might be called a diagnostic-prescriptive approach to developing comprehension. They abandoned their quest in the light of their own research findings, which showed that children generally did not demonstrate systematic strengths and weaknesses in different subskill areas (for example, by doing well on finding main points, but poorly on understanding metaphor). Instead, children tended to do well in all the subskill areas or less well in all the subskill areas: the apparently different 'subskills' turned out to intercorrelate very highly. But what did stand out was vocabulary knowledge: word knowledge and word knowledge in context factored out as somewhat separate from the other putative 'subskills' of inference, identification of main points, interpretation of metaphor, and so on. The implication for pedagogy is clear – if vocabulary and inference factor out as two skill areas, it may well be beneficial to consider different but complementary strategies for supporting and extending the development of those skill areas.

In considering their recommendations, the Panel also made the useful observation that the pedagogical implications for teaching vocabulary may be age-specific: this is because in early reading instruction, most of the words encountered tend to be known to the reader and already part of his or her receptive vocabulary. The opposite is the case for older children – in the higher grades it is to be expected that students will be meeting unfamiliar words in the books they read at school and therefore lexical or etymological (as opposed to phonetic) strategies for dealing with new words are much more important. Another very important finding is that some researchers have found that high- and low-ability readers respond differently to different types of instruction related to vocabulary development. The implication here is that teaching strategies may need to be tuned to the ability of the readers. For example, it may be that for able readers, incidental exposure to many new words through listening to plenty of stories is very effective for building and extending vocabulary. But for poorer readers with more modest word knowledge, word-building strategies and dictionary work to support exposure to new vocabulary will be much more valuable than a simple incidental exposure strategy. In a celebrated paper, Keith Stanovich argued that there is a 'Matthew effect' in reading and that, as in the parable of the talents in the gospel of St Matthew, when it comes to reading, the rich get richer while the poor get poorer (Stanovich, 1986). This may not be a cognitively inevitable state of affairs, but it is certainly an inescapable statistical fact: every year, below average readers mature at a below average rate, i.e. they gain less than one year in reading age, while above average readers mature at an above average rate; only average readers mature at the rate of one year of reading age per year. Again, there appears to be a clear implication from research – put resources into the development of early reading achievement. The only rider I would add is the crucial one about the need for balance – early reading is not just about phonics: children who read early and gain early independence are able to cope with a wide range of texts because they already have good vocabularies, have an interest in the world around them and usually have a broad initial grounding in school-related knowledge. A child who can decode but who has no interest in books is as learning-disabled as a child who has an interest in books but who cannot decode.

Research into vocabulary growth certainly fits the general pattern of a 'Matthew effect'. A number of studies have concluded that vocabulary instruction of various types has an impact on comprehension, and the positive effects showed up at both elementary and middle-school levels. But these effects are often ability related: Robbins and Ehri (1994) demonstrated that storybook readings helped teach children meanings of unfamiliar words. However, children with a larger initial vocabulary learned more words. The good news is that hearing a text read aloud can help to mitigate reading ability effects: many children of all abilities enjoy listening to stories, but there is evidence that weaker readers may profit more from having new vocabulary introduced orally than will stronger readers.

The nature of the interaction during storybook reading may also be significant: three studies found that approaches emphasising student-initiated talk and active participation were associated with greater gains in vocabulary knowledge. Similarly, repeated readings for younger children, together with question and answer sessions during reading, were associated with greater gains in vocabulary. Dole, Sloan and Trathen (1995) worked with high-school students on an 'alternative' vocabulary treatment programme: teach students how to select relevant words, learn the words on a deep level and discuss them. These students outscored students taught with the traditional approach in which readers did not learn this criterion or discuss the words in context. Similarly, 'pre-instruction', pre-reading activity involving discussion or the direct teaching of new words has been shown in a number of studies to improve vocabulary acquisition and comprehension. Getting students to define difficult words improves vocabulary acquisition, as does asking students to produce a revised version of the text. Various small-group activities have also been found to improve vocabulary development. Pair work on vocabulary can be useful, and small-group reciprocal peer tutoring has also been associated with improved vocabulary.

There is converging evidence that computer support for vocabulary development may be worthwhile (although for pre-school learners one study found that the cognitive demands of keyboard use may disrupt very young children's ability to use word-identification software). Reinking and Rickman (1990) found that 6th grade students receiving computer instruction of difficult text words with electronic text scored higher on vocabulary measures than students reading printed pages with dictionaries or glossaries. Davidson, Elcock and Noyes (1996) used a computer that gave speech prompts when the learner requested them; 5- to 7-year-old students improved on three measures of vocabulary with these prompts. The NRP report on these studies did not quote any differences for boys compared with girls, but we know from other sources that boys particularly are motivated by computer support for learning. Since boys are generally behind girls on reading, this may be a factor that argues even more strongly for the use of technology to support vocabulary development.

One further area of research into vocabulary development concerns the use of multiple approaches, particularly those associated with teaching vocabulary in context. The NRP review reported that 'rich, extended instruction and multiple exposures to words' and a 'mix of definitional and contextual approaches' worked better than either method used alone (p. 4-23). In an earlier publication, Marty Ruddell (1994) reviewed many of these approaches, and produced a useful list that can help to guide instruction. Some of the key insights from her review of research are the following:

1 Vocabulary knowledge is not an all-or-nothing matter: a word is understood in stages. For example, the reader can:
   - read and pronounce a known word;
   - learn new meanings for a known word;
   - learn new words for known concepts;
   - learn new words for new concepts;
   - clarify and enrich understanding of known words;
   - use a word in his or her own writing.

2 Children learn new vocabulary better if the learning is active and social (e.g. by performing little drama skits using the new word, or drawing maps with a partner of semantically related words).

3 Children can learn new vocabulary from context, but:
   - they are more likely to do so if they quickly use the new word in their own writing;
   - they are less likely to learn vocabulary spontaneously from high school textbooks, since these are generally too difficult;
   - they are less likely to learn from context if they do not read widely and regularly.

The general conclusion is clear: vocabulary should be taught both directly and indirectly, and teaching about vocabulary should be integrated into other types of reading instruction. In addition, the deeper the processing the better: the more connections a reader makes with other reading material or with oral language, the greater the effect.

Comprehension development – what we have learned from research into cognition

Teaching approaches that encourage close attention to texts have been advocated for at least a hundred years, and comprehension exercises of one sort or another have been with us for nearly a hundred years. What is much more recent is cognitive research that has attempted to explore the nature of a reader's processing of information during comprehension. The National Reading Panel identified Markman's research (1978, 1979) as a watershed, since her work established for the first time that many readers appeared to have very poor skills in monitoring their own reading comprehension. Most adults who are fluent readers monitor their own reading comprehension without thinking about it, and adjust their reading behaviour according to what they are, or are not, understanding. They go back and reread difficult texts, and spend additional time processing difficult words, especially those words that are unfamiliar or that have infrequently encountered letter strings (such as *fugue* or *antirrhinum*). But young readers are much more tolerant of ambiguity or inconsistency. Perhaps because so much of what is encountered in their world seems inconsistent or is only partly understood, young readers, and particularly less proficient young readers, are (to an adult, at least) remarkably relaxed about dealing with nonsensical or contradictory information in a story. Animals that can see their prey even though they are in total darkness, for example, are not a problem for young children: perhaps they simply update their schema to accommodate what for us would be a contradiction. Or perhaps (a more likely explanation in the case of poorer readers) text processing is carried out mostly at the phrase level, and therefore consistency checks with the reader's internal models of the world just don't get done, or are only done on an infrequent basis. What was particularly important about these early cognitive studies, though, was that they paved the way for studies that showed that readers could be taught strategies that enabled them not only to monitor but to enhance their comprehension.

The rationale for such teaching came from two sources. The first was a cognitive perspective on the reading process that argued that comprehension was a dynamic process involving the purposive construction of meaningful representations of text in working memory (along the lines suggested in our analysis of the work of Kintsch in Chapter 3). The second was a belief that readers processed text in ways that could not just be described using cognitive models of processing, they could be predicted and – given appropriate teaching – improved. The fundamental assumption here was that the normal strategies for comprehension monitoring and self-regulation in reading, as in the case of Markman's students, do not provide a basis for understanding and learning which is as effective as that which is possible using explicitly taught comprehension strategies based on an understanding of cognition and delivered by a teacher who demonstrates, models or guides the reader on the acquisition and use of such strategies.

The evidence that strategy instruction leads to improvements in comprehension is impressive: the NRP team reviewed published studies in relation to a range of criteria, including that of having a control group and some sort of random assignment of readers to treatment conditions, and identified 203 studies that met the criteria. The Panel then grouped the studies thematically, and identified broad areas of comprehension instruction in which there was converging evidence that a particular approach led to improvement (p. 4-42). The areas were:

- comprehension monitoring;
- cooperative learning;
- curriculum integration;
- graphic and semantic organisers (including story maps);
- question answering;
- question generation;
- summarisation.

Table 4.1 gives an edited overview of the more detailed categories of comprehension that were reviewed by the NRP. The number of studies reviewed ranged from 38 (multiple strategies) to just one (psycholinguistic), but it is not the case that there is a linear relationship between the number of studies in a particular area and the importance of the findings: the multiple strategy papers, for example, differed greatly in terms of the nature of the groups researched and in the nature of the strategies used. What is most important is to recognise the very strong evidence from 206 carefully selected studies that comprehension does not simply develop spontaneously (if it did, the control groups would have done just as well), and that a very broad range of teaching strategies was helpful in bringing about improvement. We shall not comment here on every study in Table 4.1, but it is important to point out the significance and distinctiveness of some of the research that is represented in those 15 broad areas.

Table 4.1 Categories of comprehension instruction and their effects

Type of instruction	Nature of effect in research findings
1. Comprehension monitoring	Readers taught to monitor their own understanding were able to judge how well they comprehended, and to alter their strategies as a result.
2. Cooperative learning	Readers who learned to work in pairs or groups and were taught to listen to and understand their peers were able to help one another, to focus on and discuss reading material, and to do better when assessed.
3. Curriculum-related instruction	When reading strategies were taught in cross-curricular subjects ('content area' subjects), the strategies became integrated into instruction, and into students' repertoires, and this led to improved achievement.
4. Graphic organisers	Readers rarely spontaneously use text organisation aids such as these, but they can improve both comprehension and subsequent recall.
5. Listening activity	A number of studies have shown that reading while listening is beneficial, and can improve comprehension and recall.
6. Mental imagery	There is strong evidence that imaging and mnemonic strategies can help readers recall key words and information.
7. Multiple strategies	A number of comprehension strategies have been tried in combination, and have been shown to be even more effective in combination than alone.
8. Prior knowledge	Activating prior knowledge before reading has been shown to have a number of benefits, including greater participation and higher motivation, as well as building stronger scaffolding for new vocabulary and new conceptual learning.
9. Psycholinguistic	An area of limited research, but one worth developing: looking closely at particular parts of speech can develop sensitivity to genre and to how arguments are built up in certain types of text.
10. Question answering	Answering comprehension questions may be a reader's least favourite task, but instruction in how to do it effectively pays dividends.
11. Question generation	For many teachers and their students, a much more useful and challenging task than question answering: question generation can be effective because you don't need to have all the answers from the beginning, plus many readers are capable of producing better questions than those generated by their teacher.

Table 4.1 Continued

12. Story structure	Getting readers to focus on text structure can be a very valuable prop to helping them understand a text at the macro level, and subsequently to be able to write within a broader range of genres. Knowing a text's structure also facilitates recall.
13. Summarisation	Not easy, but if it's well taught it is an incredibly useful skill, and one that can improve recall at both the text and word level.
14. Teacher preparation	When teachers learn strategies and pass them on, readers improve (see Chapter 9, below).
15. Vocabulary-comprehension relationship	Reading comprehension depends upon word knowledge; when teachers work on word meaning, readers' comprehension improves.

Adapted from NRP (2000).

First, let's consider the landmark studies of Judith Langer on the value of pre-reading activities in terms of activating prior knowledge, teaching vocabulary and preparing the reader to learn more effectively. Langer (1981; Langer and Nicolich, 1981) developed a technique for identifying prior knowledge which Langer called PreP (Pre-Reading Plan). This was a three-phase model for eliciting and classifying prior knowledge: first students generated initial associations; next they discussed and classified what they collectively knew; finally they reformulated their knowledge, clarifying what they now knew as a result of the group or class discussion. The results of research into activating prior knowledge were impressive: Langer showed that readers who engaged in prior knowledge elaboration learned more and retained more than those who did not, even though the teacher specifically refrained from introducing any new material herself during the elicitation phases. Langer argued that eliciting and organising prior knowledge makes the approach to new learning more meaningful and activates schemata (the cognitive frameworks) onto which new knowledge will be mapped, so that the teaching, when this does begin, will be much more effective. Langer also demonstrated that prior knowledge was a better predictor of learning than IQ, which suggests that if teachers elicit, clarify and organise prior knowledge, and thereby increase provisional understanding, processing and recall for all students will be increased. The explanation of why the pre-reading strategies are so effective is in harmony with our discussion of schemata in Chapter 3: if comprehension and recall are based on hierarchical and associative networks in the brain, and a class discussion of both the associations and the hierarchies shared by members of the group is brought into the open, then those with fewer associations and less well organised strategies will benefit most, but everyone has an opportunity to extend and update their own schemata before the new knowledge, vocabulary and concepts are encountered.

Next, and this is a point that is fundamental in the approaches advocated by the National Literacy Strategy (NLS) in England, teacher demonstration of how to read more attentively has been shown to have great potential for enhancing readers' understanding. As with Langer's PreP, the key element here is shared collaborative discussion of cognitive strategies. The most cited studies on the value of teacher demonstration of process have been those of Gerry Duffy and Laura Roehler (Duffy et al., 1987; Duffy and Roehler, 1989). There were four aspects to the approach they recommended. First, the teacher explained and demonstrated a strategy (in the case of reading, it might be the construction of mental images of what you are reading in a text, for example, or the practice of formulating your own questions prior to reading). Second, the students modelled publicly their attempts to apply the strategy, with the teacher monitoring, commenting and inviting the students to contribute to the process of clarifying what the strategy looked like in action in the context of an authentic reading task. Third, the teacher gradually gave less and less feedback to the students, thereby shifting the responsibility for activating and using the strategy to the students. Fourth, and crucially, the teacher prompted the students to use the strategy on occasions right through the school year, so that, although the students were encouraged to apply the strategy autonomously, this was not left entirely to the students. Thus the teacher demonstrated not only how to apply the strategy, but modelled how to recognise opportunities for applying it in authentic contexts.

The emphasis on teacher demonstration leading to shared exploration then to scaffolded application of new learning is very much in harmony not only with NLS, but with the current neo-Vygotskian movement in the UK. Vygotsky's *Thought and Language* (1986) offered the crucial insight that learning was a socio-cultural phenomenon, and what followed from this was that the focus for research into learning should be the adult–child relationship, and not simply the child. The logical extension of this was that we should examine closely the role of the adult as an expert from whom the child is learning. The often-quoted 'Zone of Proximal Development' is relevant here, since this is the distance between the child's current developmental level and the level that an expert can help the child to reach. David Wood and his colleagues carried out important studies in the 1970s that extended our understanding of how the Zone of Proximal Development actually works, through their work on scaffolding.

Wood (Wood, Bruner and Ross, 1976) used the metaphor *scaffolding* to describe the teaching support that enables the child to bridge the Zone of Proximal Development gap. Scaffolding is the process by which the teacher (though it could be another adult or a peer) organises learning that is unfamiliar or beyond a learner's ability in such a way as to assist the child in carrying out the new task. In Wood's original study, young children were encouraged to carry out parts of tasks that were within their ability, and the adult 'filled in' or 'scaffolded' the rest. Scaffolding is quite a complex process: it is not simply about generally supporting the child.

Scaffolding involves (Wood, Bruner and Ross, 1976; Wood and Middleton, 1975):

▶ activating and maintaining the learner's interest;
▶ and then (crucially) reducing the number of choices available to the child;
▶ keeping them on task;
▶ highlighting critical aspects of the task;
▶ but also controlling their frustration; and
▶ demonstrating the whole process to them.

The importance of a teacher monitoring carefully the progress of individuals is crucial here: tutors who had been specially trained to identify accurately the learner's level of achievement were not only better at gauging progress – their approach led to better learning. One further point on scaffolding: it can be unwise to dismantle it too early. Scaffolding becomes unnecessary once the learner has reached the point of having a shared perspective with the teacher. In order to be able to apply the new learning independently, the pupil needs to be able to apply the new understandings in unfamiliar contexts, and to take the role of the teacher in asking appropriate questions of himself or herself and others. This is a major transfer of responsibility, and it will not happen rapidly or spontaneously for the whole class. Variability in pupils' ability to draw inferences and to reason logically will affect how rapidly they can do without the scaffolding.

Two key themes in the research encapsulated in Table 4.1, then, are pre-reading activity and teacher demonstration. A third major element is the importance of small-group work on reading. The classical study which had a significant impact on classrooms in the US and which also stimulated a great deal of additional research into small-group work in literacy development was that of Palinscar and Brown on reciprocal teaching (Palinscar and Brown, 1984). The central idea behind reciprocal teaching was to develop an approach to using texts to promote learning in a way that actively engaged students in the process of constructing meaning while promoting the conscious use of effective comprehension strategies. This procedure was designed to involve teachers and students in a dialogue about text material, during which four comprehension strategies were actively employed. These strategies, argued Palinscar and Brown, were spontaneously applied by good readers, but not by average and below-average readers. Middle-school children (equivalent to Year 7 in England) who were extremely poor readers were instructed how to take turns asking questions about what they were reading, summarising the text and making predictions about what would be said in the next section of text. Teachers first modelled this behaviour, thinking aloud as they did so. After several weeks of practice over about 20 lessons, students scored significantly higher on tests of reading comprehension than control-group students who had been given intensive reading practice but who had not practised reciprocal teaching. Scores of the reciprocal teaching group on science and social studies tests also went up, and these differences lasted at least eight weeks after the experiment ended, which suggested that the children were transferring their learning to new reading contexts.

The strategies which are encouraged in reciprocal teaching are as follows

1 *Summarising* – developing the ability to identify the most important information and to communicate it in a succinct fashion.

2 *Questioning* – involves students in generating their own questions, in thinking about what they don't know, need to know or would like to know about a passage. The aim here is to promote purposeful reading and a sense of personal meaning-making.

3 *Clarifying* – the key skill here is monitoring one's own comprehension, identifying when there has been a comprehension breakdown and then taking the necessary action to restore meaning.

4 *Predicting* – requiring students to utilise given information and background knowledge in order to form a hypothesis about the text type and where the text was likely to lead. Predicting encourages thoughtful, strategic reading.

When introducing reciprocal teaching, these four strategies were directly presented, explained and modelled by the teacher. Once students were familiar with the strategies, they were invited to take the role of the teacher and conduct their own reciprocal teaching dialogues with their peers using new text material. At this point the teacher's role shifted from providing direct instruction to monitoring progress and providing feedback. As they became more confident, students were given greater independence from the teacher, working in pairs to coach one another, ask questions, summarise, predict, clarify and think aloud about what they were reading. This small-group work therefore became a key element in bridging the gap between teacher-directed instruction and independent reading. A large number of research reports are in agreement: reciprocal teaching has been successfully taught at every level from primary school through to college, but the research indicates that this procedure may be particularly effective with less proficient readers and is especially effective with expository texts.

At this point it is worth taking a moment to consider why, if reciprocal teaching activities are so worthwhile, teachers everywhere have not adopted them as a fundamental part of their classroom planning. Perhaps the answer is related to one of the less publicised findings of Palinscar and

Brown, which was that good readers had much less need of such scaffolding. Another classic study of how good and average readers cope differently with poorly organised texts illustrates the point. Marshall and Glock (1978–79) looked into how well college-age students coped with expository texts in which there was not only dense information, there were also problems related to information structure: in some passages, information was poorly ordered and the structure of the information was inadequately signalled. In order to carry out their research with the full range of students, Marshall and Glock worked with student populations from both an Ivy League university and a junior college (equivalent to a UK further education college). Originally, the intention had been to simply pool the data from the two groups, but, out of inquisitiveness, the researchers analysed the results from the two populations separately. The results were astounding: for the Ivy League students, it made no difference whether the passages that had to be memorised had subheadings or not, or even whether the paragraphs were presented randomly. These very skilled readers were able to cope with the missing or poorly ordered information, and did just as well as when they were given the coherent and well-signposted texts. In fact, there was some evidence that they recalled the disrupted texts better because these passages had required deeper processing. But there was an enormous difference in the case of the junior college students. This group performed adequately with the coherent texts, but fared far worse on comprehension and recall of poorly organised and poorly signposted texts.

The vast majority of teachers are good readers, in relative terms at least. In relation to the Marshall and Glock study, they are therefore likely to be towards the Ivy League end of the continuum in terms of their being able to cope with difficult or disrupted texts. By the same token, therefore, teachers may not find it easy to understand intuitively just how crucial it can be for average and below-average readers to be given support in developing reading skills and strategies to cope with such texts. It is important to review the lessons that can be learned from the Marshall and Glock study: first, we should, if possible, give poor readers well organised, clearly signposted texts; second, we should give all readers, but especially weak readers, scaffolded support and guided practice in learning how to deal with poorly organised and poorly signposted texts, especially texts that they are likely to meet and have to cope with independently; third, a 'natural' approach to reading development (for example, just having a wide range of texts and plenty of discussion) may be fine for good readers but could be disenfranchising and disempowering for the very readers who are most in need of reading development.

In concluding this section, let us review the key findings from cognitive research that relate to developing comprehension:

▶ Children will develop fluency if they do lots of independent reading, but comprehension is less likely to develop spontaneously.

▶ Class teaching of strategies for approaching challenging texts is valuable.

> Reciprocal teaching, with the pupil taking the role of the teacher in peer-led discussions of texts, is valuable.

> Developing critical literacy is just as important for weaker as for stronger readers.

The specific implications for the teacher from research were outlined in an authoritative review by Michael Pressley (2000). He argued that we now have a pretty clear idea of what strategies need to be encouraged, partly because these strategies are the ones good readers use, and partly because other studies have shown that if the strategies are well taught poor readers improve. Pressley recommends the following strategies:

> Teach decoding, with an emphasis on morphology.

> Teach the use of context cues and monitoring meaning.

> Teach vocabulary.

> Encourage extensive reading.

> Encourage students to ask their own 'why?' questions of a text.

> Teach self-regulated comprehension strategies, e.g.
>   – prior knowledge activation;
>   – question generation;
>   – construction of mental images during reading;
>   – summarization.

> Analyse into story grammar components.

> Encourage reciprocal teaching.

> Teacher modelling of strategies + scaffolding for independence.

Developing comprehension across the curriculum

One of the most widely-cited UK research studies of reading across the curriculum in schools in England, and which came to be regarded as a champion of shared exploration of texts through small-group activity, was *The Effective Use of Reading* project (Lunzer and Gardner, 1979). The project looked at a number of aspects of using and developing reading, in both primary and secondary schools, and included an 18-month classroom observation study of how much children read in lessons in school. What the team found was that at both primary and secondary level, reading accounted for between 10 per cent and 15 per cent of the time-sampled minutes of a child's day, but that most of the reading in school occurred in small bursts of less than 15 seconds with very little intensive reading. And there was often very little interaction with text. For example, in one observed lesson, a fluent Year 7 reader who was doing a reading comprehension exercise spent less than two minutes out of 45 actually reading the text. It turned out that a reading comprehension exercise was mostly about writing, since she spent 25 minutes composing and writing down her answers. Furthermore, she had no interaction with any of her peers while doing the exercise, and no feedback during the lesson in order to scaffold any comprehension monitoring behaviour.

The wider implications of what was happening here are important. For a good reader, reading easy material, the lack of interaction and lack of feedback is unfortunate, but for a weaker reader, it is disastrous. As we have already discussed in relation to Markman's work, proficient readers can monitor their own comprehension, and detect and repair their own comprehension difficulties, but weaker readers cannot. So from this point of view, a comprehension exercise done without interaction or feedback might function simply as a test, confirming the level of a reader's ability, but not offering any scaffolding or input to improve it. So it is difficult to avoid the conclusion that traditional comprehension exercises are likely to be a waste of the pupil's time if they are easy, and frustrating and unproductive if they are difficult. In any event, with this analysis in their minds, the *The Effective Use of Reading* team set out to consider the alternatives, and to explore and evaluate these. What they finally argued for, and obtained further funding to explore, were DARTs activities (Directed Activities Related to Texts; Lunzer and Gardner, 1984; Davies and Greene, 1984). Some of the best known DARTs activities are cloze (or various types of word or phrase deletion), sequencing, prediction, highlighting or underlining, diagram completion and segmenting the text. They have much in common with the strategies advocated by Michael Pressley above, and there is thus strong evidence that they can be very valuable for developing comprehension.

There were two reasons why Lunzer's team devised DARTs. One was a wish to encourage small-group reading strategies; the other was the need to support readers in meeting the challenge of getting information from school texts, particularly when the text structure was non-narrative. As we discussed in Chapter 3 above, most novels, folk tales and oral tradition stories tend to have a deep structure that in key respects corresponds to the canonical 'story grammar' forms identified by Mandler and Johnson (1975) and Applebee (1978). But the majority of information texts do not have a story structure, and this makes for a double problem for the reader: a textbook will tend to have not only unfamiliar vocabulary and concepts, it will be likely to have a structure that is unfamiliar and complex, and this will make comprehension, storage and recall all the more difficult.

Is there a generic 'non-narrative' text structure, that tends to occur widely in most text books, or do information books tend to draw upon a large variety of possible text structures? In answering this question, Lunzer and his co-workers drew upon the seminal work of Meyer (1975), who had provided an analogue to story grammars based on analyses of non-fiction passages. Meyer's central premise was that if narrative structure was not the glue that held ideas together in expository text, this coherence had to be accomplished through two other types of linkage which she called *lexical* and *rhetorical predicates*. The lexical links were mostly to do with how semantic relationships were established, while the rhetorical links related to the way the argument was developed. For example, problem-solution and cause and effect are relationships that are shown through rhetorical predicates. Using Meyer's approach as their starting point, Lunzer's group worked with teachers in a variety of subjects across the curriculum to identify generic text types. Their classification system for texts was broader and not as complex as that of Meyer, and neither was it in some respects as rigorous, but it had two great merits: teachers could use it fairly reliably, and the text types that were included in the classification system were directly related to particular types of DART activity. The text types and DARTs are listed in Table 4.2.

Table 4.2 Text structures and suggested DARTs activities

Text type	Suggested DARTs activities
1. Narrative	Underlining, labelling, diagram, completion, prediction, sequencing, question generation.
2. Structure or mechanism	Underlining, completion, diagram completion, flowchart, sequencing
3. Process	Segmenting, tabulation, flow diagram, sequencing, prediction, diagram, question generation.
4. Principle	Tabulation, hierarchical diagrams, completion.
5. Theory	Tabulation, underlining.
6. Problem-solution	Segmenting, labelling, completion, prediction, diagram construction.
7. Historical situation	Underlining, listing, flow diagram, diagram completion, prediction.
8. Classification	Labelling, tree diagrams, segmenting, ordering, tabulation.
9. Instructions	Flow diagram, tabulation, sequencing.
10. Theme	Listing, diagrams.

Adapted from Lunzer and Gardener (1984).

No one owns DARTs. Although the acronym came from the University of Nottingham, all DARTs are variations on classroom activities which have been around for decades. When readers do a DART activity, they begin by reading the text in a pair or small group. Having one group member read the passage aloud to their partner can be a crucial first step, since this can often encourage more close attention to the text than if one student is reading to the whole class. During the DART activity, discussion and sharing of ideas is crucial, and if the DART is working as it should, a very important thing happens – the processes of comprehension, of gaining meaning and drawing inferences from a text, are brought out into the open, and it is from this that one reader can learn from another how to become a better or more thoughtful creator of meaning.

How does this development of comprehension come about? Consider the following example: if readers are doing a cloze or deletion exercise on their own, filling in blanks in a text, they may appear to be reading closely, but no modelling of the process of being a fluent and thoughtful reader occurs. The reader is either capable of doing the exercise or not, depending on his or her own prior knowledge, reading ability and degree of motivation. But if two readers are reading the text and have a discussion about what the missing word might be, one reader can lay bare the process of being a fluent reader for the other. The moment when this happens is not when one person says, 'I think it should be *this* word', but rather when another reader asks the question, 'And *why* do you think it should be that word?' and the first reader then starts pointing to words in the text, and saying how he or she drew inferences, and used the evidence available in the text. This is where the processes of comprehension are opened up to scrutiny, and it is from this that another reader can learn to be a better reader. But both readers gain from this experience: just as teachers learn a topic more deeply if they have taught it, so readers become more reflective as they are required to explain to another person how they gained meaning from a text.

This modelling of how to be a thoughtful reader does not necessarily happen, of course. If one reader is dominating or bullies the other, the demonstration of the process of constructing meaning does not occur – but this demonstration is the goal. As teachers, the challenge facing us is to make these processes public, and to give students the metacognitive skills to monitor their own reading behaviour, so that they can be aware that this making public their own reading and thinking processes is an important part of developing their own reading skills. In Chapters 5, 6 and 7, we shall offer some examples that will demonstrate these processes in action.

DARTs – how to prepare the text and how to set up the small-group activity

The final sections of this chapter offer some examples of how to set up DARTs activities in class and how to prepare the texts for them. The list is not exhaustive, but it does give some guidance. Many teachers have found that the best way to develop confidence in using DARTs is to agree with a small number of colleagues to experiment with some DARTs lessons, and then to meet up to evaluate how they have been going and to exchange good ideas and pitfalls to avoid a few weeks later. The key point, however, in all the activities that follow, is to ensure that everyone understands that the emphasis is not purely on getting meaning, it is on making explicit the process of getting meaning.

Deletion (1) – single words:

> Give the students a copy of the text from which some single words have been deleted (generally it is beneficial to retype or scan in a text, since then you can avoid giving a clue to word length). Take out words (but not too many) that are in some way critical to the meaning (often 10 or so is a working maximum). Ask your pairs to agree replacements for the missing words that are syntactically and semantically (and possibly stylistically) apt. Unless the text is a scientific one, the usual approach is for the students to have a worthwhile discussion and to justify their decisions rather than to guess the exact word. Compare students' insertions with the original passage.

Deletion (2) – phrase or sentence:

> Deletion DARTs can involve deleting just one key phrase or sentence, provided that it generates plenty of opportunity for hypothesis formation (for example the title of a piece, a key date, the last line).

Deletion (3) – leaving only a skeleton:

> Give the students, for example, the first and last paragraphs of a passage and ask them to read these and then comment on what they think the missing pieces are about and why. This can be a useful technique to prepare for the reading of the passage as a whole.

Underlining or highlighting the text:

This is a simple idea as old as schools, although it has become more vivid since the invention of the fluorescent highlighting pen. It just involves asking the students to underline, highlight or indicate in the margin in some way bits of the text that deal with one issue rather than another, or to identify patterns and connections that seem to be there. Two very useful examples of text marking are (a) getting students to highlight sections they understand/don't understand in a text, and (b) getting them to highlight in different colours facts versus opinion. The physical marking is a prop for close attention and the chat involved is a preparation for whatever broader discussion is to come. Highlighting using colours often brings out issues of text information structure, and can be very useful in handling difficult information texts. Being given permission to say that you don't understand is often much appreciated by readers, and of course this is a key factor in comprehension monitoring.

Selective substitutions:

Give the students a text and tell them that some of the words/phrases/sections have been replaced by less good alternatives. The reader's job is to look through and recast any parts in any way they feel would help. The range of possible strategies for substitution – semantic, aesthetic, syntactic, logical, surrealist – are considerable.

Prediction:

This takes deleting all but the skeleton one step further. Divide the passage or short story into instalments (choosing the stopping place with care) and give them out one at a time. Ask your groups to work out what they think is going to be the next instalment by thinking about what has happened in the one they've got. The important question to ask about a particular prediction is: where is the evidence for it? Then compare predictions with what was actually written. This works best with texts with a strong narrative line, but it can be effective with non-fiction texts in which information is released a little at a time. Prediction can also be effective with a mixture of small-group and large-group talk using an OHT or data projector.

Sequencing:

> This involves serious doctoring of the text. Make copies of it and cut
> these into pieces (perhaps paragraphs or half-paragraphs or stanzas).
> Don't make too many pieces, otherwise it can become tricky to
> organise (10 is usually the working maximum). Then give all the bits
> to your pairs (use an envelope!) and ask them to assemble the bits
> into an order that makes sense to them. The idea is to focus
> discussion on the structure of the text. (Note – open windows can
> play havoc with this DART!)

Finding boundaries:

> This is sequencing the other way round. Ask the students to divide
> the text into what they think are its sections, describing what makes
> one section different from the next. It's made easier if you tell them at
> the beginning the number of sections you think there are and let
> them work from there. (It's possible to use this technique to work on
> a single paragraph, though that is usually a more demanding
> application of it.) Boundary marking can be brilliant with a difficult
> poem, since it does not require full understanding; equally, it can
> work well with a complex information text.

Drawing and diagrams:

> This simply means asking the students to present some of the
> information in a text in some visual form (e.g. a drawing, a flowchart,
> a table or a Venn diagram). This technique could be used, for
> example, to focus attention on the relationship between characters in
> a story, or their points of similarity and difference. It may also be
> useful for reassembling ideas in an information text as a way of
> preparing for note-taking of various kinds. (Note – making a flowchart
> often requires a high degree of understanding of a text; this can often
> usefully be preceded by a simpler DART, for example text chunk
> boundary-marking.)

Question-setting:

Instead of giving the reader a set of comprehension questions, turn the usual procedure around by asking the students themselves to make up a small number of questions to which they would really like answers. It's more difficult than it sounds to put this across, and students will usually tend to go for questions of the banal kind to which they are accustomed. Classifying questions to which the answers are

(a) on the lines

(b) between the lines

(c) beyond the lines

may provide a useful temporary crutch.

There are a number of possible routes after they've worked out their questions. One is to pass one pair's questions on to another pair to see if they can answer them. Another is to collect all the questions in and get a couple of bright sparks to make a list of the five questions most often asked, then next lesson discuss these as a class.

Alternatively, students can work in pairs to make a poster of their questions, with a key question in the middle and others radiating out from it. These posters can then be presented to the class and discussed. When this activity goes well, the students will say 'Wow! I've just realised – we thought we were just discussing questions, but in fact we've answered all our questions, and a lot of other people's!'

Wide angle questions:

This is a safe start for students in pairs. Give them, say, three questions to discuss on the passage, poem or short story. They must be questions to which there is no obvious single right answer and of a kind that will encourage a ranging over the text as a whole. Try and make the questions a bit eccentric. So, for example:

- 'Is this the right title for the passage?' (Or if there is no title: 'Can you think of a good one?)
- 'What kind of book do you think this extract comes from?'
- 'Can you think of anything the writer has left out here?'
- 'What idea of the writer (like age, sex ...) do you get from this piece?'

Give a time limit: no written answers, but a quick report-back session involving the whole class and discussing how evidence was used is useful.

Responding to statements:

> This is a superior version of multiple choice and a fairly painless way of focusing discussion on critical issues in a text. Make up a short list of statements (some controversial and/or contradictory, perhaps one or two to do with the writer's intentions) that can stand as overall comments about the piece. Put the statements on card so that they can be put on the table and manipulated. Ask your pairs to work through them and decide which two or three they consider to be most important/appropriate. A simple 'prioritising' system can then show the consensus of opinion in the class as a whole; a class discussion can start with those who chose unpopular statements justifying their decisions.

And finally ... some alternatives to precis and summary:

> Here the written material (or some of it) is re-presented by the students in their own words, possibly after earlier work with some of the techniques mentioned above. For example, a textbook section or descriptive piece might be condensed and 'translated' into a news bulletin or short newspaper article; a piece with a non-user-friendly structure or tone might be rewritten to mesh more comfortably with the needs of a given target audience; or characters from the text might be asked to justify their actions or outlook in a short written statement.

A final word

Clearly there is more that could be said about the relationship between research and developing comprehension, but the intention in this chapter has not been to detail and review all the thousands of studies in the field, but rather to offer some granularity on the theoretical underpinning of approaches to developing comprehension. The approaches described above are not simply highly motivating and fun – they have the equally important merit of being based on what we understand the brain to be doing as it tries to make sense of texts, particularly school texts, in the context of learning tasks, and particularly the type of task that is important in school.

In Chapters 5, 6 and 7 we shall see many of the principles described in this chapter exemplified in classroom practice, and in Chapters 8 and 9 we shall see how the research reported in this chapter impinges on issues of assessment and of teacher professional development.

Chapter 5

Literacy development in the primary classroom: fun, phonics, fluency, fantasy and developing reading for meaning

Colin Harrison with Geraldine Kotsis

.

Introduction

What is argued in this chapter is that reading development in the first six or so years of formal schooling needs to be based on a confident ability to decode, but that learning to decode print is not the most important goal of primary education: the most important goal is gaining access to the words, stories and information that the print represents. For this reason, the teacher's first priority is not the choice of phonics teaching strategy, but the choice of texts, and the pedagogical, social and environmental contexts that mediate those texts to children. Decoding skills may be the ladder to meaning, but as teachers we must also take responsibility for what children are going to encounter once they get to the top of the ladder. If children do not have positive experiences with books, then even if they have the ability, they won't want to make the climb. So the first part of this chapter will talk about fun.

When Liz Waterland (1985) wrote her revolutionary book *Read With Me*, which became the bible of the reading apprenticeship movement in England in the 1980s, she did so not because she wanted to avoid a systematic approach to teaching letter–sound relationships. She did so because, as a successful teacher, and one who taught phonics as part of her work, she was distressed to encounter children who came into her class able to read, but unwilling to pick up a book. Matters came to a head when a boy joined her class from another school. He was a pleasant child, but he did not want to read, and would never voluntarily pick up a book. 'What book were you reading when you left your last school?' she asked. 'Book Six,' was the reply. Here was a boy who could climb the ladder, but who had never found anything interesting at the top, and Liz Waterland understood how important it was to seek to remedy this potentially disastrous situation and to bring literature and fun back into reading.

Fun first and fast

Growing up is a difficult, dangerous and occasionally very frightening business. In *The Uses of Enchantment*, Bruno Bettleheim (1989) argues that fairy tales provide what is potentially an enormously valuable source of support for children in coming to terms with their fears, and with violence and unhappiness in the world, and suggests that, as infants and as developing adults, children can revisit fairy tales and come to understand more fully why events in those stories turned out as they did. In sharp contrast to the palliative fluffy-coated offerings of many children's television programmes and the arbitrary violence of computer games, fairy tales can provide a site for dealing in a detached and therefore very safe way with some of our deepest anxieties and fears. And the fears and dangers are real: Cinderella does live in abject poverty and misery; Little Red Riding Hood does get eaten by the wolf; and Jack is involved in a terrifying escape from a giant whose aim is indeed to grind up his bones to make flour for bread. But the heroes and heroines triumph, and do so despite having failings such as being negligent of the time, straying from the path against a parent's wishes, or stealing. In doing so, the characters demonstrate their humanity, and their similarity to generations of children who have read, listened to and been frightened by their stories. And as Bettleheim reminds us, these stories, particularly those versions told by the brothers Grimm, do not belabour and patronise the reader with explicit moralising; they work on a much more subtle level, introducing powerful themes such as sibling rivalry, emerging sexuality and dishonesty in contexts that are distant enough to be unthreatening to the individual reader, but that are nevertheless universal in their relevance. In their own lives, children are as powerless as Cinderella, Little Red Riding Hood and Jack in *Jack and the Beanstalk*, but as they read or listen to fairy tales, they can enjoy the vicarious triumphs and begin to respond to the messages that lie behind the metaphors and images in the tales, and accommodate at least some of them in their own lives.

And this is why we introduce stories to children. Not to teach them phonics first and fast. Not to help them to pass tests. And certainly not to boost the school's or the school system's average test scores. As has been emphasised since the first page of this book, reading is important because it teaches you how to live. Fairy tales teach that a devalued person may come to be valued, that danger has to be faced and dealt with, and most importantly of all that the fears that seep into our dreams at night and that hide in the dark shadows under our beds can be conquered.

Why are these matters so important in a book on developing reading? The answer is twofold: first, because testing regimes and performance management systems may neglect these issues, so we need to remind ourselves again and again of the real purposes of learning to read; second, in thinking about how to develop comprehension, we need to remind ourselves that not everything needs to be explained. For Bettleheim, it was crucial for both parents and teachers to understand that we should *not* dwell too determinedly on morals to be learned and errors to be avoided, because if the morals are dwelt on prematurely or too deeply by adults, the child will almost certainly not bother to undertake the journey of making personal meaning for himself or herself. This is exactly what Pennac was talking about in relation to developing the concept of Bovarysme, which we discussed in Chapter 1. Sometimes the book can safely be left to do its own quiet work – that, after all, is why the author wrote it in the first place.

Of course I am not suggesting that teachers should not encourage discussion of a fairy tale, a story or a poem – quite the opposite. But for Bettelheim, there are boundaries around the personal space of the child that a teacher (or in some circumstances even a parent) should not cross, simply because to do so, tempting though it might be, would be ineffectual. Those are the spaces for the child to explore in their own time, and within their own rules of engagement. And the first rule for most children (and indeed for most of us, most of the time) is this: reading must be fun.

Teachers of children in the early years of schooling have permission to make reading fun. It's the rest of us who are in danger of forgetting this principle, even though to do so makes our job many times more difficult. Of course, fun is not about spending 14 hours a day watching cartoons on television – to do this is almost the antithesis of fun, although it is worth asking what makes cartoons addictive for children so that we can ask whether there are some lessons to be learned from what film-makers know that we might have forgotten. Fun is about feeling happy, about feeling comfortable, about excitement, anticipation and release of tension (in a game being won, a rescue at the end of an adventure, the solving of a problem or through the punchline of a joke), and about being fully engaged in an activity. Table 5.1 lists my attempt to capture some of these feelings, to make it easier for us to consider just how many are present in the reading contexts that we create for those whom we teach (the list works just well at university level as in the infants school). The list was informed by what I have learned from children and from teachers. It all seems so obvious from an infant school perspective – but very far from what is on offer in many classrooms for older children. I would argue that to recreate in school the conditions that have encouraged many children to become readers in their own homes (but which are not available in a great many homes) would be a tremendous gift, one that will be eagerly accepted by the majority of children. These include having a comfortable location where reading can take place, perhaps with a carpet and a bean bag or two as well as chairs to sit on. Also necessary are fiction and non-fiction books on a wide variety of subjects (many children and their parents are often willing to pass on at least some of the books that were enjoyed in primary school when they leave to begin secondary school-ing), with easy-to-read books as well as more challenging books, high-interest 'dip-in' books such as joke books and annuals featuring the latest TV or film characters, as well as classical fairy stories and children's novels. Finally, and most importantly, the challenge for the teacher is to make this comfortable place where you can sit down and enjoy a book the most sought after place to be in the school. I love to visit schools in which teachers reward children who work well with a five or ten minute visit to the book corner, or reward individuals who deserve it with an opportunity to read anything they choose in the book corner. The teacher can also let those who deserve it choose a name for the book corner (so long as it is a fictional place name, of course!).

Table 5.1 Contexts for reading: the feelings associated with 'fun' and 'not fun'

Fun (usually feels like 'play')	Not fun (usually feels like 'work')
This makes me feel happy	This makes me feel sad
I feel comfortable	I feel uncomfortable
I am winning; I can do this	I am losing; I can't do this
I want to be here	I don't want to be here
This is interesting (this connects to other things I am interested in)	This is boring (this doesn't relate to the things I am interested in)
There are surprises (tension + release of tension)	There are no surprises (no tension; no release of tension)
I am alone if I want to be and with others if I want to be	I can't choose whether I'm alone or with others
I am very engaged in this – I am giving it my full attention	I am not very engaged in this – I am not really giving it my attention

Motivation and fun are closely related, and one project that combined the two with great skill was the Curiosity Kit project, a reading development project that attracted both government money for its development and research council funding for its evaluation (Lewis et al., 2000). The project's goal was simple – to evaluate an idea for generating enthusiastic readers in the 8–10 age range, particularly among a group that is notoriously difficult to motivate: lower-achieving boys. The goals of the project did not stop at the classroom door – they went further, and also targeted parents and other family members – again, particularly focusing on males. This was quite a challenge, but the project was spectacularly successful and has been widely copied, in the UK at least, and I was able to get first-hand knowledge of how popular Curiosity Kits were because I was one of the evaluators.

A Curiosity Kit is essentially a book bag that the child takes home and shares with his or her family for one week. But it is more than simply a reading book bag. First, the Curiosity Kit was contained in a sports bag, so for a boy to carry it was less potentially stigmatising than to be carrying a dinky reading folder of the sort associated with the first year or two of formal schooling. Originally the project begged and borrowed some rather impressive bags from a business sponsor (sponsors come in very handy if you are launching a book bag project), but in the second phase of the project the team opted for sports bags with a less desirable designer logo – it was less attractive to other, non-project children! Second, the Curiosity Kit contained a number of items all related to a theme likely to be of interest to difficult-to-motivate readers (Formula One motor racing, an internationally famous soccer team, fishing as a hobby, Batman, a national sporting hero, a currently popular children's movie, etc.). The items in the bag were a children's high-interest easy-reading book on the theme, a magazine on the theme published for the adult market, a laminated card containing a list of suggestions on how the kit might be used particularly encouraging male family members to share and discuss the items with the child who had borrowed the kit, and an artifact or toy (e.g. a goalkeeper's glove in the soccer kit, a model car in the Formula One kit).

The Curiosity Kits were distributed in the following way: there were 30 kits for the class of 28 children, and every Friday afternoon the children chose a new one to take home, to be returned the following Friday. The class teacher soon discovered that she had to arrange a very rigid booking system for determining which child got to take home which Curiosity Kit. To begin with, the project attracted mild levels of interest, but as word spread among the families, the pressure to obtain a particular kit became intense, and it was often led by the child's male family members, with children coming up to the teacher on Monday morning, urgently asking to reserve a particular kit ('because my dad wants it' or 'because my brother says he'll beat me up if I don't bring it!'). In the end, being permitted to make an advance booking for a Curiosity Kit became one of the most important parts of the teacher's reward system in the project classes, and no one except the teacher seemed to notice that anything unusual was happening. But it was: traditionally, in the UK at least, most dads and brothers don't regularly read with younger family members, but in this project that changed. What the project showed was that it was only tradition that was preventing this from happening more widely, and that, when offered the opportunity, males were perfectly willing to read with the young children in the family. In the UK at least, the majority of adult males read a newspaper every day; men are not non-readers – they just don't tend to read with younger family members. But to do this could be crucial in supporting the development of wider reading among males of all ages.

One of the reasons girls are thought to read more and more success-fully than boys is because in most countries the teachers of young children are female, and so girls see a female modelling the process of being a reader while boys do not. This trend is prevalent in every one of the 35 countries that participated in the 2003 PIRLS study of reading achievement of ten-year-olds (Ogle et al., 2003): in every single country, girls outperformed boys. So for boys to see models of older males enjoy-ing reading is potentially very significant, and for them to have the fun of sharing reading with dad or a brother is even better. I am not wanting to argue here for an approach to developing reading at the expense of girls' success or enjoyment: the Curiosity Kit evaluation found that girls enjoyed the kits, and regarded them as an interesting extension of oppor-tunity to read. The avid girl readers simply carried on reading their novels at the rate of one a week but added Curiosity Kits to what they were already doing. For some poorly motivated girls, the Curiosity Kits defi-nitely increased motivation, so the themes (which included plenty of less gender-specific topics such as wild animals or travel) appeared to be attractive to both sexes.

In this section I have talked about fun, and about the relationship between fun and motivation. Fairy stories are fun when the danger, excitement and resolution are shared and enjoyed in the safety of a class-room or the comfort of a home. Choosing your own books to read is fun, because freedom to choose gives the reader the power to create the world they want to in their own head, and to people that world with the char-acters with whom they want, for a little time, to share their lives. Clearly there is much more to be said than will be said here about how to use lit-erature to build a classroom in which books and the love of books are central, but the key point remains – if we can make reading a pleasurable and positive experience, children will choose to read, and if they choose to read they will become fluent readers.

Developing fluency is essential, and for this reason we shall devote a section of this chapter to the topic, but before that I am going to take a little time to review the implications for the middle primary years of what we know about the teaching of phonics. The reason for this is that some aspects of phonemic and phonological awareness are still developing in most children up to the age of ten.

Phonics – the work continues

I have argued strongly that phonics is not the most important part of learning to read – gaining meaning is the most important part. But this does not mean, even with good teaching, that children have stopped developing in relation to their understanding of letter–sound relationships by the time the move into Year 3, which in England is after three years of formal schooling.

These days, it is pretty well universally acknowledged that most children learning to read in English will benefit from phonics instruction. What I wish to emphasise in this section is the research evidence that tells us that (a) children's use of analogies for decoding is still developing up to age nine or ten, and (b) that the teaching that supports children in constructing more complex analogies is best developed by linking the teaching of reading with the teaching of spelling. Children's developing ability to use analogies for word recognition was studied in detail by Usha Goswami (Goswami and Bryant, 1990; Goswami, 2002). What she reported was a systematic and subtle picture that not only included readers generalising from knowing 'hoot' to be able to pronounce the word 'toot', or 'flight' by analogy with the word 'light'; it also included being able to work out the word 'wink' from knowing the analogous word 'tank'. The child who is fully independent as a reader finally reaches the stage where he or she can use higher order rules to decode difficult words such as 'cipher', using an analogical rule that makes the *c* soft because it precedes the letter *i*. There are a number of pedagogical issues here.

First, Goswami argued that young children's use of analogies is spontaneous. She pointed out that, given sufficiently large reading vocabularies, children work out for themselves that there is much greater spelling-to-sound consistency in the 'rime', that part of the word that follows the initial consonant (for example the letters – *eak* in *beak*, *leak* and *tweak*) than there is in the case of most vowels or vowel clusters taken on their own (the letters – *ea*- are pronounced differently in the words *beak*, *bread* and *steak*). The least predictable letter, the vowel *a*, to take the most extreme example, is pronounced seven different ways (as in *cat, call, car, cake, care, bread* and *leap*). But its pronunciation is much more predictable within a rime unit (*cat, bat, fat, chat,* or *call, ball, fall, tall*). Pronunciation is still not 100 per cent predictable within a rime unit, but in the case of the letter a, predictability goes up from 51 per cent for the letter considered in isolation to 77 per cent when it is considered within a rime context. All this, suggests Goswami, argues for the importance of children's being aware of how rime units work, since such awareness will help them not only to decode through using analogies, but also to predict and therefore become more proficient at spelling.

But it's only part of the story. Goswami also argues that just because most children spontaneously become aware of the stability of the rime, this does not mean that analogical strategies should not be taught explicitly. Such strategies should be taught, not least because most children are still not able to work out some of the more complex ones until the age of eight or nine. Also, just in case anyone overgeneralises from her findings, Goswami makes it plain that just because the rime is an important unit of analysis, this does not mean that teachers should avoid encouraging children to segment the rime and to delve inside it. Clearly the more advanced analogical strategies such as generalising from *tank* to *wink* involve segmentation within the rime unit.

The final point to remind ourselves of is that related to fluency – children are only going to be able to use analogical reasoning for decoding or spelling if they have a large enough reading vocabulary, one that will enable them to develop a repertoire of analogical strategies based on acquaintance with hundreds (or thousands) rather than dozens of words.

Fluency

In their chapter on the teaching of beginning reading, the US National Reading Panel team argue strongly that '... phonics programs that emphasize decoding exclusively and ignore the other processes involved in learning to read will not succeed in making every child a skilled reader' (NRP, 2000, p. 113). They go on to suggest that what is needed to achieve this goal is a programme that develops fluency. The Panel quoted with approval the findings of the National Research Council report, *Preventing Reading Difficulties in Young Children* (Snow, Burns and Griffin, 1998a), which concluded that 'Adequate progress in learning to read English (or, any alphabetic language) beyond the initial level depends on sufficient practice in reading to achieve fluency with different texts' (p. 223).

What, then, are the procedures that research recommends should be put in place in order to develop fluency? The first message is that *guided repeated oral reading* was effective in improving reading fluency (NRP, 2000, p. 191). Conducting a meta-analysis of fluency research proved to be difficult because sample size was small in many of the studies reviewed, but overall the highest impact of guided oral reading was on accuracy in reading. Next came the impact on reading fluency itself – which was generally taken to mean speed in word recognition, accuracy in word recognition and appropriate expression. Finally, but very importantly, there was some impact of guided oral reading on overall reading comprehension.

There were some between-group effects reported in these fluency studies: broadly speaking, any type of repeated reading assisted fluency, but

for some poorer readers especially, teacher feedback on oral reading performance was particularly helpful. Similarly, reading aloud while listening
to the text being read was helpful for some weaker readers. There was a general trend for poorer readers to benefit more from oral feedback on their
reading than did stronger readers, though this might sometimes have been
a statistical artefact – poor readers have more room for development and
thus might be more amenable to improvement. Another point noted by
the Panel is that stronger and weaker readers might benefit differently from
practice in oral reading: weaker readers might benefit in terms of faster
word recognition while more confident readers might improve their
prosody (intonation and pitch).

Oddly enough, studies of uninterrupted sustained silent reading were
disappointing in terms of research evidence for their worth. Many studies
suffered from weak methodology – few of the studies monitored carefully
how much reading the students actually did and so it was difficult draw
confident conclusions based on experimental data. The correlational evidence that plenty of silent reading leads to improved reading achievement
is very strong: the Panel found 'literally hundreds of studies' that showed
that those children who read most had better fluency, better vocabularies,
better world knowledge and better comprehension than those children
who did not. This finding held good at secondary as well as primary level.
So why does it matter that most of these studies were correlational rather
than experimental? The answer is simple – in correlational studies, you
can't be sure there is causation, and even if there is a causal factor, you
can't be sure in which direction the causality is working. It is possible that
better readers simply choose to read more, in which case encouraging
weaker readers to read more might not necessarily improve their reading.

What is needed in this area, then, is better research, though it is not a
simple matter to evaluate a sustained silent reading programme. You need
to have a programme that is in place for a substantial period of time; you
need to have a valid and ethically defensible alternative treatment for the
control group (but if it's another reading activity, and that activity is worthwhile, it might deliver just as much improvement as your silent reading
programme); and finally you need to monitor carefully just how much
reading takes place, and you need to be confident that you can relate this
evidence to good data on reading fluency, vocabulary knowledge and reading comprehension ability at both the start and the end of the programme.
That is a tall order. Perhaps the gains from silent reading are difficult to
measure because they build up slowly and incrementally. Perhaps, too, the
gains in reading fluency, vocabulary and comprehension that come from
being an avid reader are very difficult to separate from those that accrue
from those other aspects of human development that so often accompany
being an avid reader – namely being imaginative, being thoughtfully interested in others and being interested in the world around you.

The magic of fantasy

One of the themes that runs through this book is that reading is not simply about developing word recognition, fluency and comprehension. It is about developing the whole person, and so understanding reading comprehension involves understanding what a holistic approach might mean in practice. One extraordinary example of teaching that produced startling gains in both reading and writing but which involved every aspect of the emotional, cognitive and linguistic development of children was reported by Jenny Tyrrell in her book *The Power of Fantasy in Early Learning* (Tyrrell, 2001).

Jenny was working with a class of five- and six-year-olds, and saw at the beginning of the year that she would be facing some serious and delicate challenges. Among the children she would be teaching were six boys who had barely made any visible progress in their previous year in the school, six children for whom English was an additional language, one child with a serious heart condition and one child, a girl Jenny calls 'Joanna', who had elected not to speak in her previous class (though her parents assured the school that she did talk at home). In order to capture the children's interest immediately, and to establish that literature was going to be important in their work, Jenny began the year by introducing *We're Going on a Bear Hunt* by Michael Rosen and Helen Oxenbury. This gripping, suspenseful, rhythmical and beautifully illustrated story took on a new dimension when Jenny's daughter visited the class and said, 'You know what we should do, Mum, we should make a Bear, a big Bear, and put him in a cave in the corner.' This they did, making use of a child's dressing-up bear suit stuffed with newspaper, and a face (also stuffed with newspaper) made from a pair of tights, with eyes, nose and smiling mouth made from felt carefully stitched into place. The bear was hidden in a 'cave' in the corner of the classroom, made from black fabric. It took a few days before the children, who had been introduced to *We're Going on a Bear Hunt* on their first day, gradually began to peep behind the black cloth, and announced to their teacher that there was a bear in the classroom. This is a part of the story that unfolded:

For about a week, Joanna, the child who would not speak, watched. I had decided not to force speech on her, but to wait for her confidence to develop. I talked to her but never invited a response. She began to relax, to smile, to touch. Then one day she crawled into the cave and began to speak to the Bear. This was repeated three or four times a day. She would stay with him for about five minutes and Bear would smile at her and hug her. It might sound as though I have launched into a complete flight of fancy, but that is in fact what she did;

snuggling up to the newspaper-stuffed suit, putting floppy arms around her, and telling him the things she would not tell anyone else. I used to watch and listen, but from a distance. I am a good eavesdropper. It's a very valuable accomplishment in a classroom. One day I noticed a difference in Joanna's speech, a uniformity in her words, a rhythm ... she was reading. There she was sitting on the Bear's lap reading Hairy Bear *fluently. Closely followed by* Can't You Sleep Little Bear? *I looked into the cave. 'Did he like the stories?' I asked. 'Yes, he loved them,' she replied. I crossed my fingers, took a deep breath, and asked, 'Will you read me a story?' Joanna smiled, nodded, moved over and I crawled in with her and Bear. Fortunately peace was reining in the rest of the room. From that day on her confidence grew, along with her ability to communicate verbally with me. She also began to talk a little with her classmates. They had all become accustomed to ignoring her, not through any kind of malice, but with the matter-of-factness of six year olds. 'Well Joanna doesn't speak' is what they used to say, but not any more.*

It was, I think at this point that I realised that there was a powerful force at work in my classroom.

(Tyrrell, 2001, pp. 7–8)

With care for the children's psychological well-being and a deep understanding of the powerful forces at work, Jenny let the bear live in the classroom for the rest of the year. He became a focus for sustained activity in science, spelling, reading, geography, mathematics and group problem-solving. Here's an example:

I thought it would be a rather good idea to get Bear writing to the children, so one morning, after some kind soul had left him a small piece of chocolate cake for the night, there was a message on the blackboard:

Fnk U 4 the brn hny

The children thought this was great and stood around trying to make out what it said. 'Thank you for the' was easy, but 'brown honey', was a bit more difficult to figure out, although it caused a lot of amusement when the children realised that it was chocolate. This simple idea was the beginning of an era in the Bear's education because the children decided that he needed to be taught to spell. They gave him lessons during the day and he practised at night. His mis-spelled efforts each morning gave us a language focus for our easel sessions. They all got very good at analysing his errors and showing him the correct form ... with the desired outcome that they became focused on spelling too.

(Tyrrell, 2001, p. 13)

Over the course of the year, the Bear helped the children to learn, and he also became a focus of love and affection. He even played an important role when one child had to deal with the devastating death of his little sister and became a temporary companion and patient listener to the whispered words of a grieving brother. Of course the children all knew that the bear wasn't real and that he was stuffed with newspaper. But the unspoken shared suspension of disbelief in the class enabled the role of fantasy to do its work and to provide a space where imagination could develop and where learning could flourish.

Many teachers will read the inspiring story of the Bear and applaud Jenny Tyrrell's creativity and professional skill, while making the tacit assumption that what she did is not generalisable to their own classroom context. But Jenny believes that any teacher, in any educational system, can build upon young children's innate enjoyment of make-believe and plan their teaching to utilise this powerful force, and I share that belief.

Reading for meaning – how DARTs can help

In Chapter 4 we looked in some detail at what research has to say about developing reading comprehension and in particular at the need for the active processing of text, and we suggested that DARTs activities can be very beneficial in encouraging that processing and thus encouraging reading for meaning.

Many teachers in the UK are familiar with DARTs activities. As we have attempted to establish in Chapter 4, there is nothing magical about DARTs; they are simply a convenient basis for grouping together a number of activities for encouraging close reading of text, usually in a small-group context. One of the key messages of this book, however, is that when we encourage children to engage in DARTs activities, we need to be really clear about the underlying pedagogy and rationale for the approach. A constructivist approach to group work and problem-solving, in which the students are given responsibility for taking forward their own learning, is worthwhile in its own right and in many educational contexts. Encouraging talk about stories and about information texts is good. But the point which I want to make as clearly as possible is this: even if highly motivated children are discussing text, there may be absolutely no benefit in terms of reading development unless the readers discover for themselves or are offered by someone else a model of how to go more deeply into the text. If there is no model of how to get more deeply into meaning then children who are doing DARTs may simply be enhancing fluency through reading practice but not developing comprehension at all.

I have observed children doing DARTs on many, many occasions and I have also discussed with very skilled teachers tapes and transcripts of children engaged in DARTs activities, and we all agree on one thing – getting more deeply into a text is not easy: you need models of how to do it, and you need a discourse with which to do it. The good news, however, is that this can start at any age.

I once asked a group of a hundred teachers in Scotland at what age they thought children could demonstrate higher-order reading skills. Their answers were very interesting. The secondary teachers said, 'Higher-order reading skills such as synthesising information from different sources are really challenging. Very few of our students can do this until the final two years of secondary schooling, and even then it is probably only those who are going on to university who can do it well.' The primary school teachers had a different view. They said, 'Higher-order reading skills, such as bringing together information from different books are very challenging; very few children can do this until the last two years of primary schooling.' There were some teachers of beginning readers in the audience. They said, 'Reading between the lines and bringing together information from different books is very difficult. Very few of our children can do it in Primary 1, but most can do it before the end of Primary 2.' Needless to say, when I went on to put the same question to university teachers, they thought that very few students ever demonstrated higher-order reading skills before the final year of their undergraduate course! For me, the implications of these differences in professional perspective are profound. My interpretation of these very different answers is as follows: first, there are such things as higher-order reading skills; second, nearly all readers can be taught to develop them; third, there are significantly greater challenges as readers get older, but these are associated more with the demands of complex and challenging reading material rather than with the cognitive load associated with processing multiple texts.

For many teachers of children in the early years of schooling, developing their own resources to support the improvement of higher-order processing of text has proved to be a difficult challenge. The primary curriculum is so crowded, and in many parts of the English-speaking world the curriculum constraints have been such that teachers have found themselves with neither the time nor the flexibility to develop children's reading using the resources they would wish to bring into their classroom. In recent years, many primary teachers in England have told me that they have felt that they were reeling under the weight of constraints and learning objectives associated with the National Literacy Strategy, and yet of course those who have written and are responsible for the implementation of the strategy would not wish this to be the case, and would not want teachers to be teaching objectives in a manner unrelated to the larger goals of reading for fluency, fun and comprehension. It certainly is possible to teach reading development in context, and the examples that follow in this chapter and the next are all taken from the classrooms of full-time teachers working in normal school contexts.

Because the DARTs activities were developed out of the Effective Use of Reading project by a new team, and a project called 'Reading for Learning in the Secondary School' (Lunzer and Gardener, 1984; Davies and Greene, 1984), many teachers have understandably made the initial assumption that DARTs activities work best with older children. But as I was attempting to illustrate with my anecdote from the Scottish Teachers' Conference, just as higher-order reading skills can be developed at any age, so DARTs activities, provided that the content and tasks are appropriate, can be successfully used with any age group. The examples of DARTs activities that follow in this chapter were devised and trialled in an inner-city primary school in Glasgow. The teacher who developed them, Geraldine Kotsis, had a Primary 2 class (aged 6 at the start of the school year), whom she split for much of the reading development work into three ability groups. Initially, she thought that only the most able readers would be able to tackle DARTs. She was wrong. What she discovered was that children's understanding was often ahead of their writing ability and that many of the DARTs that she devised for the most able readers were in fact popular with the whole class, and she was able to support the less confident readers and writers by reading them the text and helping them to write down the oral answer which they had given her.

I am going to illustrate Geraldine's approach by presenting some of her DARTs. I have deliberately chosen ones that were used with very young readers in order to make the point that DARTs work for all readers – even those whose reading skills and vocabulary are just starting to develop. But if they can be used with the very youngest readers, and can be shown to encourage both reading for meaning and higher-order reading skills, then the case for using these approaches with all age ranges can be made more strongly. Secondary school teachers have sometimes asked me in anguish, 'How can I teach these children my subject when they can't read?' Well one answer is to look at how a teacher works with a class in which to begin with no child can read, and to learn from her.

What is the best way to develop reading strategies with beginning readers? Geraldine didn't know; many of the fiction and non-fiction reading tasks she wanted to set her class involved locating information, and so she let the children work out for themselves how to do this and at the end they would have a short discussion on how difficult or easy the task had been and how the group (or the whole class) had located the information. She encouraged the children to talk about their strategies to one other and to let them learn from each other's ideas. This was a perfect strategy from a theoretical point of view. The children had fun; they enjoyed working together; whatever strategies they used were acceptable. But children who did not have appropriate strategies were not left behind in this class. The regular shared discussions on how the children had undertaken and completed the DART were absolutely crucial. It was in these discussions that the processes of becoming a fluent and thoughtful reader were laid bare and modelled for the less experienced. It was here that more advanced strategies were discussed by the children, using language with which they were familiar, and with these developing discourses anchored to real texts with shared reading purposes. This is precisely what I referred to earlier when I said that reading development does not occur spontaneously simply because children are reading and discussing texts. There needs to be a demonstration of close reading and there needs to be a discourse of close reading and both of these were occurring in Geraldine's class every week.

DARTs with younger readers

The first DART which Geraldine developed involved *The Cat in the Hat* (Dr Seuss, 1957). This delightful book can, of course, stand on its own. Generations of readers have encountered this book at an early stage of their journey in learning to read and Geraldine's class enjoyed this book with her, sharing in the fun and the rhymes and the dangerous behaviour of the cat in the hat, and the rescue from near disaster by the cat's wonderful tidying-up machine. Geraldine devised three DARTs on *The Cat in the Hat*. The first, completing a Cat in the Hat picture, was aimed at the more able reader group, but it went so well that the other children wanted to join in and this DART was eventually shared with the whole class.

The children were already very familiar with the story of *The Cat in the Hat*, since they had read it several times in class. What the children had to do was to follow the text closely as the teacher read it out loud, and then to mark in any way they chose the key information that would prepare them for the second part of the task, drawing the objects that the cat was juggling on the partly completed picture started by the teacher. The children discussed how to mark up their page, and some began with circling key words, others used ticks or underlining. One child, Aimee, first circled a word but then switched to putting a tick at the end of each line containing an object. Her ticking was not perhaps the optimal strategy since it became automated and carried on down to the end of the text. However, in Aimee's picture that forms the second part of the DART a number of objects on the Cat's list were recognisable: the books, cake, fish (complete with 'No No' speech bubble), the little toy man and the red fan. Aimee also chose to add to the drama of her picture in a way the other children did not by including speech from the Cat, who is saying, 'Look at me Look ...'

There are a number of positive points to note about this DART. It was based on a text the children had all read and knew well; it involved close reading with a preliminary task that required additional close reading but which gave opportunities for choice and discussion in relation to how we highlight key information, but which did not put a heavy load on comprehension (the reader had to mark the key words, such as *rake* and *fan*, but was not asked to copy, spell, define or memorise them). The drawing task also involved going back to the text to check on the words circled or ticked, thus making a series of text-to-picture connections. Finally, Aimee's addition of speech from the fish and the Cat added to the immediacy of the drawing and cemented a firm bond between picture and meaning. This was not meaningless 'colouring in'; her work on this DART showed that Aimee saw her picture as a representation not only of the objects in the Cat's poem, but of the drama in the story and irony of the imminent disaster as the balancing act ends in catastrophe.

Over the next week, the class did some further DARTs on *The Cat in the Hat*. One was a speech bubble completion DART, with the children invited to discuss how to fill in thought bubbles placed over the characters' heads, as they sat, bored, looking out of the window at the opening of the book. This produced lots of discussion about both character and repetition, with the children eventually choosing text such as 'I wish it would stop raining; I do, I do, I do,' or 'I wish it would stop, stop, stop.'

The final DART on this book was another speech bubble task, this time related to the point at which the mother is about to return. Again the children were creative, and showed insight into the children's characters, in one case subverting the teacher's expectations and writing text aimed at the cat, not at the other child, as one boy used the speech bubble to address the cat with the phonetically transparent insult 'You are styoobed cat!' What both these final DARTs show is the impressive distance children can travel in understanding the relationship between a person's words and their personality, particularly when that person is in an emotionally charged state, in the first case bored, in the second case apprehensive.

Another DART that was approachable by the weakest readers, but which nevertheless produced some very thoughtful responses, was that on Martin Waddell's *Owl Babies* (Waddell and Benson, 1994). In this wonderful book, three worried owlets await the return of their mother from a food-hunting night flight. Never has the plight of young ones who miss their mother been more hauntingly or more beautifully told than in this book, which the children had read, reread and enjoyed before the DARTs work began. This first DART demonstrates how a creative teacher can link art and collage work to reading in a way that is not only valid, but which

Figure 5.1 Aimee's DART on *Owl Babies*. The first task was to read the text, paying careful attention to the information on what the nest was made of and who was inside it

invites an attentive consideration of both the owls' habitat and the notion of 'house'. As Figure 5.1 shows, the children were given a cut-out tree as well as the text. They had to lift up this first page and construct on the inside page that represented the inside of the tree a collage of the owls' habitat (Figure 5.2), paying careful attention to what it was made of and the owls inside. The children had been given a box containing different materials, including strips of brown and green paper that could be used to represent the twigs and leaves in the story, feathers, and a number of non-relevant materials such as strips of paper in other colours, felt, sand and sea-shells. Every child produced a carefully crafted collage, and the class all discussed which materials would be best for their nest before they began their work.

Aimee's nest shown in Figure 5.2 has 'twigs' made of brown paper, together with others drawn by her, 'leaves' of green strips of paper, some of which have been augmented with veins drawn by her, some other, darker strips of paper, some yellow and some cream-coloured feathers. The baby owls, with Sarah, the largest owl, in the centre of the three, are next to their mother, and all are smiling – mother has returned. The owls were drawn with particular care: each was drawn in pencil, then carefully shaded in brown crayon, and then small cream-coloured feathers were added to each owl.

Figure 5.2 Aimee's second task was to construct a representation of the nest, using drawings, glue and collage materials

As with the *The Cat in the Hat* DART, what could have been nothing more than a 'draw a picture' activity in the event became an entry point for shared close reading of the text and a class discussion of materials, nests, animal habitats and the difference between a home and a house. The children coped well with the activity, and even pointed out to their teacher that their drawings reflected the relative sizes of the owls (reflecting the real-life hatching of owl chicks, which usually occurs over a period of days, leading to larger differences in size than is the case with most other birds).

A follow-up DART focused on character development, and invited the children to contribute an extension to the book, with each of the owl babies having a chance to say something to their mum upon her return. A speech bubble was to contain these final words. This task produced lively and thoughtful discussion, and demonstrated a sensitive understanding on the children's part of the differences between the three owl babies: Sarah practical and reassuring, Percy anxious but hopeful and Bill who felt only pangs of love and panic at his mother's absence. The children showed that they were capable of close reading and of the beginnings of a literary response (listen for the Scottish accent in the phonetic spellings of these six-year-olds).

Dylan wrote:

> Sarah – I was sensible for my brothers mum
> Percy – Mum I was scerd I fot you wher lost
> Bill – I was always sain I want my mum

Aimee wrote:

> Sarah – Mummy we all sat on my bransh
> Percy – I was wured
> Bill – I missed my mummy

Sinead wrote:

> Sarah – Mummy we were all worried But I saed it is going to be OK so we
> all sat on my brash
> Percy – We were scerd too
> Bill – and I didt forget you

Geraldine did one particularly helpful thing in helping her group to prepare for doing this concluding DART: she not only initiated a preliminary
discussion of the characters of the three baby owls and got the children
looking closely throughout the whole book at the text containing direct
speech, she also taped that discussion and then played it back to the class.
There could hardly be a more valuable example of a teacher demonstrating
the principle of modelling thoughtful and attentive reading behaviours:
Geraldine guided the discussion in ways that made public the processes of
getting meaning and deeper understanding of the text and the characters
that the text introduces, so every child, even the poorer readers, could gain
access to both the deeper meaning and the discourse of exploring that
meaning. Then, in replaying the tape, the children had an opportunity for
the meanings and discourses to become more deeply embedded through
rehearsal, but there was also an opportunity for a third level of meta-
discourse – reviewing what had been learned and talking about the strategies that were used and discussed in the taped part of the lesson.

Bringing it all together: teaching principles for reading development in the primary school

The intention in the previous section was not so much to present DARTs that could be used as they stand in other contexts (although they could be used very effectively) as to emphasise what it is to construct DARTs that are fully engaging, and to talk about how a good teacher ensures not only that close, engaged reading occurs, but that the children get to model publicly and see modelled publicly examples of thoughtful reading behaviour from which they can learn and which they can take into other reading contexts, including their own small-group reading discussions. In Chapter 6, we shall take this process one stage further, and look at some multi-activity DARTs, but also at transcripts of lessons in which this modelling is happening, and in which first teachers and then students model good (and poor) reading behaviours and lay them open for inspection and discussion.

To conclude this chapter, though, we shall review in bullet-point format some of the teaching principles that have been signalled in this chapter and the chapters that have preceded it and that are particularly relevant for the primary years:

For vocabulary development:

- Make use of what children already know.
- Use all the senses when introducing new words.
- Use drama to develop vocabulary.
- Offer meaningful opportunities for using new words.
- Encourage children to teach each other.
- Model curiosity about vocabulary to the whole class.
- For older children teach about word derivation and introduce etymology.
- Use a wide range of texts.

For fluency development:

- Encourage lots of reading.
- Make reading fun.
- Make reading comfortable.
- Value fairy stories.

◗ Reward children with stories, poems and time for reading.

◗ Develop a Curiosity Kit.

◗ Model being an avid reader in your class.

◗ Give children opportunities to choose what they read for themselves.

◗ Encourage peer-to-peer reading.

◗ Provide opportunities for personal response.

◗ Use a wide range of texts.

For comprehension development:

◗ Don't assume that comprehension will develop spontaneously.

◗ Activate prior knowledge.

◗ Use question-setting techniques prior to reading.

◗ Use pre-reading, prediction and hypothesis formation strategies.

◗ Encourage self-monitoring of comprehension.

◗ Encourage visualisation of words and meanings.

◗ Use DARTs, but ensure that modelling of comprehension process occurs.

◗ Use reciprocal teaching approaches.

◗ Provide opportunities for personal response.

◗ Use a wide range of texts.

A final word

It is on the theme of the need for a wide range of texts that we shall end this chapter. In an interesting book that compared US basal reading schemes with those from continental Europe, Bruno Bettleheim and Karen Zelan (1981) made an impassioned plea for real books as the basis for early reading experiences and instruction. They said:

> *It is high time that children and teachers were freed of the yoke and the blinders that are the direct result of teaching reading as if its ultimate purpose is the acquisition of decoding skills, and as if the only way to become able to recognise a word is to be exposed to it innumerable times. The truth is that words are learned easily and fast if we are interested in what they mean to us. If we want our children to grow up literate, reading must be exciting from the beginning, and never become a chore.*
>
> (Bettleheim and Zelan, 1982)

As we have argued in this chapter, Bettleheim and Zelan put the case that reading and human development are intimately connected, and that if this is so, children must not be denied the opportunity to develop through exposure to the best literature and information texts available. Reading development is about helping children to become people:

> *The first literature probably consisted of myths, which tried to explain the nature of the world and of man; it was literature through which man tried to understand himself. Out of myths grew poetry, and later science, the sources of the 'two cultures' that are still two avenues for understanding ourselves and the world. If we wish to open the world of literacy to our children, what they are asked to read should from the beginning help them to understand themselves and their world.*

Chapter 6

Case studies of reading development at secondary level

Colin Harrison, Alan Dewar and Steve Willshaw

Introduction

Case studies are useful when you are looking at complexity. As Yin (1994) noted, 'In general, case studies are the preferred strategy when "how" or "why" questions are being posed ... and when the focus is on a contemporary phenomenon within some real-life context.' And these are just the questions we are asking in this chapter – not 'what does research tell us that it might be useful to know?' but rather 'how do we implement that knowledge?' and 'why are we doing it in the first place?' So in this chapter we are not so much seeking a scientific basis for generalisation as considering three case studies that between them provide conceptualised examples of reading development in secondary schools and drawing out the implications for understanding and extending that practice.

The case studies have the following the themes:

▶ How to set up DARTs – modelling reading behaviour.
▶ Dealing with challenging students and inconsiderate texts.
▶ What makes a good reader? Leaving space for readers to set their own goals and to make text-to-life connections.

All three case studies build upon principles set out in earlier chapters but exemplify them in the messy reality of the classroom. Within each case study I have tried to permit the voices of the teachers and students to be heard in the belief that it is in the discourse of the participants that a case study gains much of its compellingness.

How to set up DARTs – modelling reading behaviour

In this first case study the intention is to offer an example of how to model DARTs (Directed Activities Related to Texts) in front of a whole class. The reason for doing this is important: in Chapter 5 we looked at some of the principles behind constructing DARTs with examples taken from texts for younger children (for the good reason that Lunzer and Gardner, 1984, and Davies and Greene, 1984, provided us with many examples of DARTs for older readers). But as I indicated earlier, DARTs have not always realised their potential, and I think that the reason for this is that while readers have often been willing to engage in text-focused discussions, they have not always had a clear enough idea of the kind of conversations that should be taking place in small-group or pair work. The solution to this is to bring some of those conversations to the front of the class and open them up for analysis, modelling the discourse of a text-based DART and then, in whole-class discussion, modelling the meta-discourse of a discussion about the quality of the reading activity that took place while the readers were completing the DART.

I have seen this done in different ways in primary schools, but hardly ever in secondary schools. Our primary colleagues are sometimes more aware than their secondary counterparts of the need for students to see and discuss multiple examples of good practice before they can internalise and take on those behaviours themselves. The example that follows was with Year 8 (twelve- and thirteen-year-old) pupils in an English lesson in a rural comprehensive school in Lincolnshire. The lesson had a three-part structure. First, the teachers who were team-teaching the lesson modelled doing a DART badly. Second, they modelled doing the same DART carefully; on both occasions the students in the class made notes on the reading behaviour of the teachers and these were discussed as a class. Third, all the pupils did a new DART, and after they had completed it, one pair of pupils came to the front and modelled the conversation that had taken place while they had been doing the DART. The whole class then discussed this. Clearly the goal was to present publicly three models of doing a DART, and three opportunities for critiquing the reading strategies of those doing the DART.

To begin with, then, the two teachers (let's call them Mr W., the wise and intelligent Head of English, and Mr H., a somewhat eccentric but enthusiastic guest in the classroom) introduced a DART to the class and gave the students a brief opportunity to do it in pairs. The teachers then modelled doing the DART in front of the whole class, hinted that it was not going to be done well, and asked the pupils to observe and to note three things that Mr W. and Mr H. might have done better. The DART activity was to read in a textbook an information sheet on the city of Rome, and to locate three examples of each of the following that a visitor to Rome might experience: (a) wonders of the ancient capital, (b) treasures of the Renaissance, and (c) examples of 'how the city buzzes with life'. The pupils had in fact done this task two weeks before, so it was reasonably familiar to them. It soon became clear that Mr W. and Mr H. were way off target in locating three 'wonders of the ancient capital':

Mr H.   *Rome. What have we got to do exactly?*

Mr W.   *Haven't you been to Italy?*

Mr H.   *I have been to Italy. Yes.*

Mr W.   *Well, this is going to be dead easy. A wonder ... I've got it! That tower thing. The Tower of Pisa's a wonder. I was amazed. Have you got that down? ... Oh, yes, while we are still on wonders it says here the shopping is wonderful.*

Mr H.   *The stores make for wonderful browsing.*

Mr W.   *We're nearly there now, what else?*

Mr H.   *What about the Sistine Chapel, that's really famous?*

Mr W.   *I remember a joke about the Sistine Chapel. These two women were on a bus and Alan Bennett was on the seat behind them, and one of them said to the other 'Who painted the roof of the Sistine Chapel?' and the other one said 'Wasn't it Underwood's of Batley?'*

The two teachers selected the Leaning Tower of Pisa, the shopping in Rome and the roof of the Sistine Chapel as their three 'wonders of the ancient capital', and wrote down their answers into PowerPoint, including the occasional misspelling, so that everyone in the class could read them; none of these choices was correct. They carried on in this vein, selecting the Coliseum as an example of a treasure of the Renaissance, and the buses of Rome, mugging and the Trevi fountain as examples of how the city of Rome 'buzzes with life'.

One reason for having teachers modelling how not to do a DART was that it gave permission for the pupils to enjoy themselves pointing out how poorly the teachers had performed, and to be critical in ways that might have been cruel if aimed at their peers. As the pupils gave their very detailed evaluative comments, Mr H. typed them up for everyone to read on the screen:

Mr W.   *OK, right. Did you spot anything that we did wrong? Good – some of you have been making notes. David, what did we do wrong?*

David   *You were not reading the text, and your spellings are all wrong.*

Mr W.   *Right. That's two things, so let's stick to the first one. We weren't reading the text. No, we were talking about lots of different*

	things; we were talking about our experiences we have had, or we had heard about, so we were getting our information from what we had heard about Rome rather than what was in the textbook. OK, let's try Alicia.
Alicia	*At the beginning you didn't sound like you knew what you were doing.*
Mr W.	*Right. So did we get off task or were we just not listening to the information?*
Alicia	*You said you didn't know what you were doing.*
Mr W.	*Right ... We just kind of sorted it out for ourselves ... Simon?*
Simon	*You said that the Leaning Tower of Pisa was a wonder, but it's not in Rome.*
Mr W.	*Right; so we were factually wrong, mainly because I was not reading the text properly. Obviously the Leaning Tower of Pisa is in Pisa not Rome. Rachel?*
Rachel	*It sounded like you were guessing all the time. You weren't using the textbooks to find the information.*
Mr W.	*Right. Brilliant. Laura?*
Laura	*It says that you should pick out three things for each section but in some sections you have only got two things.*
Mr W.	*Brilliant, yeah. We didn't follow the instructions very well, did we?*
Calum	*You didn't look very closely at the text because there is a lot of information you need in the textbook.*
Mr W.	*Right we didn't use loads of things in the text. In this dense piece of text there is all sorts of information in there – in the photos, the maps and the cartoons. We used some of it badly and some we didn't use at all ...*

In all, the pupil feedback on the teachers' poorly done DART elicited critical comment from 14 different students in the class. After complimenting those who had made comments, Mr W. moved the discussion onto one of the thornier problems of comprehension in the original passage:

Mr W.	*What about what was in the 'wonders' section and what was in the 'treasures' section? Oh yes – if you look at the task, can you say why the teacher would not be happy with our response to that question?*
Sam	*In 'treasures of the Renaissance' it says things like 'gold goblets' and things, and the Coliseum is a building.*
Mr W.	*You're kind of on the right lines, would you like to expand on this?*
David	*By 'wonders' it says 'of the ancient capital' which means Rome. So this means things like the Coliseum. And then the 'treasures of the Renaissance' is going to be the Sistine Chapel.*
Mr W.	*Yes you've got it. 'Sistine Chapel' is a Renaissance treasure – a wonderful thing of the Renaissance – a great masterpiece. What it is trying to get you to understand is the difference's between the things that were built by the Romans at the time of Christ and things that were built in the 1500s or so.*

The hardest part of doing a DART is engaging in a conversation about exactly how a close reading can bring about a clearer or deeper understanding of a text, and this is precisely what Mr W. does in this final part of the discussion. Some of the children in the class would not have realised initially that 'ancient' implied the time of the Romans and 'Renaissance' was comparatively much more recent. At the same time as acknowledging that the teachers did not do this initially, Mr W. is modelling how to have this deeper conversation.

In the second attempt at the DART, the two teachers worked much more carefully. In their conversation they mentioned explicitly making use of the subheadings in the text to guide their understanding, discussed the etymology of the word *Renaissance*, discussed discarding irrelevant material, used the map that came as part of the text, discussed the commonalities in architecture in the photographs of Renaissance buildings and brought together insights from different parts of the brochure in order to help decide which points to note down as answers.

Mr W.	*OK. We are going to stop there. I'll get out of my chair to show I'm not in role any more. OK. We are going to do the same thing again but hopefully you can see the things we did right this time. So, Kirsty?*
Kirsty	*You were working together as a team.*
Mr W.	*Yes. That's good. Helen what else were we doing right?*

Helen	*You were checking spelling by using the text.*
Mr W.	*Yes, good, Sabrina?*
Sabrina	*You were both asking questions with each other so you both knew what you were doing.*
Mr W.	*Yes, that's very good, well spotted. Samantha?*
Samantha	*You were concentrating.*
Mr W.	*Yes well done. We were concentrating and not telling jokes, singing songs or looking out the window like we were on Friday afternoon. Rachel?*
Rachel	*You were confirming with each other.*
Mr W.	*Yes that's similar to another point. Can I ask you, can you remember anything in particular, can you think of what we were saying when you wrote that down?*
Rachel	*I think you were saying things in the text, checking it.*
Mr W.	*OK. I'll put it down, because it ties in with the checking the text – going back to the text. I'll put it in as it's so important. Ross?*
Ross	*You were taking your time, like before you were really quick and this time you took much longer.*
Mr H.	*That's a great point. Someone I once worked with said this to me. 'This is what you should do to be a good reader.' I'm going to write this down: 'READ FAST THINK SLOW'. So in a sense, look what is in the text, but then go back and think about it. There is nothing wrong in reading fast to begin with. That's what you tend to do when you're in class. But then go back and think about it.*
Ross	*That's what I tend to do.*
Mr W.	*Well that's good, that's something to remember then. We will take a few more points then we need to move on. Simon?*
Simon	*You looked all over the page this time.*
Mr W.	*Yes. We used all the information available this time. We used the pictures and information this time to make sure they were in the right places. Stephen?*
Stephen	*You were always looking for more proof.*
Mr W.	*Yes, that ties in with the confirming bit we had earlier.*

The discussion continued, and again there were a total of 14 contributions before Mr W. brought things to a conclusion by reminding the class that the main goal of the teachers had been to check their own understanding by going back to the text and discussing exactly what it meant. There was some overlap in the student's points, but the class discussion elicited a really worthwhile list of behaviours that exemplified attentive reading. The list was as follows:

> Good readers work as a team.
> Good readers check their spelling as they go.
> Each member of a small group asks questions of the text.
> Every one concentrates.
> Good readers go back to the text to check their answers.
> READ FAST – THINK SLOW.
> Use all available sources of information, including pictures and subheadings.
> Discuss vocabulary, breaking words up if you can.
> Discuss difficult ideas: generate hypotheses, then look for proof.

In the final part of the lesson, the group did their own DART based on two 150-word parallel passages, one about the North Pole and one about the South Pole. Their task was to read the passages and then, working in pairs, to consolidate the information from the two passages into a single table. The first part of the task, and in many ways the most difficult, was to decide on the headings for information in the table. Mr H. and Mr W. circulated round the class and persuaded one pair, Katie and Stephen to do an 'action replay' of their planning conversation. The class was asked to make notes on what Katie and Stephen said for subsequent whole-class discussion. With some hesitation, Katie and Stephen made a laudable attempt to recreate their initial planning discussion. Here's an extract:

Katie	*What do we have to do?*
Stephen	*Look at the text and put the headings about the information for the North and South Pole.*
Katie	*OK. So if we put* Weather *in so we can compare the differences. Um … what do you think?*
Stephen	*Yes. What about* Animals?
Katie	*What about the* Location? *In here it says that they have different geography.*

Stephen	*What about* arctic flowers?
Katie	*OK. So we have got more than three. So which ones do you think we should keep?*
Stephen	*Keep* The weather, *yes.*
Katie	*And* Location, *we don't really need the animals so we will take that out.*

In the event, while Katie and Stephen did try very hard, a good deal of the discussion and thoughtful revision that informed their initial attempt did not get repeated in their 'action replay'. Nevertheless, their classmates had many helpful comments to make on how the two had been working. Mr W. first gave everyone two minutes working in pairs to review what they had seen, and then elicited these evaluative comments from the class:

David	*They decided what's important.*
Hannah	*They were helping each other.*
Alicia	*They re-thought their ideas because they had too much information.*
Mr W.	*Yes. They prioritised.*
Phoebe	*They made sure every thing was right before they finished.*
Mr W.	*OK – they did a check through before they finished.*
Simon	*They kept talking to each other.*
Mr H.	*It's tough to do it when being videoed, with that extra pressure. They shared ideas, great. What Katie did not do this time, which she did when we were first listening to them, was – she suggested* polar bears *as a title and because they had not read much of the text, they soon revised that idea as it was not such a good suggestion. Why did you drop polar bears?*
Katie	*Because it was not important and there wasn't much information about them in the text any way. It talked about animals but not polar bears so we changed it to* Animals *instead.*

This then was the final part of the lesson, modelling the meta-discourse of DARTs. Although this final extract is brief and these Year 8 children were getting tired, we can see in the extract the attempt of the teachers to go beyond a public demonstration of the process of doing a DART (valuable though that can be), and to make public the process of reflection on how thoughtfully and carefully the DART was done, and to articulate the ways in which Katie and Stephen modelled good comprehension skills and strategies. In this case the reflection foregrounded the following strategies:

▶ prioritising;

▶ collaborating;

▶ cross-checking;

▶ concentrating – they kept going;

▶ discarding a lower-order category in favour of a superordinate one.

The purpose of this case study of DARTs in action has been to emphasise the crucial importance of these two stages in inducting readers into making good use of opportunities for small-group discussion of texts. Readers need (a) to be active witnesses of many examples of how to discuss text, and (b) to encounter many examples of how to be constructively critical of those discussions. It is only when both these stages are woven into lessons on comprehension that significant reading development is most likely to occur.

Dealing with challenging students and inconsiderate texts

My own belief is that, broadly speaking, governments and policy makers get compelled by research while teachers are won over by case studies – by vignettes of good practice that have the ring of truth about them and that inspire us and make us want to change what we do, irrespective of whether a statistically significant F-ratio suggests that 'science' is on our side. Daniel Pennac's book *Reads Like a Novel*, which we talked about in Chapter 1, is an incredibly compelling case study of how to get poorly motivated readers motivated. How did he accomplish this? In an interview reported in a French government website (France Diplomatie, 2000) Pennac said: 'The written word ... creates a shock from which one never recovers.' But that does not happen simply because books are made available, important though that is. What Pennac did as a teacher was first to acknowledge that he was dealing with 35 individuals, and the intellectual challenge for him as a secondary school teacher with a culturally and socially heterogeneous group of 16-year-olds is not to 'teach' but '... to create a dynamic within the group without ever denying any one of the individual personalities of which it is composed.' This is a huge task, but if it is not accomplished, or if the teacher gets it wrong by giving too little or too much attention to the pupil as an individual, the atmosphere of the class is destabilised, teaching becomes a 'blind mechanical device' and learning occurs only for the 10 per cent of 'good' pupils. The case study we are going to consider next forms a bridge between Pennac's literature classes and this chapter's focus on the realities of reading development. In it we meet Kathleen Reed, whose aim is to teach both literature and reading strategies that will be beneficial to her students across their social studies classes, but who was working in a context that had much in common with that of Pennac's Parisian suburbs – where many of the students live in the outer circles of society where aspirations are focused on survival rather than college or a highly paid job.

In preparing background material on this chapter last year, I put 'inconsiderate texts' into Google. What I was after was the authoritative word on who first used or popularised the term 'inconsiderate texts' (my money was on Bonnie Armbruster, from the National Reading Research Center, *circa* 1984). I pulled up a wonderful essay by Kathleen Reed (1999), at the time a teacher at an alternative high school and a student at the University of Colorado at Denver. Her essay was a think piece on cognitive factors in learning, woven into an engagingly frank account of the bleak realities of her class on Modern World Literature that brought together '13-year-old teen moms and 21-year-old ex-gangsters'. But reading that world literature did not seem to be an option: many of these students were reading at 2–4 years below grade level. Other courses taken by these students seemed, mysteriously, to involve no reading and no assignments. All the reading that these students should have been doing in their other social studies courses (she had been landed with the task of grading the papers of those courses, since she was the English teacher ...) seemed to have been based on 'inconsiderate texts' – texts that were either poorly signposted, poorly structured, poorly written or written with little scaffolding to support the needs of below-average readers.

So what did she do? First, Kathleen Reed sought from the history department information relating to all the other courses these students would be studying and then headed to the library. Her plan was to support the students by bringing in a wide range of primary and secondary source material, and to scaffold their learning by having the students reading and evaluating this material in her Modern World Literature class. She spent the weekend seeking out historical novels, biographies, diaries, anthologies, encyclopedias, atlases and copies of newspaper clippings, magazine articles and picture books. These students were going to have a great experience: this was going to be cross-curricular teaching at its best. But this wasn't an Advanced Placement class – these were below-average students with low aspirations, and to the students all these varied resources were perceived as 'inconsiderate' texts. The students reacted as students do, one with a succinct summative evaluation of the resources Kathleen had provided: 'This sucks!' another with a plaintive, 'I read it, but I don't understand any of it,' and a third group by showing their level of engagement with the voluminous piles of material by falling asleep. Kathleen Reed felt panic:

> *I could feel myself losing inward control.* This isn't supposed to be happening! *I could feel my adrenal glands releasing the cortisol and all the resulting physical reactions to stress (Jensen, 1998). My large muscles were tensing, beginning with my stomach. I could feel each and every platelet as it clotted. The blood coursed through my veins so rapidly, I just knew an artery would burst. Even now, the summer after the dreaded event, I'm sure I remember feeling a large number of neurons shedding branches like leaves in a windstorm.*
>
> (Reed, 1999)

Kathleen's reaction to the rejection by her students of the resources for learning was in two parts – both of which were scaffolded by her reading in the psychology of learning and cognition, in particular by some of the ideas on challenging students' perceptions of learning that are in Rhodes and Dudley-Marling's book *Readers and Writers with a Difference* (1996). The first part of her new plan was to get the students thinking about reading strategies that they might need to bring to bear on this difficult material, so she set about constructing a list of strategies, with the idea that by reminding them of what strategies they had available, it might 'kick-start their memories about what good readers do.' There are dozens of lists of reading comprehension strategies, some of which put more emphasis on 'think-aloud' and small-group discussion. This is the kind of list that would be generated from the research literature:

▶ What do I know?
▶ What do I want to know?
▶ What have I learned?
▶ Do I use fix-up strategies?
▶ Do I talk out loud about information that confuses me?
▶ Do I make comparisons?
▶ Do I connect what I read to what I already know?
▶ Do I form mental pictures?
▶ Do I make and revise predictions?

The plan of introducing a discussion of reading strategies was in my view a good one, not least because, as we saw in Chapter 4, such strategies have been found to be most useful for less confident readers. But at this point, Kathleen Reed saw a weakness in how she was intending to introduce the strategies, and began to develop the second part of her plan: she imagined her most challenging students leaning back in their seats and rolling their eyes as their teacher took them through a long list, and doing everything they could to indicate to their classmates that this stuff was not for them. What was needed was personal challenge and group engagement. The second part of the plan was therefore to have the students work together in small groups of three or four, with each group containing at least one competent reader, and for the students themselves to plan and deliver a poster presentation on reading strategies that could be helpful if you couldn't understand the text that you were reading. These presentations would, Kathleen hoped, produce at least as full a list as the one she had prepared. The presentations would have two other benefits: first, the students would be collaborating in their learning, and collaborative learning has the potential to move every member of the group well beyond the point that they would have been capable of reaching on their own; second, the students would have fully activated their prior knowledge of reading strategies, which would put them in a stronger position to learn from their peers or from the teacher about other potentially useful strategies.

Needless to say, the students' initial reaction to what they were being asked to do was lukewarm, but Kathleen had two other important pieces of information to share before the groups began their work: only one member of each group would have to make the presentation, and there was to be a reward for the group with the list that most closely resembled that of the teacher. This did the trick, and the groups set to work, gradually building up their enthusiasm and finally producing a set of posters that went up all round the room and stayed there until the end of the school year.

One other thing happened that Kathleen Reed had not been anticipating: because it mattered who had the longest list, the students started critiquing each other's presentations:

'Hey that's bunk.'

'That's something you do before you start reading!'

'I never do that until I'm done, fool!'

They got especially fired up over ideas they felt were something other groups 'just made up to make this list longer,' or not 'something you'd really do'.

'Miss, Miss! Cross that one out, that's weak.'

(Reed, 1999)

The session was fun and it worked. As Reed puts it in summing up what was learned:

> *The memory of the lesson and the poster are real models for what Mayer is talking about when he says, 'The self-regulated learner must appropriately control his or her learning processes by selecting and organizing relevant information and building connections from relevant existing knowledge (1992).' I was able to point to the strategies when students were confused and ask, 'which one of those have you tried,' which gave us a place to start for dialogue about each student's learning.*
>
> (Reed, 1999)

There are so many helpful examples in this case study of good teaching that exemplifies some of the important principles of learning and cognition that we have identified in earlier chapters in this book that it is worth listing them:

▶ Acknowledge that learning is a social as well as a cognitive activity.

▶ Directly encourage collaborative learning.

▶ Use explicitly taught reading strategies with weaker readers.

▶ Activate, classify and critique prior knowledge.

▶ Use the richest range of reading resources available.

▶ Set tasks that respect the knowledge already possessed by the group.

▶ Set tasks that involve an authentic purpose.

▶ Set tasks that involve an authentic audience.

▶ Intrinsic motivation is best, but in its absence, consider extrinsic motivation.

What makes a good reader? Leaving space for readers to set their own goals and to make text-to-life connections

Our third case study takes a different approach to supporting students in becoming more reflective readers, but it has much in common with Kathleen Reed's approach in that it involves collaborative learning, a respect for what students already know, and an attempt to make that knowledge explicit and then to build upon it.

In Alan Dewar's class of 15- and 16-year-olds, the purpose of the reading activity that I am about to describe was to try to help the students develop by using their own language and conceptual frameworks for describing and monitoring their progress as readers. Alan's school is a community college in a depressed former mining town in a semi-rural area of the Midlands of

England. The area has high unemployment but a strong sense of community, and the school is highly regarded in the area. Within the county, this school is close to average in terms of student achievement and the numbers going on to college, but higher than average in 'value-added' as measured by the county's statistics.

There were two parts to the enquiry: part one involved getting the students to think about what made a good reader and about what it might be for them to improve individually as readers. Part two was a follow-up on part one, approximately six months later, in which students discussed whether or not they had improved. Part one involved team-taught lessons for the whole class given by Alan and me in October and November, and part two was set up by Alan on his own, with the students' conversations tape-recorded. We began in October by asking the students to work in pairs, and getting them to try to say what they thought it was to be a good reader. A month later, we presented back to the group the results of what they had said, and encouraged them to reflect more deeply on what it might be for them to improve as readers, drawing upon their own ideas and those of their peers. The following April, we asked them to reflect on whether they had indeed improved as readers, again drawing upon their earlier reflections.

As teachers, Alan Dewar and I tried to support the students in using their own preferred language and concepts; we wanted to encourage deep and critical reflection, but we also wanted to see whether this could come about without superimposing our own discourse. Our reasoning was that, provided we as teachers were clear in relation to the goals we wanted to achieve, we should encourage the students to use their own preferred terminology which might be more comprehensible to them and to their peers than the discourse of psychology. Naturally, we accepted from the outset that everything that is said in a classroom is situated discourse, constrained by the authority structure of schooling and mediated through the discourse of schooling; even so, we tried to monitor and restrict our intervention in so far as the introduction of specialist terminology was concerned.

What came out of the October lesson is presented in Table 6.1. The students were told that the activities were intended to help them develop as readers and that their own views and opinions were very important and would be valued. The students were asked to work in pairs, in friendship groups, to list their own answers to the question, and later to share their responses with another group. The students wrote down their own ideas, putting a bullet point for each, and then, if they wanted to add a further point to their list following discussion with another group, this point would be indicated with a plus sign. There was plenty of discussion and sharing of ideas between the students, and some further ideas were added to their lists during whole-class reporting back. After the whole-class discussion, the students were encouraged to give thought to a further question: what does a good reader do that other readers don't? The aim here was to revisit the first question, but to do so by projection into the minds of their peers. We wondered whether the students might introduce into their answers some strategies that they thought others might find useful but which they did not themselves use.

Answers to this second question were written down, shared and added to in the same way as for the first question. At the end of the lesson, all the answers were collected in, and typed up into a single consolidated table, as shown in Table 6.1. This is the form in which we presented the information back to the group at the beginning of the November lesson.

In the event, as Table 6.1 makes clear, most of the students' ideas were based around comprehension and fluency. The freedom to use their own preferred language, though, permitted some interesting personal constructions of good reading behaviour to emerge. Good readers not only have good understanding, they can 'place themselves in the text' and will 'try to live the story'. A good reader will not only 'understand the deeper meanings of the text', but will 'let concentration mingle with the book'. A good reader will not only be fluent, he or she will demonstrate certain personal qualities in their reading: a good reader will like sharing what he or she has read; a good reader is confident, dedicated and careful, as well as being willing to re-read when necessary.

One other aspect of response on which many students commented was enjoyment. All three of the boys-only groups put enjoyment in their list of what makes a good reader, and interestingly none of the girls did this. But three groups containing girls put enjoyment in their list of what good readers do that other readers don't. We interpreted this as perhaps indicative of the salience of motivation (and in the case of many boys fairly low motivation) when it comes to reading, and therefore a factor that the boys were particularly aware of when considering what it was to be a good reader. For the girls, enjoying reading was clearly a factor as a point of difference between good and poor readers, but it did not appear until the second list, and in the case of Luke and Maxine only as an additional point.

Alan and I privately applauded this emphasis on the students' perception of reading as a matter of disposition and personal distance between themselves and the text, because these were factors over which the students might feel they had some control and therefore some opportunity for change and movement, but we also noted with some concern that there was very little emphasis on reading strategies in the students' lists. Looking up words and re-reading were certainly reading strategies, but there was little evidence of other cognitive strategies such as pre-reading, question setting, hypothesis formation or monitoring comprehension. Nevertheless, in planning the follow-up, we kept faith with our determination to value the students' own conceptions and encouraged discussion of these without introducing new terms or strategies of our own.

Table 6.1 What makes a good reader?

Students (Y11)	What makes a good reader?	What does a good reader do that other readers don't?
Jane, Sonia	• Someone who understands what words mean. • Someone who can concentrate. • Chooses own books. • Can look up words which confuse them. + Someone who doesn't skip words.	• Looks up words. • Reads for long periods of time. • Re-read if they don't understand. + Read every word, because key words could be missed out. + Understand plot and characters.
Michelle, Hester, Sarah, Katie, Charlotte	• Someone who can read a book and understand it. • Someone who has enough knowledge to understand the words in front of them. + Imagination. + Patience.	• Read something more carefully. • Most good readers enjoy reading. • A good reader tries to understand it. • A good reader lets concentration mingle with the book. + Dedication.
Ruben, Mark, Jamie, Jonathan, James	• Prepared to read. • Takes time. • Reads fluently. • Enjoys it. • Likes sharing his/her reading with others. + Understands the text. + Can describe what is happening.	• Expresses his/her opinions. • Spends more time reading. • Can interpret it better. + Understands the deeper meanings of the text. + Can write about the text.
Russell, Brett	• To make a good reader the person needs to read with comprehension, and also needs to be dedicated to it. • They need to read regularly, and may even have a schedule for it.	• A good reader can understand the plot, characters and theme of a text better than other readers do.

Table 6.1 Continued

	● A good reader will place himself/herself in the text and try, where possible, to live the story. ● They will read a whole book in a short space of time. + Enjoys reading. + Spelling good. + Imagination. + Good vocabulary. + Confidence.	● Enjoys reading. ● Feels as if they're part of the text. + Better understanding of the plot. + Reads often.
Kirsty, Kelly	● Dedicates time to reading. ● Likes reading. ● Understands the text. ● Feels as if they're there. + Good vocabulary. + Imagination. + Confidence.	
Luke, Maxine	● Understanding. ● Imagination. ● Patience.	● Dedication. + Read carefully. + Enjoy it. + Try more to understand. + Read it all (don't skip bits).

In the November lesson, we began by presenting the students with the information in Table 6.1 and encouraged small-group discussion of what the class as a whole had concluded. We then presented the students with the task of reflecting on their own possible improvement as readers, inviting them to list some questions that they might ask of themselves and then come back to later in the year in order to check on how they had improved as a reader. One group of boys and one group of girls asked to tape record their November discussion, so that they could listen to it later in the year. Table 6.2 shows the results of this second exercise. Many of the questions the students set themselves related to fluency and understanding, but there were some interesting changes of emphasis. Jane and Sonia's first question was about motivation, and they were among the five groups out of seven

Table 6.2 What questions might you ask of yourself and then come back to in order to see how you improve as a reader?

Students (Y11)	What questions might you ask of yourself and then come back to in order to see how you improve as a reader?
Jane, Sonia	● Do you enjoy reading? ● Can you read more fluently? ● Have you gained any knowledge about new words through reading and can you use them in your own work? ● Can you concentrate on your reading? + Do I understand what I read?
Michelle, Hester, Sarah, Katie, Charlotte	● Do I find it easy to read aloud? ● Have I got the patience? ● What is my concentration span like? Has it improved? ● Do I understand the things I read? ● Has my reading improved at all?
Ruben, Mark, Jamie, Jonathan, James	● How often do you read a book? ● What type of book do you read? ● Do you enjoy reading? ● How long do you spend reading each reading session? ● Where do you read? ● Do you think you understand most types of text?
Russell, Brett	● Do I understand the text? ● Do I understand the author and his/her viewpoint throughout the text? ● Do I enjoy the reading? ● Do I simply read the words, or do I read with understanding? ● Do I read the text regularly?
Kirsty, Kelly	● Do I enjoy reading? ● How much time do I spend reading?

Table 6.2 Continued

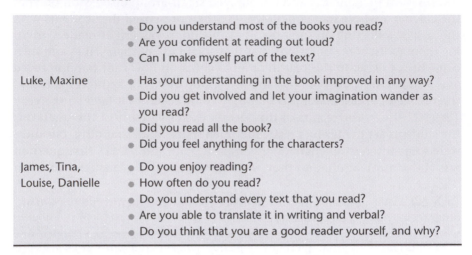

	• Do you understand most of the books you read? • Are you confident at reading out loud? • Can I make myself part of the text?
Luke, Maxine	• Has your understanding in the book improved in any way? • Did you get involved and let your imagination wander as you read? • Did you read all the book? • Did you feel anything for the characters?
James, Tina, Louise, Danielle	• Do you enjoy reading? • How often do you read? • Do you understand every text that you read? • Are you able to translate it in writing and verbal? • Do you think that you are a good reader yourself, and why?

that on re-reading their October list put enjoyment as a factor they might wish to monitor as an indicator of whether they had improved as a reader. Jane and Sonia also wanted to focus on vocabulary development. Michelle's group put concentration span and patience into their list (a number of their teachers would have heartily applauded these goals!). But Ruben's group also stressed reading stamina ('how long do you spend reading each session?'), as did Kirsty and Kelly. Luke and Maxine, who had put 'imagination' and 'patience' in their original list, included perhaps the most lyrical personal goal: 'Did you get involved and let your imagination wander as you read?' We found this emphasis on personal response, which we felt was also present throughout the groups (in our view, there were affective goals in the points made by every group on Table 6.2), suggested that collectively the students had a holistic perception of what it was to be a good reader – that being a better reader was not just about skills and intellect, but about how you felt about reading, and how you felt towards the book and the characters in the book.

Alan encouraged the students to reflect on these issues during the months that followed. In April, as the students approached the conclusion of the two-year course leading to the exams that mark the end of statutory schooling in England, Alan asked if any were willing to volunteer to tape record a conversation in a teacherless small group about their progress as readers. No boys volunteered, and the seven girls who volunteered asked if they could all work together in a single group. The girls were familiar with using a tape recorder in English lessons and recorded a 20-minute discussion. Alan is regarded by his peers, both within his school and beyond it (he was elected chair of the county association of Heads of English departments), as a dedicated and very effective English teacher, the sort who spends many hours on lesson preparation and on giving detailed formative commentary on students' written work, and he thought that he knew these students well. But after listening to the tape, he told me, 'I learned more from this 20-minute tape about how I can respond to and support the development of these seven readers than I have done from the 12 pieces of written work in their portfolios that have been collected over 18-months.' The girls' discussion ranged fairly widely, from fluency and concentration span to their personal reading habits and the gulf between these and the texts they were required to read for school. At the same time, however, they revealed some powerful insights into Shakespeare, the politics of reading and the nature of education.

The first question the girls addressed was about whether they had improved as readers. Alice answered first, and her answer produced an audible shocked reaction from the other girls. This 16-year-old had been reading 'Noddy and Ladybird books', the sort of book many parents buy for pre-school children, in order to find material that was at her preferred reading level:

Charlotte *How have we got better?*

Alice   *Since we made the last tape I've read extra books; my reading has got a lot better. I've been reading Noddy and Ladybird books...* [Audible intake of breath from the others] *I have! It's just helped me; it just gets you, when you're speaking it, when you're reading it, more fluently, instead of story-like 'de-de-de-de'.*

Alan and I both felt that Alice would never have admitted in front of the whole class that she had been reading the books of her much younger sister, but in the privacy and security of a group of her peers this could be said. This environment also permitted the girls to reveal, in talking about whether or not their concentration span had improved, that they had not been reading the books on which they were about to be examined:

Charlotte *What's your concentration span in school, then?*

Sarah   *Ooh ... about two minutes. To tell you the truth, I haven't read any of them books we're supposed to be doing ... 'cos they're so boring. You cannot expect me to read a book that is so boring.*

Sarah also makes it clear that she is not unwilling to read, and was happy to read 'normal books'. But not only did she see Shakespeare as impossibly difficult, she saw being required to read Shakespeare as a government-initiated torture:

Sonia	*I can read out loud better ... I enjoy reading ... I concentrate on it if I find it interesting ...*
Sarah	*I'm more confident in front of the class. My concentration span is improving. But understanding the things that I read is still very confusing for me. I don't know what I'm reading ... I just do it. Especially with Macbeth. Normal books I can read and really get into. But these Shakespeare books I can't get into at all. I don't think we should be made to do it at all ... I've improved on reading aloud ... because people make me at home ... My concentration span varies: when I'm reading at home, I can read for like – oh, I don't know – five minutes. But when I'm at school reading all these stupid government GCSE-Literature-you've-got-to-do-it-or-else-you'll-not-get-any-grades ...*
	[The girls interrupt to cheer. They laugh.]

One thing was clear – these girls might not have liked Shakespeare, but they had become vocal and confident young people, with strong opinions and a developing awareness of the fact that reading and politics are firmly related. They were also aware of the fact that reading connects to their lives and that they had a social responsibility in relation to reading:

Sonia	*I promise you, I read every day. This is Sonia. Because I read the paper. It's the only thing I find interesting to read, the paper, because –*
Charlotte	*Because it's true – real life, it's crime. We're going to learn more from society if we read the paper. But not* The Sun, *'cos that's a Tory paper.* The Mirror. The Daily Mirror. *Not* Macbeth! *Not Shakespeare! Not Hamilton – er – Hamlet! Not* Romeo and Juliet!
Sarah	*You do realise that you're pointing your pencil at the tape recorder!*
	[They all laugh.]

Now the girls were on a roll. But as their invective against the set texts of school gathered momentum, they also revealed that they were becoming interested and critical readers, with a sense that newspapers are not value-free and had a political purpose. The discussion of the difference between the 'natural' reading of newspapers and the 'unnatural' reading of school texts continued and began to focus on another opposition, that between recalling the text and commenting on character:

Sonia *It's one thing, you see, in that you might read a book, and you might find that you understand the plot and the structure, and you might get to the exam, and you've bloomin' got a question on characterisation, and you don't understand that at all. Or you're doing viewpoint, in something, and you don't understand that.*

Charlotte *We learn about characterisations, viewpoint, structure, atmosphere and plot ... but ... and style. But do we really understand it? This is what I'm asking you, Professor ...*

[The others giggle, then say]: *Shut up! Shut up!*

Suddenly (they hadn't seen me for nearly six months) came a powerful expression of the girls' awareness of the arbitrary and potentially invalid nature of reading assessment procedures. Sonia and Charlotte demonstrated an awareness of the discourse of English literature essays and used it confidently, ending with the ironic rhetorical question to a distant authority. But in fact, as their conversation shows, and despite their protestations, these girls had an interesting perspective on the character of Macbeth.

Charlotte *If you retell the story, it proves that you've read the book, and understand what you're reading –*

Sonia *– and you know what the characters are doing, because, say Macbeth kills somebody, he's killing somebody because he wants – he's got ambition, he's angry, he's been drinking. All the usual reasons you kill people.*

Let us just consider for a moment what the girls are saying about murder. Most commentators on the death of Duncan have dwelt on Macbeth's ambition and the bloody dagger that invites him to commit murder. But to the girls in this town, no lessons from teachers or literary critics are necessary to explain why a man gets murdered in the middle of the night – it happens when people get drunk and when men are angry and drunk. But were they reading Macbeth in order to help them understand murder, or to help them pass exams? The girls had no doubt:

> Charlotte *If you're writing about what Shakespeare has written, you know what the characters are like. You know how it says, you're not supposed to write like a social worker, and you know the characters like that –*
>
> Sonia *Surely, if you're writing like a social worker, you're showing that you understand what the characters are going through, and therefore you understand what Shakespeare's making them do.*
>
> Charlotte *This shows how education has changed. Before, you used to go to school to learn things for life. Now you just go to learn things for exams, and do things that you're never going to use in your life ever again. So what is the point? ... [pause] ... Listen to this, right? What you really need is: you go to Switzerland, you go to a finishing school. And that's all we need to learn – to be polite, well mannered, and to respect our elders. That's all we need to get through life. And it's not what you know, it's WHO YOU KNOW!*

These young women, and the other students in their class, had only three months before the point at which they could choose to leave school, and in many respects the 'What makes a good reader?' exercise revealed a disturbing chasm between the goals of the education system and the needs of the individuals whom the system is intended to serve. These students were, like their counterparts in the alternative high school in Colorado, acutely aware of and articulate about the elitist nature of the education system in western countries, with its discourse of inclusivity and its mechanisms of alienation. In this respect this case study could be read as dispiriting and depressing. But my intention in including it has been carefully considered, and I suggest that the case study has plenty of relevance in relation to the overarching aims of this book.

First, the discussion demonstrated a willingness on the girls' part to see reading as an important part of their lives, something they thought was relevant to them, that was related to their self-confidence and at which they wanted to improve. Second, they saw reading as something that related to the world beyond school: 'We're going to learn more from society if we read the paper,' said Charlotte. Third, as the comment on Macbeth and murder showed, the girls were making text-to-life connections, and they understood that a key purpose of reading was to enable you to '... understand what the characters are going through.' As a group, the girls were dismissive of the aims of the education system in relation to passing examinations, and the cheer that greeted the rhetorically powerful phrase 'all these stupid government GCSE-Literature-you've-got-to-do-it-or-else-you'll-not-get-any-grades ...' was triumphant. Of course some of the girls went on to do very well in those exams, but the point remains that if one of the most profound goals of an English teacher is to encourage students to 'Read, in order to live,' there was evidence on this tape that this goal was being achieved.

In this case study, there were a number of pedagogical principles revisited that relate to our understanding of reading development and which connect with the themes highlighted in the first two case studies and in earlier chapters:

- Respect and make space for students' views of themselves as readers.
- Encourage a holistic response and 'living the story'.
- Don't underestimate students' willingness to make text-to-life connections.
- Work on dictionary and vocabulary skills for everyone.
- Make connections with newspapers and other easy reading.
- Don't overestimate students' preferred 'easy reading' level.
- Try to make reading enjoyable for everyone.
- Get students to set personal goals for reading improvement and to revisit them.

These case studies have each highlighted examples from the classroom of ways to make explicit, to encourage and to deepen reflection on reading and reading comprehension. Implicitly, each case study has also been about encouraging criticality in a reader. This theme is one that has been given increasing attention by academics, and because of its importance we shall devote the next chapter to the development of criticality.

Chapter 7

Developing critical literacy: text, discourse and the collaborative construction meaning

Introduction

What is critical literacy, and why is it so important in relation to under-standing reading development? The answer is that language practices are becoming ever more important in determining, reproducing and sustaining the power relations that dominate and control our society, and since many of those language practices operate in ways that are implicit rather than explicit, it becomes a matter of great importance to be able to locate, iden-tify and critique those practices. As Norman Fairclough, who first popularised the term 'critical language awareness' (CLA), put it:

> It is changes of this sort that make critical approaches to language study of particular contemporary relevance, and make CLA an urgently needed element in language education. CLA is, I believe, coming to be a prerequisite for effective democratic citizenship, and should therefore be seen as an entitlement for citizens, especially children developing towards citizenship in the educational system.
>
> (Fairclough, 1992, p. 3)

Of course the use of the term 'critical' is not a new one as applied to society and the culture industry. As Siegel and Fernandez (2000) argue in a very useful essay on critical approaches in the *Handbook of Reading Research, Volume III*, the critical theory of the Frankfurt School in the late 1920s and early 1930s was perhaps the mainspring of this approach to historical, sci-entific and cultural analysis, particularly as it was interpreted through the writings of Jürgen Habermas. The crisis that precipitated the need for criti-cal theory was twofold: on one side was the increasingly rationalist and positivist path down which philosophy and linguistics were moving, which was tending to reduce philosophy to a branch of logic with a separation of facts from values; on the other side was a concern about the relationship between theory and society, with science moving down pathways of knowledge that were only a decade away from splitting the atom, but which had no structural connection with either human betterment or the world of ethics. The urgency of the crisis was felt keenly in the University of Frankfurt itself, since the rise of Nazism forced the members of the Frankfurt School into exile in the US. The effects of critical theory began to spread from continental Europe into philosophy, sociology and literary theory during the 1960s, as Marxist and subsequently neo- and finally post-Marxist critiques began to permeate these fields.

In the field of education, the impact of critical theory began to be felt first in the sociology of education, particularly through the influential work of two English authors, M.F.D. Young and Paul Willis, whose books *Knowledge and Society* (Young, 1971) and *Learning to Labour* (Willis, 1977) opened many people's eyes to questions related to the authority of knowledge and theories of cultural reproduction, and to challenges to those analyses. Around the same time the liberation theology of Paulo Freire was also beginning to have an impact, particularly on those involved with the education of adults. Freire's most influential book, *Pedagogy of the Oppressed* (1970), is in some respects a synthesis of Christian principles from the Sermon on the Mount ('But I say unto you, Love your enemies, bless them that curse you, do good to them that hate you, and pray for them which despitefully use you, and persecute you': Matthew 5: 44) and Marxist principles of worker solidarity. Freire saw not only poverty but also the colonial government of his native Brazil as contributing to oppression in ways that damaged not only the oppressed but also the oppressor. What was needed, argued Freire, was a pedagogy of liberation that had the potential to break up and replace the structures of dominance and dependence that existed in Brazil, but which other commentators have felt are increasingly present in the current globalised economy. What was needed was not an armed struggle against oppression, but a deeper understanding of the fact that oppressor and oppressed existed in a dialectical relationship which was self-sustaining because it was not questioned or understood. Both oppressor and oppressed are dehumanised, but through a process of critical analysis, *concientização*, we can become able to perceive social, political and economic contradictions, and to engage in a struggle for liberation against these oppressive forces. And a key site for this struggle was pedagogy.

For Freire, a critique of the concept of 'illiteracy' was a key focus for this liberation theology. He argued that illiteracy was not the product of an individual's failure or the failure of their family; it was rather a historically constructed product of society that had a structural bias to produce inequality. Strategies for reducing 'illiteracy' therefore had to begin, not with literacy programmes for adults, but with a critical examination of the conditions, and especially the linguistic conditions, that produced those inequalities:

> *Consistent with the liberating purpose of dialogical education, the object of investigation is not persons ... but rather the thought-language with which men and women refer to reality, the levels at which they perceive that reality, and their view of the world in which their generative themes are found.*
>
> (Freire, 1970, p. 78)

If 'illiteracy' is one key concept that has to be seriously reconsidered from a critical theory perspective, perhaps the other most important lexical casualty of critical theory is 'truth'. There are dozens of possible routes into an analysis of truth, but one of the most useful from the point of view of contemporary cultural history is that of Foucault (1977). The concept of truth has in the past 50 years been reconsidered by philosophers of science, theologians, logicians, critical theorists and cultural theorists, among many others, but one reason for briefly considering Foucault's account is that he explicitly links his analysis to language and to society. Foucault developed a theory of power that saw power as pivotal in all social relationships and in constructing all types of discourse and all forms of knowledge. Truth, by contrast, was no longer the absolute that we had grown used to perceiving it to be:

> *Truth is a thing of this world: it is produced only by virtue of multiple forms of constraint. And it induces regular effects of power. Each society has its regime of truth, its 'general politics' of truth, that is, the types of discourse that it accepts and makes function as true, the mechanisms and instances which enable one to distinguish true and false statements ...*
>
> (Foucault, 1977, p. 131)

What Foucault goes on to argue is that what we call 'truth' is a construct made up of political and economic forces within a society – there is no universal truth, but rather there are truth-generating apparatuses within a society, and within all societies.

As Siegel and Fernandez point out, the reading field has been relatively slow to take on the perspectives of critical theory, and the main reason has perhaps been the essentially positivist discourses of psychology, and particularly the version of psychology most privileged by governments and research grant-awarding bodies. Governments that fund research want unequivocal answers to 'what works?' questions, and critical literacy may not be welcome where it challenges conventional beliefs related to the confidence we can have in relation to the findings of 'scientific' research into literacy.

Critical literacy is different from literacy. Literacy, as most governments understand it, increases educational achievement levels, improves the job-market skills of the population and cuts down crime. Critical literacy does none of these things: critical literacy challenges what schooling is attempting to achieve; it makes people more likely to be confident and articulate workers, who are ready, when necessary, to challenge their bosses about working practices, about the ethics of production, about redundancies; and it makes those in prison able and more likely to complain about their conditions. It's not easy to evaluate the effects of adult literacy programmes, because those who have been failures within or who have been failed by the education system hate tests. But it is not difficult to detect the efficacy of a critical literacy programme: those in power become uncomfortable.

Critical literacy and media studies

Texts are pieces of social action and critical language awareness attempts to lay bare some of the assumptions and value systems that have helped to construct that social action. Media texts, for example those produced by television, radio or newspapers, have their own value systems, their own grammars and their own discourses, and we are still in the early stages of developing tools for analysing these and certainly still in the early stages of bringing them into the classroom. But the need to do so is urgent, and I shall illustrate it by a single example: the media coverage of a singular tragedy – the events of September 11 2001. On that day, for most of us, the events of a normal working day gave way to a period of time – for some many hours, for others many days – in which the media, and particularly television, dominated our consciousness. Normal living was suspended for most of us as we were transfixed by the images and messages, myths and stories, facts and conjectures, interviews and commentaries. The indescribable trauma, pain and loss is instantly and fully evoked every time I recall, not a visual image, but an inadvertent metaphor uttered by a child whose school was only a few blocks away from the World Trade Center. What the child said to her teacher was 'the birds are on fire'.

It was difficult enough as adults to attempt to come to some sort of understanding of what happened on that day, but as teachers and as parents, many of us faced professional challenges that we felt ill-equipped to meet, as we sought to answer questions, to deflect questions, to find some kind of explanation, to find some sort of appropriate space to deal respectfully and properly with those events, conscious as we did so that in the playground (and, *sotto voce*, in the workplace), within two or three days, 'jokes' relating to those events were already beginning to circulate.

One response to the professional challenge faced in such a situation, a response that I would argue is worth considering because it gives back to the teacher some sort of moral leadership at a time when a moral vacuum leaves space for every kind of racist and fanatical reaction, is to consider a straightforward media studies approach. I am going to reproduce below a posting that I made to the National Reading Conference e-mail list, just two days after September 11 and which argues for such an approach. I thought very carefully before I pressed the 'Send' key, but two thoughts encouraged me to do so: first, if we have a moral responsibility to teach, then that responsibility is even greater at times of crisis and when others are asking for help; second, the theories of semiotics and media analysis are complex and subtle, but the tools of analysis – the questions one needs to ask – are simple and readily put to work, but the answers they produce can be very revealing, and as with all critical analysis, to generate answers begins to put the power back into the hands of the consumer and to reverse the power relations that are so unbalanced when we become the helpless absorbent surfaces on which the media messages are projected.

This is what I wrote:

One perspective which has not been mentioned thus far in the discussion of texts around which to focus conversations which might have the potential to help young people to come to terms with the terrible events of Tuesday (September 11th) and its aftermath is that of media studies. Clearly, to even make this suggestion is to risk offending many people, since to begin any sort of analysis of the visual and media texts would, for most groups, be felt to be inappropriate at this time. But, I would wish to align myself with those who argue that currently (in what we are pleased to call the developed world), it is through these visual and multimedia texts (especially newspapers, TV, and, increasingly, the Web) that we learn, and learn to form our opinions and beliefs. The results of undertaking even a very limited analysis of what is presented to us by the media are nearly always problematic, and difficult for a teacher to handle. Yet, how much more difficult would it be to engage in critical literacy discussion of how TV and other media have meditated our understanding, our representations, and our views ... first of what happened, and second, of how we understand what happened, and third, of how we behave in light of what happened, individually and collectively. Right now, it is the time for care, for hugs, and for making kids feel less afraid. But maybe later, when it's time to ask questions about how we try to understand, teachers (and they will have to be very sensitive and perhaps brave teachers) will think about adopting a media approach. Media analysis begins with simple questions:

▶ *What did we see?*

▶ *Why were we shown this?*

▶ *What were some of the effects of its being shown this way?*

▶ *What might have been some of the effects of its being done differently?*

These questions can apply just as much to a family video of a wedding as to real-time TV coverage of a catastrophe. But (unless the teacher takes a very strong editorial line), such analyses tend to lead inevitably to one thing – to students gaining thoughtful, critical, and better-informed personal understanding of the events that occurred. They also gain understanding of the ways in which it is impossible to represent 'reality' without editorial bias – and this leads to a more informed understanding of how meaning is made for us in our world by the media, and ultimately to an awareness that we can play an active part in constructing meaning for ourselves. In the past two days (which seems like years – and I am acutely aware that I am not an American, and come as a guest when I visit your country), adults and children in England have seen some terrible scenes repeated and repeated, and used as a visual backdrop to talking-head interviews. Someone decided to do this. Someone decided to show images of people in some communities in the world celebrating the tragedy with laughter and delight. Someone decided that we should see an interview with two New Yorkers who were looking for a lost loved one, but who said to the microphone, 'Why are we hated this much?' How might people's feelings be different if they had – or had not – seen one or more of these images? I cannot say, but I do feel that media analysis can help students to make personal sense of the world, as they reflect on what they have witnessed in the media, and on how those images were gathered, edited, juxtaposed, and broadcast.

(Harrison, 2003)

Media studies undertaken in the way described above would be challenging for the students and for the teacher, but I would want to argue that since in many respects the media define our culture, we have a responsibility to give our students tools for deconstructing and understanding the mechanisms by which and through which that culture comes to be represented.

The promise of multiliteracies

Much of what has preceded this chapter has emphasised the development of the individual reader. Critical language awareness, by contrast, is often discussed in a wider social or civic context. The work of the New London Group, of which Norman Fairclough was a member, emphasises citizenship and the relationship between texts and cultures rather than just texts and readers: '... we want to extend the idea and scope of literacy pedagogy to account for the context of our culturally and linguistically diverse and increasingly globalised societies; to account for the multifarious cultures that interrelate and the plurality of texts that circulate' (New London Group, 1996). A crucial factor in considering this new pedagogy is that it needs to be extended to accommodate a plurality of literacies – including the variety of text forms associated with information and multimedia technologies.

In many respects, a multiliteracies approach to education ought to hold the promise of democratisation. After all, if tens of millions of people are using the Internet daily, if tens of millions of people are sending text messages on their phones daily, if it takes only a tenth of a second for an Internet search engine to search over 3,000,000,000 websites and to locate getting on for a million results evoked by the term 'critical literacy', then surely this suggests that the promise of democratisation of knowledge and the production of knowledge is being realised. Doesn't it? The answer is yes, but there are two major problems: first, for many marginalised or disadvantaged groups, that promise is only slowly being realised, or is not yet being realised at all; second, the apparent democratisation of knowledge and the 'conversationalisation' of discourses can mask a process of radical change that is essentially market-driven and whose values are neither made explicit nor readily open to challenge.

On the first of these points, cultural commentators have noted that technology is expensive, and that the means of technological production remain in the hands of an elite few, with the result that the problems and inequalities caused by economic status recur or even multiply with technology. As Colette Daiute (2000) pointed out, 'Because literacy development depends in large part on having extensive, engaging exposure to print and involvement with communication technologies is print intensive, students who do not have access to these technologies may be at a disadvantage.' This is indeed what the ImpaCT2 project found (Becta, 2002). In England, in 2001, 90 per cent of 15-year-old school students had a computer in their home, but there was nevertheless a significant correlation between socio-economic status and computer ownership, and an even stronger relationship between socio-economic status and access to the Internet.

Where that access is available, however, it can make an important difference. Daiute quotes the words of a young student, Ryman, whose access to the Internet changed the availability of information not only for him, but for others:

> *The library had like two books, and I was the one that had the computer at*
> *home and could get access to the Internet, and I went online and got all the*
> *information that they [students in my groups at school] needed, and also I*
> *typed everybody's papers for them, cause not a lot of kids have computers.*
>
> (Daiute, 2000)

But Daiute also argues that some of the accounts of the democratic nature of communication in cyberspace are overoptimistic, in that when technology is made available to poor and low-income groups, children are encouraged to learn to use them in 'deskilled' ways. Such students may be taught word processing skills (and, we might add, put on programmed learning systems whose goals are to increase those basic skills), while their more affluent peers are using the computer for personal research and the development of critical thinking. On a more optimistic note, though, Daiute (2000) reviewed a number of studies that remind us that cyberspace does offer potentially democratic environments, where colour, gender and nationality do not necessarily declare themselves, and where there is a tremendous range of authentic audiences and possibilities for communication in a wide variety of formats.

For Ernest Morrell (2002), in a recent article in the New Literacies department of Reading Online (www.readingonline.org), critical pedagogy and literacy development came together around the concept of popular culture. For it was there that students could explore aspects of literacy that accommodated a broader range of social contexts than those normally accessible within the dominant culture of the school curriculum, and this was very important for groups that have traditionally felt themselves to be marginalised by that curriculum. Morrell suggests that the critical teaching of popular culture is one way to make connections that are relevant to all students in diverse urban classrooms.

Starting from the premise that hip-hop culture is the representative voice of urban youth, Morrell aimed to design a classroom unit that would give a critical literacy space within which to consider and discuss rap music as part of the consciousness-raising that is an essential component of critical pedagogy. Morrell presented a lecture on poetry that linked individual poems to specific time periods of historical and cultural importance (the Elizabethan age, the US Civil War, etc.) and then invited the students, working in small groups, to prepare a presentation linking a rap song chosen by the group to a short talk on its historical and literacy context. The presentations would then be critiqued by their peers. What happened of course was that not only did the students generate thoughtful, socially contextualised commentaries on the rap songs they chose as important; they were inspired to create their own poems to serve as a celebration of the event. The students 'moved beyond critical reading of literary texts to become cultural producers themselves, creating and presenting poems that provided critical social commentary and encouraged action for social justice' (Morrell, 2002). Providing an opportunity for the students to engage in critical literacy within a school context that valued their out-of-school culture proved very successful, but it also met the criteria of critical pedagogy in that it called for critical dialogue between students and between the school and non-school discourses.

The concept of applying critical pedagogy to multiliteracies goes well beyond extending the range and provenance of written forms that become subject to critique. In his chapter in the *Multiliteracies* volume that framed the theories of the New London Group, Gunther Kress (2000) argued that currently existing theories of meaning and communication cannot adequately describe or characterise the communication landscape of our contemporary world. First, he suggests, verbal communication involves much more than lexis and grammar; it involves, for example, the pragmatics of social distancing in ways that link word and image ('I look down on him ... I look up to him') that are nowhere described in current theories of semiotics. Second, theories of semiotics as they currently stand do not possess characteristics that make them capable of taking account of exponentially increasing change in relation to form and meaning; still less do they have causal or teleological mechanisms that might explain or enable us to predict that change. What is needed, he suggests, are new theoretical tools that move beyond definitions predicated on competence and use, and into areas that model and understand the mechanisms of transformation and design. Kress goes on to argue that all texts are multimodal, and gives a fascinating example of this through a semiotic analysis of a bottle of mineral water on a supermarket shelf.

As we walk along the shelves of a supermarket, argues Kress (2000, p. 188), we not only 'read' the text on the label of the bottles, we 'read' the bottles, noticing their shape (will they fit in my fridge? how would they look on the dinner table?), noting whether they are glass or plastic, coloured or colourless, are decorated with fake royal crests or vignettes of an idyllic Scottish countryside. This 'reading', suggests Kress, is a semiotic practice in which it is the meanings as much as the water which are 'consumed'. And the 'delightfully still' water from the Hampshire Downs calls up further sets of associations, one set related to the shock of learning that the water had been 'protected for millennia from the environment' (Kress hadn't realised that the environment was something from which he needed such protection!), and one set related to his personal associations with Hampshire (the novels of Hardy, the music of Elgar and the voice of John Arlott, the cricket commentator). All these form part of what Kress called 'the reinforcing mesh of meaning'. On such a multimodal analysis, the 'meaning' that is communicated by the bottle is hugely extended. Kress goes on to develop numerous other examples of multimodal communication, involving other objects, body language and pages from children's drawing and writing, and school textbooks. His overall message is clear – a critical literacy that takes on multimodalities is going to be essential, but it is also a form of semiotic cultural practice that engages all the senses and will therefore necessarily involve a great deal of complexity and negotiation, since the analytical tools that will do this work are still in the process of being designed.

In his essay describing four innovative programmes that exemplify some of the principles of multiliteracy, Courtney Cazden (2000) cites a metaphor from an Aboriginal language that has been used to frame and organise the curriculum of Yirrkala, a community school in a remote region in the Northern Territory of Australia. The word is *ganma*, and it refers to the places where fresh and salt water meet, and metaphorically ganma is where two cultures meet. The fresh water represents the indigenous culture, and the salt water is the white knowledge and culture, and the place where they meet is school. The fresh water cannot harm the ocean, but the salt water can potentially flood the land. However, if the two are kept in balance, a rich and diverse culture can develop. Very briefly, and while recognising that these summaries can give no more than the flavour of the programmes, Cazden's four case studies establish the following points:

▶ In Boston, a six-year-old girl, Jiana, from a traumatised background, comes to first grade in a school that prides itself on its respect for difference, and a sympathetic teacher and fellow students enable Jiana both to develop her language skills and her personal voice, partly through their accepting Jiana's novel approach to Sharing Time, which she adapts from a 'true' news story time to a 'fake' fantasy and fictional personal narrative time.

▶ In a Californian community school, a programme involving English teachers and Mexican-American mentors supporting students' personal writing portfolio is successful in building the confidence and identity of Juan, a Hispanic student.

▶ In a Sydney high school, students with a multiplicity of home languages (including Vietnamese, Greek, Arabic and Chinese) were encouraged to study their home language in school as part of the official curriculum for at least four years, and although time for English in the curriculum was decreased, proficiency scores in English increased.

▶ In a school in Alice Springs that was subsequently closed, a Concentrated Language Encounters programme developed a radical curriculum focused substantially on Aboriginal issues and critical language awareness; attendance was remarkably high.

Somewhat ruefully, Cazden reports that all four programmes have either been closed down or threatened with closure. The crucial point in the four accounts of educational practices in different parts of the world in which two cultures meet is that ganma is never simply about curriculum or about students – it is about teachers, and their willingness to seek balance in the cultural dialogues that determine the role of the teacher, the language of the teacher, and the business of schooling. An attempt to develop a curriculum that respects the culture of the individuals in the class is always likely to involve risk, negotiation and tension, but Cazden reports examples in his innovative settings of students from minority cultures developing critical literacy and flourishing in environments that respect their home culture and do not inadvertently or wilfully attempt to ignore or marginalise that culture.

Coda

In this brief chapter we have explored some of the key concepts related to the term 'critical language awareness' and other related terms that involve engaging students in a critical dialogue with texts. I've tried to suggest that such explorations need to be undertaken in ways that privilege multiple literacies, multiple voices and multiple cultures, and I'm acutely aware that I've left much unsaid. I've not made space for talking about the eminently worthy Reading and Writing for Critical Thinking project which has trained 12,000 teachers, and its journal *Thinking Classroom: A Journal of Reading, Writing and Critical Reflection* which has made such a strong impact in post-Communist countries, though I shall talk about it in the final chapter of the book.

But I hope that I have made one point very clear – namely that critical literacy is not just about generating new discourses; it is about the potential of those discourses to produce human betterment, democracy and emancipation. It's about those in power becoming uncomfortable.

Chapter 8

Evaluating response to reading: can there be such a thing as postmodern assessment?

Introduction

The goals of this chapter are simple, though their implications are complex. These are:

- to express some of the problems facing reading assessment in the areas of ethics, statistics and cognition;
- to identify a coherent theoretical basis for a review of the principles that should address these problems;
- to derive a set of principles from that theoretical base;
- to identify some of the chief implications for practice that come from those principles.

There are good reasons for considering assessment in a book on understanding reading development. The chief one is that because assessment drives the curriculum, it is important to consider how best the forces that do this might be made to operate in benign rather than malignant ways, and enhance reading development rather than stifle it.

I have no problem with the principle of accountability. In a publicly funded education system, we, the teachers, must accept that we have a responsibility to those who have been elected to run that system to deliver the best education we can using the resources available. Of course we have other responsibilities too, and these include a moral imperative not to stand idly by if our employers bring in policies that are damaging to our students. And there is little disagreement among educationists that 'high-stakes' assessment damages children. In England there is some evidence that the tide is beginning to turn against national tests in a country that has the most tested children in Europe: following a recent survey that reported that 10 per cent of seven-year-olds have been reduced to tears and have lost sleep over the national tests, parents' organisations are starting to withdraw their children from school at the time of the tests (BBC, 2003). The news report quoted a survey that showed that over 10 per cent of 11-year-olds refused to go to school to sit the Key Stage 2 national tests. We also know that tests damage teachers: in England in 2003 we had the tragic case of a headteacher being sent to prison for three months after pleading guilty to forging test results of 11-year-olds. While many fellow teachers will have felt sympathy for the enormous pressure that led this person to commit such a crime, the chair of the school governing body did not take such a view, and was on record as saying: 'I am pleased he got a custodial sentence and I hope that this will send out a clear message to schools everywhere.' And just in case anyone in the US is complacent about teachers cheating in tests, a paper by Jacob and Levitt (2001), who developed a clever mathematical model for spotting unusual answer strings and test score fluctuations, reported that 4–5 per cent of all classrooms in the Chicago Public Schools district indicated teacher cheating on standardised tests.

In the context of this chapter, though, student anxiety and teacher cheating are not the primary issues. At least as important as these ethical issues are the other fundamental problems with high-stakes testing, namely that it rarely does the job of assessing reading effectively, and its backwash effects actually hamper reading development. Richard Elmore, the distinguished school accountability specialist from Harvard, wrote a critique of the high-stakes testing built into the 2002 US Elementary and Secondary Education Act that had the dramatic title 'Testing trap: the single largest – and possibly most destructive – federal intrusion into America's public schools' (Elmore, 2002). It is worth quoting from his paper at some length:

> *Under the new law, the federal government mandates a single test-based accountability system for all states – a system currently operating in fewer than half the states. It requires annual testing at every grade level, and states must disaggregate their test scores by students' racial and socioeconomic backgrounds – a system currently operating in only a handful of states, and one fraught with technical difficulties. The federal government further mandates a single definition of adequate yearly progress, the amount by which schools must increase their test scores in order to avoid some sort of sanction – an issue that in the past has been decided jointly by states and Washington. Finally, the law sets a single target date by which all students must exceed a state-defined proficiency level – an issue that in the past has been left almost entirely to states and localities.*
>
> *Thus the federal government is now accelerating the worst trend of the current accountability movement: that performance-based accountability has come to mean testing alone. In the early stages of the current movement, reformers*

had an expansive view of performance that included, in addition to tests, portfolios and formal exhibitions of students' work, student-initiated projects, and teachers' evaluations of their students. The comparative appeal of standardised tests is easy to see: they are relatively inexpensive to administer; can be mandated simply; can be rapidly implemented; and deliver clear, visible results. But relying only on standardised tests dodges the complicated questions of what tests actually measure and of how schools and students react when tests are the sole yardstick of performance.

If this shift in federal policy were based on the accumulated wisdom gained from experiences with accountability in states, districts, and schools, or if it were based on clear design principles that had some basis in practice, it might be worth the risk. In fact, however, it is based on little more than talk among people who know hardly anything about the institutional realities of accountability – and even less about the problems of improving instruction in schools.

(Elmore, 2002)

This comprehensive indictment echoes some of the points made four years earlier by one of the top educational statistics experts in the world, Lee Cronbach, who with his colleagues (Cronbach et al., 1997) called into question the fundamental assumptions of generalisation from the statistics on individuals to high-stakes decisions relating to schools and whole districts.

Of no less importance in challenging the approach of governments to high stakes testing was the position statement of the American Evaluation Association, whose task force on testing spent a year reviewing all the available evidence before coming to its conclusion that 'High stakes testing leads to under-serving or mis-serving all students, especially the most needy and vulnerable, thereby violating the principle of "do no harm"' (AEA, 2003). The task force stated that 'The consequences that concern us most are increased drop out rates, teacher and administrator deprofessionalisation, loss of curricular integrity, increased cultural insensitivity, and disproportionate allocation of educational resources into testing programs and not into hiring qualified teachers and providing sound educational programs.'

The AEA task force came up with what was in my view a devastating list of the challenges that need to be met before high stakes testing is routinely administered. It sets the agenda for change in a professional and productive manner, not by rejecting but by specifying the complex nature of the task ahead if such assessments are to be conducted in a theoretically sound and ethically just manner. The new procedures need to address:

▶ how gaps in educational achievement between minority and non-minority students are effected;

▶ the amount of student and teacher time taken away from other valued school goals and activities;

> the extent to which improvements in test scores are reflections of actual and valued student learning;

> the extent to which curriculum is narrowed, and how, by the test;

> the impact on non-tested subjects;

> the impact on English language learners, special education students, high mobility students and students with special talents;

> drop out rates;

> the fairness, accuracy, validity, reliability and credibility of the measures of content and thinking skills that students are expected to master;

> the extent and form of cheating to increase scores;

> the accuracy, fairness and disclosure of scoring procedures, cut score setting and methods of aggregation;

> incidence of disciplinary action or termination of teachers as a direct result of high-stakes testing;

> monetary and non-monetary costs of high-stakes testing practices and policies;

> ethical issues, such as access to student records and student, teacher and parent rights to know.

(AEA, 2003)

So, given this somewhat daunting list, where should we begin? My answer would have to be with the eighth point – the fairness, accuracy, validity, reliability and credibility of the measures of content and thinking skills that students are expected to master – because we still have a major job on our hands simply assessing comprehension. The problem has been elegantly expressed by Christina Hellman (1992), namely that it is incredibly difficult to get at our own or anyone else's psychological processes as we or they deal with text and struggle to reach some sort of understanding:

Cognitive processes are ... largely impenetrable to the human processor and, sad though it may seem to the cognitive scientist, it must so be. The inherent constraints on the mind's ability to recognise its own processes have an important ecological value in that they prevent us from an infinite regress of processing processes and instead help us to tune in our limited attention on activities going on in the environment.

This basic impenetrability makes investigation of discourse comprehension a constant methodological challenge.

(Hellman, 1992)

We cannot assess reading directly. This much is clear. But as I have attempted to argue elsewhere (Harrison, 1995; Harrison, Bailey and Dewar, 1998) the inaccessibility of cognitive processes is only part of the challenge we face in considering reading assessment. The rationale for offering what I have called a postmodern analysis was simple: if the government seeks to take control of assessment, as it did under Margaret Thatcher in the late 1980s, then it behoves us at the very least to be in a position to propound a principled argument setting out how such assessment might be managed, and that in turn implied a declaration of principles. And in seeking a principled theoretical foundation for assessment, it proved impossible to avoid taking a postmodern position.

A postmodern view of assessment

I want to suggest that two important aspects of postmodernism, a rethinking of the nature of scientific enquiry and a rethinking of the concept of meaning in text, have very significant implications for reading assessment. 'Postmodernism' is not a philosophical position that we can choose whether or not to adopt. It is a term for the state of our culture. As the philosopher Jean-François Lyotard put it, postmodernism: '... has altered the game rules for science, literature and the arts' (1984, p. xxiii). The condition of our society and culture is 'postmodern', and our task is therefore not so much a matter of deciding whether or not to accept a 'postmodern' position as to try to understand its implications and to decide how to act on them.

In his essay *The Postmodern Condition*, Lyotard (1984, p. xxiv) defined postmodernism as an 'incredulity towards metanarratives'. By the word 'metanarratives', Lyotard was referring to the grand socio-historical narratives, one of which portrays science as a dispassionate march towards objectivity, and it is such grand narratives which postmodernism calls into question. A postmodern account of science would note the many ways in which science has had to reinvent its own rules – in post-Newtonian physics, in metamathematics and in quantum theory, for example – as a result of which many scientists have become incredulous towards superordinate concepts such as 'truth', 'scientific accuracy', 'objectivity' and 'expert'. These new systems of thinking have replaced a single notion of 'science' with a more flexible one: the single metanarrative has been replaced by a series of locally applicable discourses, and the scientist's role is to select from these as appropriate.

How does all this relate to reading assessment? Very directly, since we can apply the argument to the question of which models or paradigms of assessment should be accepted as valid by the authorities (scientific or governmental). Traditional models (those of the 'metanarrative') are those which emphasise efficiency, performance and improvement not of individuals directly, but of the state. Assessment is a 'modernist' project: a project that focuses on 'improvement' at the system level rather than at the individual. In the case of reading assessment, the 'metanarrative' involves large-scale national testing of skills and knowledge, using norm-referenced procedures. Within such an approach, testing would be part of a national programme for not only educational but also economic improvement. A postmodern view, by contrast, calls into question the validity and authority of such national testing programmes. It questions the extent to which it is valid to assume that it is even possible to test reading attainment on a national scale, and it would certainly question the assumption that test data can present an 'objective' picture of reading standards, given that so many subjective decisions have to be made to produce national test results.

Where does all this leave us? A postmodern analysis would lead to three specific implications: that we acknowledge the potential of local system solutions if global system solutions are difficult or impossible to achieve; that we acknowledge the importance of the individual subject, given that the concept of 'objectivity' has to be recognised as problematic; that we acknowledge the importance of accepting as valid a range of methodologies, given that it is no longer possible to bow to the authority of a single, grand scientific metanarrative. These principles – of local rather than global, of emphasising the subjective rather than the objective, and of valuing a range of methodological discourses – appear to have a good deal of potential in reading assessment, and we shall go on to make use of them after considering for a moment the impact of postmodernism on literary theory.

Postmodernism brought about a fundamental rethinking of the nature of authority in science, but it also brought about a number of parallel seismic shifts in the field of literary theory. One useful way into postmodern literary theories is through the writing of Mikhail Bakhtin (Medvedev and Bakhtin, 1978; Bakhtin, 1973). Bakhtin's topics ranged widely, but one constant theme was a challenge to the notion of a 'monologic' concept of meaning. Instead of a fixed or passive notion of meaning, Bakhtin emphasised its 'dialogic' nature, and argued that language was a series of acts of communication, each of which takes place in a unique social, cultural and ideological context. One clear implication of this position is that 'meaning' is not something to be regarded as immutable. The 'meaning' of a word is not fixed, because 'meaning' is a social as well as a linguistic phenomenon, as a result of which it varies subtly within each context of production and interpretation. Bakhtin's view of the concept of meaning as dynamic rather than static also extended to literature. He argued that not just words but whole texts were 'dialogic'. Dostoyevsky's novels, for example, are not 'monologic', they do not offer a single, unified authorial view of the world. Dostoyevsky's novels, suggested Bakhtin, introduce and celebrate a 'polyphonic' range of points of view, expressed through the various characters, and between which the author does not adjudicate. Instead, the reader is faced with the difficult task of struggling to come to an active, personal and individual interpretation of meaning, and to engage in a personal search for unification.

Other perspectives from literary theory contribute to the demise of the author as arbiter of meaning, As Eagleton (1983, p. 74) has pointed out, in recent years there has been a marked shift of attention in literary theory away from the author (the focus of nineteenth-century criticism) and the text (the focus of structuralist criticism in the early and middle years of the twentieth century) towards the most underprivileged of the trio, the reader. Eagleton's account of the new focus on the reader develops from a description of phenomenology and hermeneutics in the early twentieth century into an explanation of reception theory and the work of Wolfgang Iser. Iser (1978) argued that the process of reading is a dynamic one, to which readers bring personal experiences and social and cognitive schemata in which predictions, assumptions and inferences are constantly made, developed, challenged and negated. Iser's theory goes further than Bakhtin's in suggesting that the text is unfinished without the reader's contribution to making meaning: it is the reader who, in partnership with the author, fills the 'hermeneutic gap' in the text, bringing to it his or her own experience and understanding, and resolving the conflicts and indeterminacies which the author leaves unresolved. Perhaps the most extreme challenge to any notion of stability in meaning and interpretation – a notion which is essential if we are to retain any hope that it is possible to assess response to reading with any validity – is that posed by the literary theories of Jacques Derrida. Derrida's *Of Grammatology* (1976) proposed a theory of 'deconstruction' of texts which was so radical that it seemed to imply not only the 'death of the author' as determiner of meaning but to threaten the death of meaning itself. According to Derrida, the reader's role is not to discover meaning but to produce it: to dismantle (*déconstruire*) the text and rebuild it another way. Derrida uses the metaphor of *bricoleur* to describe the reader's role. The reader is a handyman or do-it-yourself enthusiast for whom the words of a text, the signifiers, are no more than tools to be used in deconstructing, not constructing, the text. Deciding on a text's meaning under these circumstances is not possible – the reader can do no more than look for traces of meaning and contemplate the text's geological strata during the unending fall into the abyss of possible deferred meanings.

We would argue that the positions from literary theory outlined above are postmodern in their overthrowing of traditional notions of authority in text and meaning in similar ways to those of postmodern positions in science. As was the case with our account of postmodernism in science, we want to suggest that three broad implications follow from our analysis. The first is that we acknowledge that we need to recognise a polysemic concept of meaning; the second is that we acknowledge a privileging of the role of the reader; the third, related to the first two, is that we acknowledge a diminution of the role of the author, or to express it the other way, a diminution of the authority of the text.

The implication of these positions is that we need to move towards a model of 'responsive assessment': a set of assessment practices that are responsive to the conditions of indeterminacy and provisionality that must now contextualise our understanding of reading assessment, and responsive to the role of the reader, whom we now cast as the agent rather than the object of assessment. In constructing that model, we shall take the six theoretical imperatives and from them derive six practical imperatives. The theoretical imperatives are:

1 that we acknowledge the potential of local system solutions if global system solutions are difficult or impossible to achieve;
2 that we acknowledge the importance of the individual subject, given that the concept of 'objectivity' has to be recognised as problematic;
3 that we acknowledge the importance of accepting as valid a range of methodologies;
4 that we acknowledge the need to recognise a polysemic concept of meaning;
5 that we acknowledge a privileging of the role of the reader;
6 that we acknowledge a diminution of the authority of the author and of the text.

The six theoretical imperatives lead us to six practical principles of responsive assessment. We list them below, together with some of the ways in which responsive assessment might be put into action:

1 *First, in responsive assessment, the emphasis is switched to the classroom*, and to curriculum practices. At this point assessment can begin to serve two essential purposes which national programmes usually ignore – assessment evidence can be of direct value to the teacher, and it can be of direct value to the student.
2 *Second, responsive assessment calls for increased emphasis on teacher assessment, self-assessment and peer assessment.* We would suggest that it will be enormously important to develop a wide body of information, not only on teacher assessment, but on self- and peer-assessment, and to put in place mechanisms for sharing the information.
3 *Third, responsive assessment of reading should not only draw upon a range of methodologies, but should be negotiated with the participants.* Students should be involved in deciding what evidence of their response to reading is to be recorded, and that range of evidence should be broadened to include, for example, playscripts, logs, scrapbooks, narratives, maps, graphs, taped or videoed conversations, photographs, role-playing, interviews and displays.

4 *Fourth, it is important to increase the authenticity of the tasks that form the basis of reading assessment.* Equally important, however, is the need to attempt to capture the authenticity of response to reading that takes place within a task, and to obtain evidence of the transactions that form the reader's response.

5 *Fifth, it is important to take greater account of a reader's response.* We suggest that interviews offer a basis for exploration of response which is potentially fruitful for a number of reasons: interviews can be open-ended and dynamic; recorded data can be stored, retained and played back later for comparison and discussion; recording offers the potential for a teacher-less context for collecting evidence, over which a student or group of students can have some authority and sense of ownership.

6 *Sixth, responsive assessment of reading should acknowledge a diminution of the authority of the author and of the text.* In our view, tasks that involve the reader in active reflection on texts, with the active hypothesis formation, dialogue and engagement which are possible in small-group work, offer great potential for achieving this final goal, which positions the reader in a central and powerful role as an active and purposeful user of texts and creator of meaning.

The implications of the implications: the crucial importance of portfolio-based assessment

Portfolio-based assessment came and went. But if our own analysis tells us that it is the approach we should be using in order to bring alignment between the ethical and theoretical imperatives on the one hand and the practicalities of reading development on the other, then we should perhaps ask why portfolio-based approaches lost their way and what we might do to bring them back. From the 1980s up to the mid-1990s, in the UK, the US and Canada, and also in Australia and New Zealand, various forms of diagnostic and portfolio-based approaches to assessment were developed and broadly speaking found a great deal of support from teachers. Let's not put too much Vaseline on the backward-pointing lens of time, though: diagnostic and portfolio-based assessment required a great deal of teacher effort and organisation, and was most useful only when it was tied into a larger administrative framework that made intelligent use of the diagnostic data that had been so painstakingly gathered.

But portfolio-based assessment, and its related approaches of classroom-based assessment, foundered on the rocks of state and national accountability. As Valencia and Wixon (2000) report in their review of policy research in the assessment field, the problems came when these approaches were grafted onto statewide and national assessment initiatives. First, many teachers were both ethically opposed to mapping developmental assessments onto standardised scoring frameworks. Second, teachers were in many cases not experienced in such procedures, and inter-rater correlations in the range 0.46–0.63 were obtained on some statewide assessments which were too low to permit their being reported as reliable estimates of students' achievement. These factors, together with a coolness towards teacher-based judgments on the part of conservative administrators and politicians led to the discontinuation of most large-scale portfolio projects.

These problems were not necessarily indicative of a fundamental structural weakness in a classroom-based approach to assessment, however. In England, a highly respected and efficient system of classroom-based assessment in English language and literature at age 16, based on a portfolio of work collected over two years for the externally validated GCSE examination, was regarded as reliable and valid by universities, parents and employers. It was terminated following a year of unprecedented high achievement scores that were interpreted by Prime Minister John Major's government as unreliable, but the high scores were validated two years later when the same cohort of students broke all records in their achievement in the more traditional Advanced Level examinations.

Similarly, as Salinger (1998) pointed out, portfolio-based assessments can be made to be reliable when the teachers using them have been trained in the new procedures and those procedures integrated into district-wide moderation and calibration arrangements. Salinger reported agreement coefficients in the range 0.85–0.90 for teachers' ratings of early literacy portfolios after teachers in seven elementary schools had spent many months collaborating with researchers from the Educational Testing Service in designing a six-level literacy development scale and working through six drafts in their determination to make the scale a valid and comprehensive reflection of children's achievement.

Ironically, the first government-funded approaches to national tests in English for 14-year-olds in England and Wales piloted classroom-based assessment procedures that extended over three or five weeks on a population of 9,000 children (Vincent and Harrison, 1998). The pilot involved extensive collaboration with teachers and had flexible sets of assessment materials, including written, spoken, individual and small-group tasks, often with authentic communicative purposes (e.g. producing a community newspaper). Ninety per cent of teachers said they preferred this approach to a 'short written examination', but in the event, before the evaluation report was even submitted to government, the Secretary of State for Education curtailed the pilot, dismissing it as 'elaborate nonsense', and brought in a new regime of objective tests.

If we are successful in moving back towards classroom-based assessment – and I think there are some signs of this beginning to happen –

then the assessment should strive for alignment between curriculum and assessment, and between diagnosis and the development of the individual. The Diagnostic Procedures project in Scotland was an attempt 'to place responsive assessment at the centre of a national assessment system which has as twin central aims support for every pupil and self-referencing by each school against a set of defined levels of attainment' (Hayward and Spenser, 1998, p. 137), and ultimately I hope that this visionary project will prove to have been a template from which other nations will have been able to learn.

Computer-based assessment and the need for intelligent adaptive online assessment

At the time of writing this chapter, commercial companies, states and governments are rushing headlong into computer-based assessment of reading, and no wonder. Computers, and especially computers connected to the Internet, offer the promise of instant data on reading achievement, based on centrally standardised and uniformly administered tests. Computers also offer the promise of instant sales of test instruments, with no printing or distribution costs. To make online assessment more sensitive to the individual, an increasing number of states are declaring that their tests are 'adaptive': the computer tailors the items to the achievement level of the child taking the test, thereby, it is argued, increasing validity and reliability while reducing stress, anxiety and a possible sense of failure.

Well, that's the theory, and that's the marketing line. 'Idaho to adopt "adaptive" online state testing' ran the headline in *Education Week* (Olson, 2002) over a story that saw the chair of the state board of education saying, 'We wanted an assessment system that would provide data first and foremost to improve instruction, which in turn, would improve accountability.' But precisely what data was to be made available? The answer is – multiple-choice test results ... though and it is by no means clear just what 'data to improve instruction' would be available from these scores. And in what ways are the tests 'adaptive'? Well, broadly speaking, the computer pulls items from a bank of items, and if you get one wrong, it asks you an easier one, and if you get one correct, it asks you a harder one. The bonus for the test developer is shorter tests and fewer items; the bonus for the state is online access to statewide data on reading or maths achievement that is updated hourly. But if we consider for a moment what is happening here, the gains for the individual student from instant feedback are slight – the test that is online is no different from the old pencil-and-paper multiple-choice test that has been taken for decades. It provides no developmental profile, no reading diagnosis, no recommendations for future pedagogy. Is this the best that the massive increases in computing power – advances so great that what was fifteen years ago the whole university's computing power is now compressed into a single laptop – can offer? If the answer is yes, 'adaptive' online tests are no more than multiple-choice tests but with harder and easier items stripped away, then I confess to being disappointed.

Let's just consider for a moment how a good reader behaves when carrying out a research task: good readers:

▶ set themselves purposeful reading and writing goals;
▶ decide where they need to look for reading resources;
▶ navigate effectively towards those resources;
▶ adjudicate thoughtfully between possible sources of information, rejecting, selecting, prioritising;
▶ decide which parts of the chosen sources will be useful, rejecting, selecting, priorising;
▶ decide on how to use the sources: to edit, order, transform, critique;
▶ produce a new artefact, matched to its audience;
▶ evaluate the adequacy of their performance, revising and looping back to earlier stages of the process as appropriate.

Now my question is simple: out of the list above, how many of those tasks could potentially be carried out by a reader working on a computer. Answer – all. Would it be possible, therefore, for computers to assess such authentic reading behaviour? Answer – yes, in principle, but it would be incredibly challenging, for not only would it be dauntingly difficult to attempt to write an intelligent adaptive program that would capture and evaluate some of the behaviours listed above, in reality, as Spiro and his co-workers (1994) have reminded us, actual online behaviours are even more complex. For a good reader, goal-setting is provisional; the task being executed is therefore provisional; resource selection is provisional; and evaluation is carried out incredibly rapidly, on the basis of partial information; finally, a good reader assembles information from diverse sources, integrates it with what is already known, mapping it into a new, context-sensitive situation-specific schema, rather than calling up a pre-compiled schema.

But if we are interested in pushing forward the use of the computer into the area I would prefer to term 'intelligent online reading assessment' (IORA), then let's encourage test developers to work with cognitive scientists and artificial intelligence specialists and to begin to take reading assessment into this new and exciting domain. We are possibly a decade away from having anything approaching reading assessment of the sort I'm envisioning here, but I want to suggest that if we put online multiple-choice tests at one end of the continuum and IORA at the other, then we can at least use the two as triangulation points and measure the progress in online assessment against a more challenging and more worthwhile target.

Conclusions

In this chapter I have attempted to develop a single argument. This has been based on a review of some of the ethical, statistical and cognitive challenges facing reading assessment, which I suggest point to the need for a fundamental re-evaluation of the theoretical underpinnings upon which we construct the edifice of reading assessment. This re-evaluation uses the conceptual framing of postmodernism to derive three theoretical imperatives from the philosophy of science and three from literary theory that together lead to six practical principles upon which, I argue, reading assessment should be based. I have then used these to review briefly why portfolio-based assessment on the one hand and intelligent online adaptive assessment on the other might be helpful triangulation points on any future map of reading assessment. The argument has been compressed, and some parts of it have been much more fully developed elsewhere (Harrison, 1995; Harrison, Bailey and Dewar, 1998), but I hope that enough structure and detail has been presented to make a compelling case for responsive reading assessment and to give at least a sense of where the map would lead us, and lead us in ways that enhance rather than diminish the development of readers' skills, understanding and motivation.

Chapter 9

A whole-school approach to developing reading: policy, staff development and evaluation

Introduction

This chapter will be brief, but in it I want to make some important points about the relationship between teacher development and reading development. First, I want to review some of the very strong evidence that now exists that shows a strong relationship between teacher education and teacher professional development on the one hand and literacy improvement on the other. Second, I want to reassure those who worry that change does not occur fast enough that change takes time, has to take time and cannot be speeded up, and that we would do as well to think about the implications of this rather than to try to speed up the life cycle of change. Third, I want to say something about how digital video can encourage teacher development and its potentially pivotal role in certain aspects of pre-service and in-service teacher development.

What research says about teacher development and literacy development

Let's just remind ourselves what it took us 30 years to learn, but which we are always in danger of forgetting – namely that changing the curriculum and bringing in new teaching materials does not actually change what happens in the classroom.

As Michael Fullan, who led the Canadian team evaluating the National Literacy Strategy in England has pointed out (Fullan, 2000), improving standards in children's literacy is not simply a matter of applying the findings from research in order to develop classroom materials. Fullan was very clear that there was a 'massive failure' of reform initiatives in the 1960s and 1970s because innovations were based on disseminating materials that were adopted (or not adopted) by individuals, without systemic change at classroom, school, district and regional levels. Systemic change has to involve teachers, but it also has to be about putting in place integrated and coherent reform initiatives supported by strong and complex partnership networks.

Evidence examining the relationship between in-service professional development in literacy and student achievement was reviewed in the National Reading Panel (NRP) report produced in the US in 2000. The NRP report concluded that appropriate teacher education does produce higher achievement in students. The Panel argued that while it is possible to 'train' teachers to use particular methods to teach, it is more appropriate to educate teachers of literacy to work flexibly and with a high level of autonomy in a professional context that gives them control over a wide range of decision-making tools (NRP, 2000, pp. 5–4). Analysing the trends in research studies that looked at the relationship between in-service development and student achievement among a total of 70 groups of teachers, the National Reading Panel concluded that:

▶ Provided they are well-funded and well-supported in terms of providing time for teachers to learn, interventions in teacher education and professional development are successful in improving literacy.

▶ Improvement in classroom teaching leads directly to higher achievement on the part of learners.

▶ Teacher attitudes change as a result of successful interventions, and without such changes in attitudes, it is extremely difficult to effect changes in practice.

▶ No single method of teaching that was investigated showed unquestioned superiority, but rather an eclectic mix of methods was successful.

(NRP, 2000, pp. 5–13, 5–14)

The Teacher Training Agency in England commissioned a study of what made for effective teachers of literacy, and the report of Medwell and her co-workers (1998) is highly regarded in England. Having put in place a very stringent set of criteria against which to identify effective teachers, the team located 228 teachers from local education authorities across the country who matched the criteria, and then collected data on their beliefs, practices, organisational skills, pedagogy, assessment strategies, knowledge about literacy and professional development histories.

The *Effective Teachers of Literacy* research team followed up a questionnaire with interviews and classroom observation, and this is what was found. Effective teachers of literacy (and it is made clear that this includes writing as well as reading) showed the following characteristics:

▶ They made clear the purpose of their teaching to the pupils, and were very specific in explaining how individual literacy activities at word, sentence and text level contributed to the creation of meaning.

▶ They centred much of their teaching around 'shared' texts, that is texts which the teacher and children either read or wrote together, and these shared texts were used to exemplify the connections between whole text, sentence and word-level knowledge.

▶ They taught decoding and spelling in a highly systematic and structured way, and made it clear to the pupils why such structures were useful.

▶ They emphasised to pupils the functions of what they were learning, teaching the rules of grammar, for example, in a way which showed how such knowledge could help improve their writing.

▶ Effective teachers were well theorised: they had strong and coherent philosophies about the teaching of literacy that guided their selection of teaching materials and approaches. These philosophies enabled them to consolidate their knowledge and brought coherence to their planning and teaching.

▶ They had well developed systems for monitoring children's progress and needs in literacy, and used this information to plan future teaching.

▶ They had extensive knowledge about literacy, including a good knowledge of children's literature.

▶ They made good use of opportunities to develop their skills and understanding through in-service courses.

The effective teachers of literacy had a coherent set of beliefs that emphasised purpose, communication and an integrated approach to comprehension and composition. They connected everything up, and this was crucial – skills were important, but they were not taught in isolation. The effective teachers did not declare a strong orientation towards phonics, for example, yet they taught phonics systematically, as a means to an end, not as an end to itself (Medwell et al., 1998, p. 26). The 'validation group' (a control group of teachers, one in each of the schools studied), by contrast, ascribed greater importance to phonological awareness than to enjoyment. But the philosophy of the effective teachers of literacy was clear: first and foremost, make reading enjoyable; help children to understand that books and words carry meaning; and then teach skills systematically, but not as an end in itself.

The Medwell study also included an investigation into the literacy teaching of novice teachers who were just completing their training. What was found mirrored the findings of the main study: the most successful novice teachers had already made coherent connections between their teacher-preparation course (both university-based and school-based) and their practice in the classroom. Having a strong academic background was not enough, however: many beginning teachers had not yet reached the point at which they could transform subject knowledge into pedagogical content knowledge. The study concludes that such transformations will not inevitably come through experience, but rather need to be facilitated through contact and ideally through observation of experienced teachers, followed by opportunities for discussion, linked to target-setting for future performance (Medwell et al., 1998, p. 67).

This is an important point: there is in many staffrooms a historical antipathy towards 'theory', which in the past has been seen as not only abstract but divorced from the classroom and irrelevant to the improvement of good practice. Yet not only were Medwell's effective teachers of literacy well theorised, they regarded theory as emancipating and professionally empowering – it was what enabled them to make confident and professionally informed decisions about their literacy teaching. It was what enabled them to move beyond the role of technician or educational paramedic and into the role of professional, to become teachers who could use the National Literacy Strategy as a toolkit, not a script, and apply it with flexibility and confidence rather than obedience.

The implications here are clear:

▶ All teachers benefit from having an understanding of literacy processes, and a well-theorised understanding of how what they do as teachers leads to improvement.

▶ But theory alone is not enough – many of the novice teachers were strong on theory and subject knowledge, but they had not yet connected it to practice.

▶ Making strong connections between theory and practice does not just happen: it needs to be facilitated by providing opportunity and support over an extended period.

One other important point to make, though, is that connecting theory and practice is only likely to happen if there is genuine respect shown towards the skills and understanding of the teachers who are the focus of any change agent's activity. Over the past 20 years, I have contributed to the evaluation of many initiatives aimed at teacher professional development, and I have often been called upon to make a contribution to that professional development. In reflecting on those meetings, I have been struck by how much many of them have in common with the challenging teaching environment described by Kathleen Reed in Chapter 6 of this book. Over the years, I have come to the view that the strategy she adopted of giving her students the responsibility for their own learning is by far the best one for approaching staff development with teachers. As an example, I can recall visiting a comprehensive school in one of the toughest areas of a city in the Midlands that has more than its share of economic and social disadvantage. The school had recently failed its government inspection and was in danger of being closed down. Morale was low and suspicion towards a visitor who was supposed to be contributing to staff development in relation to the teaching of literacy was high. So the first task I set the teachers was to work in groups of five or six to produce a poster presenting all the reading development strategies that between them the teachers used with their very challenging students. When the teachers gave their presentations to the assembled staff, I wrote up their suggestions on an overhead projector slide.

In the event, I needed three slides, because the list of strategies was incredible. There wasn't a strategy that was covered in the Masters level modules on reading development taught in my university that was not present on somebody's list. And these were teachers who did not regard themselves as experts in literacy development – they assumed that the Special Needs Coordinator was the expert in literacy. The list was as follows:

▶ differentiation of material (in both directions);
▶ emphasising and explaining key words;
▶ pupils made aware of additional resources available, e.g. dictionaries, glossaries, thesaurus, library;
▶ increase use of discussion in the classroom – pair work, group work and role play;
▶ paired/group reading;
▶ the use of structured tasks that are carefully explained, e.g. cloze, sequencing, locating materials from text, scanning to find essential information, the use of tables to collate evidence from text, underlining key words or what I know, what I don't know, the use of spider diagrams, KWL – what do I know after reading?
▶ the use of word banks, display of key words on the wall, image banks;
▶ school training for teachers/pupils in target setting;
▶ being aware of the presentation/layout of the material;
▶ use of larger text, with illustrations, glossary for key vocabulary on handouts, spacing, amount of information on the page, order;
▶ class reading of texts and selecting information for discussion: use selected readers; teacher reads to class while capable readers read silently;
▶ use of alternative vocabulary/simplifying definitions;
▶ highlight key words on handouts;
▶ staff records of pupil reading;
▶ pupils have reading-spelling lesson;
▶ pupils set questions/quiz on texts for other pupils to complete;
▶ discuss issues prior to reading to tap pupil knowledge and interest;
▶ turn headings into questions;
▶ use Q&A/role play/hot seating to test pupil understanding;
▶ groupings used to support peers;
▶ use of audio/visual resources – information technology to reinforce and focus attention on the text;
▶ break down information into easier to handle activities; assign different tasks to different groups – report back;

▶ relate information to events in the real world – community, e.g. newspapers;

▶ use of open-ended questions;

▶ pairs to take it in turns to read text.

I scrapped my plan for the day and instead we devised a new plan based around this list, with teachers identifying strategies that were unfamiliar to them, setting up opportunities for demonstration and shared learning in the morning and resource preparation in the afternoon. Everyone went away with their heads buzzing with fresh ideas and a strong feeling of solidarity, coupled with a sense of professional satisfaction related to the fact that their shared knowledge of strategies for literacy development was far more extensive than anyone had realised.

There were two crucial points in the previous example: one was the need to respect and make use of the knowledge of experienced teachers if we want those teachers to develop still further; the other was the powerful potential for learning that occurs when teachers are able to come out of the classroom in order to learn from others. We know from Reading Recovery that seeing other expert teachers teaching is a very powerful learning experience for teachers who are already skilled: they report that to observe others is a transforming experience. This is a point we shall take up in the final section of the chapter on the use of digital video.

Change takes time

The issue of the time needed to implement systemic change is crucial, and it is a vital one in considering the effects of professional development initiatives for teachers, as I have argued elsewhere in a paper on the evaluation of NLS pilot work on literacy improvement at Key Stage 3 (Harrison, 1998). The research evidence available in this area has been gathered more in primary than secondary schools, but in many cases the findings are relevant across sectors. One major US study that looked at 'Schools that are beating the odds' (i.e. in which the children are below the 50th percentile in terms of economic indicators, but where literacy scores are above the 75th percentile nationally) was conducted by the national Center for the Improvement of Early Reading Achievement (CIERA). It came to one important conclusion: that it takes up to three years for a large-scale innovation to impact on schools and school achievement at the systemic level (Taylor et al., 1999).

On reflection, this is a very reasonable analysis. First, teachers develop highly individual and deeply embedded approaches to teaching their subject, and if they are going to make a fundamental shift in those approaches, they will need to go through the same processes of coming to terms with new learning that characterise the learning of their pupils. They will have an initial period of working by the book, with a partial and incomplete sense of how everything connects up and coheres. This is followed by a period of consolidation, as emerging understandings and practices are aligned with and are related to their earlier experiences. This does not happen overnight, and for such changes to become embedded in teachers' practice, and for this change in practice to affect the achievement of a whole year cohort, is going to take time, perhaps as long as three years.

What were the characteristics of schools that were 'beating the odds' in literacy achievement? Taylor's answers nearly all related to system-wide factors and to the issue of the professional development of teachers. She reported that whatever the socio-economic background of the pupils, these successful schools had:

- high expectations of pupils;
- teamwork across the school, with common training and regular meetings;
- change occurring over more than one year;
- coherent literacy interventions across all age groups;
- ongoing staff development.

Taylor also reported on the specific literacy-related practices that these schools had in common. These were:

- emphasis on the enjoyment of literature from the earliest years;
- systematic word-recognition instruction;
- repeated reading to develop fluency;
- guided writing;
- one-to-one reading support;
- regular formative assessment of progress;
- 20 minutes small-group instruction daily from classroom teacher.

These practices are clearly in harmony with the goals of the literacy strategies in England. Taylor's research also extended to older children, where there was an additional emphasis across the successful schools on the following:

- strategy instruction on reciprocal teaching and vocabulary development;
- work on transferring and applying strategies in students' own reading tasks;
- development of students' self-dependence as readers;
- development of teachers' skills in encouraging independence in readers.

The CIERA study offers the promise of lasting improvement, but not unless teachers are supported in a sustained way through staff development. Taylor's schools had monthly meetings in the first year of implementation, and bi-monthly meetings thereafter. The teachers worked collaboratively with strong support from the centre, and it is common in US interventions for some of the teacher meetings to occur in school time with cover from substitute teachers supplied as part of the innovation's funding.

The CIERA findings mirror those of the evaluation in a major Midlands city that I conducted in 1990: out of seven inner-city comprehensive schools, only two showed significant school-wide gains in reading improvement at the end of a year in which all seven schools worked tirelessly on staff development and reading development with students at Key Stage 3 (students aged 11–14). I learned at the end of the project that the two most successful schools already had a two-year history of targeted staff development on literacy at this age level. My conclusion was therefore that it was not just their strategies in the year of the project that led to success, but rather it was these strategies mapped onto two years of groundwork in the area that enabled change to connect up with student achievement.

Research suggests that unless there is strong and enduring central support for a major literacy innovation, the chances for long-term success must be in doubt. The National Reading Panel reported on some studies that did not show long-term gains, and there are serious implications here for states and governments to consider in relation to the system-wide strategies for change.

The less successful studies reviewed by the National Reading Panel included that of Morrison and his co-workers (1969), which showed no effect on literacy improvement and in which the intervention basically consisted of giving teachers packets of material. Similarly, a study by Stallings and Krasavage (1986) showed initial positive effects, but a decline after three years. Morrison's study (1969) showed that after three years, teachers who were working without sustained support eventually reverted to the methods of teaching that they had been using initially, and jettisoned the materials and approaches which had been advocated in the innovation. The results of the Morrison study should not surprise us: as Fullan (2000) suggested, innovation which is not supported by staff development is likely to fail.

In a recent interview with Michael Fullan, Dennis Sparks (2003) asked Fullan to comment on the importance of changing a school's culture, and Fullan, while agreeing that changing the culture was crucial, related his answer to the picture of four decades of reform in England represented in Table 9.1. This representation of literacy teachers in England presents a very revealing insight into how Fullan sees teachers' knowledge improving, but also the relationship between teachers' knowledge and professional autonomy. The table suggests that education in England

Table 9.1 Teacher knowledge and sources of teacher action over four decades: Michael Fullan's description of literacy teachers in England

Source of teacher action	Teacher knowledge low	Teacher knowledge high
Teacher action prescribed externally	1980s	1990s
Teacher action based on professional judgment	1970s	2000s (?)

Source: Sparks (2003).

in the 1970s was characterised by uninformed professional judgment, in the 1980s by uninformed prescription (as a new National Curriculum was imposed), and in the 1990s by 'informed prescription' as the National Literacy Strategy put a well-theorised new curriculum and pedagogy into place and gave teachers support and in-service time to come to terms with it. What he was hoping for, however, was that teachers would gradually show themselves over the coming decade able to implement the Literacy Strategy flexibly and confidently, guided by 'informed professional judgment'.

How digital video can offer new opportunities for professional development

As I have attempted to argue throughout this book, reading fluency and reading comprehension do not develop in the same way. As I have tried to illustrate in Chapters 6 and 7, while reading fluency is likely to develop if readers keep on reading, in order to develop reading comprehension readers need to experience learning opportunities in which they witness and take part in a rich and varied range of constructive interactions with texts. And in this final section of the book I want to suggest, carefully, and with great respect to every teacher, that exactly the same thing happens in relation to teacher development. As teachers teach, so, generally speaking, their skills improve, and their automaticity increases; they become, if you will, fluent teachers. But that does not necessarily enable us change to and develop, and to become more deeply theorised and more profoundly aware of how our teaching might need to develop. In order to become more professional as teachers, we need learning experiences that engage and transform us.

As a university teacher supervising those preparing to be teachers, I have often, over the years, heard secondary teachers bemoan what they see as the low levels of achievement of some of the pupils who come to them from primary schools: 'What do they teach them down there?' said one teacher; 'How can I be expected to teach my subject if the children they send me can't even read?' said another. Well one answer, of course, is for secondary teachers to visit the classrooms of those pupils. A secondary teacher who belongs to an informal literacy action-research group that meets in my department six times a year has been doing just that, and witnessing how literacy is taught in primary schools. 'It blew me away!' she told us; 'those teachers are incredible!' Liz went on to tell the group how impressed she had been at the organisational skills, the deep understanding of literacy development and impressively broad curriculum knowledge of the teachers in whose classes she had been a guest. 'I'll never let anyone slag off a primary teacher again!' was her resolution. One thing was clear to all of us – it was having been able to get out of her own classroom and into those of some other teachers that enabled that experience to take place.

So being able to witness the teaching of others can be transforming, as Liz reported, and as Reading Recovery-trained teachers have reported (see, for example, Hobsbaum and Leon, 1999). But taking every teacher out of their classroom and into the classrooms of others is not only very expensive, it is also very disruptive. This being the case, watching a video of other classrooms would seem to be a potentially viable alternative basis for witnessing the teaching of others. And digital video offers a new range of contexts and framings for observing and discussing teaching. Videotape is relatively bulky and quite expensive to copy and to distribute. Video is difficult to navigate around. It's also not easy to edit and can't be viewed without a TV and a playback machine. But the possibilities of digital video are significantly different: digital video can be stored on computers, on tape, on CD, on DVD, and can be sent over the Internet. It is navigable in the same way as any other computerised data, is easy to edit and can be shown using any relatively new computer. And digital video is already starting to revolutionise teacher education and teacher development. Let me give three examples. Information technology uses a clock that runs faster than other clocks, so by the time you read this, all three of these projects may have transmuted into other forms, but the points I want to make will still stand. The three projects are

▶ Reading Classroom Explorer (http://www.eliteracy.org/rce/);
▶ C-TELL (http://ctell.uconn.edu/home.htm);
▶ LessonLab (http://www.lessonlab.com/).

Reading Classroom Explorer (RCE) is a hypermedia environment that contains approximately 500 video clips of reading classrooms, together with transcripts, questions to ponder, further reading resources and an interactive notebook. This is how the RCE team answer the question 'why should I use RCE?'

RCE provides multiple examples of successful teachers who are teaching thoughtful curriculum to students of diverse backgrounds. Through RCE you can explore a variety of literacy practices (e.g. literature-based, phonics, whole language, emergent literacy, basals, writer's workshop, etc.). The video clips demonstrate teachers using a variety of instructional formats (e.g. small group, large group, discussion, etc.) while working with students in grades K-5 including ESL and special needs students ... Preservice teachers can use RCE not only to see multiple approaches to literacy instruction but also to compare and contrast those approaches. RCE provides opportunities for professional development for inservice teachers as they view and reflect upon the teaching of others. Teacher educators can use RCE to help bridge gaps in theory and practice by providing real world portraits of literacy teaching and learning.

(http://www.eliteracy.org/rce/whyuse.htm)

The idea is that any student teacher (or their tutor) in the US whose college is signed up to RCE can pull down any of the 500 clips and use it as the basis for discussion and teaching. Naturally, as soon as a group of teacher educators saw their first clip of a beta version of RCE demonstrating 'exemplary teaching' at a reading conference in 2000, there was mayhem: 'There's no way that is exemplary teaching!' declared one of the world gurus of reading, and a dozen academics embarked on an impassioned critique of the video, while David Pearson and Laura Roehler, the leaders of the RCE project, looked on benignly, and gave each other eye contact that said 'we have a winner here!' because, of course, what was important in that context was not whether or not the experts agreed with the team, but that an earnest discussion of the criteria that identify exemplary teaching of reading was taking place.

The basis for C-TELL (Case Technologies to Enhance Literacy Learning), which in 2003 was running in 11 US states, was to use a 'case-based' approach to literacy teaching and literacy intervention along the lines of case-based medical and legal university teaching, but with the cases delivered by a central team, using multimedia delivered over the Internet or on CD/DVD. In the authors' words:

... An extensive set of studies will use the digital, multimedia resources available at our site to study the use of a case-based approach to pre-service teacher education. We plan to accomplish three central objectives: (a) raise pre-service teachers' understanding of best practices of early literacy education; (b) increase pre-service teachers' use of best practices in the classroom when they first begin teaching; and (c) significantly raise young children's reading achievement.

(http://ctell.uconn.edu/about.htm)

The C-TELL argument is that we don't need more research into initial reading instruction; we need better research on how to get teachers delivering that instruction. And the project's goals are ambitious: over 2,000 beginning teachers will use C-TELL, they will be followed into their first jobs, and C-TELL's effectiveness will be gauged by the extent to which these teachers raise (or don't raise) children's literacy achievement.

Both RCE and C-TELL envision pre-service teachers using the multimedia clips as a resource for discussion, engagement, reflection and interaction. But fundamental to both projects is the belief that digital video will permit access to a much richer set of classroom-based examples of literacy learning than was hitherto possible in pre-service teacher preparation, and that these will significantly enhance the knowledge and understanding of those preparing to teach.

LessonLab is also a teacher development environment based on the use of digital video, but its starting point is different from those of RCE and C-TELL: as it says on the home page, 'LessonLab's mission is to understand and improve classroom teaching and learning through its software, research and teacher learning programs' (http://www.lessonlab.com/), and its motto is 'teachers making their work visible'. The underpinning framework is straightforward: LessonLab offers an environment within which teachers can watch a video of the classroom in one section of the computer screen, accompanied by various types of support material in other screen areas. These can include a lesson transcript and various other types of material, including discussion tasks and commentary on the lesson or clip from others. The main philosophical position of LessonLab is that digital video of teaching is a potentially valuable site for professional discussion and professional improvement for every teacher.

In my opinion LessonLab philosophy has much in common with the views of Lawrence Stenhouse on the relationship between action research and teacher development – namely that we improve our teaching by coming to understand it: that we become better teachers through reflection on our teaching, and through understanding the events that occur in our own classrooms at a deeper level. In this respect, the use of lessons stored in digital video in LessonLab is not so much exemplary as facilitatory. To put the issue more clearly, let me give an example from the UK. Many recent government initiatives related to teacher development in the UK have been supported by video clips of exemplary practice. This is fine as far as it goes. I have great respect for those brave souls who agreed to have a production team in their lessons, and I respect the motives of those who made those videos in order to disseminate teaching ideas and good practice. However, the implied authority structure in this dissemination model is vertical: the teachers in the video are at the top, and the rest of us are at the bottom of the cascade, and yet we know that this is not necessarily a strong model – it is incredibly hard to change anyone's practice just by showing them good teaching.

In my view what is needed (and although it is a good example, LessonLab is only one among many possible examples of this) is a flat authority structure, with teachers working alongside each other to challenge and question the models of teaching they encounter on digital video and to set these against their own practice. The model of using digital video for teacher development that I would wish to see in place I call 'Interactive Classroom Explorer' (ICE), and it aims to bring together the best elements of all three of the packages that I have just described – the extensive library of vignettes of RCE, the case-based approach of C-TELL and the flat authority structure of LessonLab.

The following is an example of what I mean by a flat authority structure: in my mind's eye is the image of a teacher sitting alongside a colleague, and they are collaborating in using ICE for professional development. On the screen is a video clip from a national project that is ostensibly demonstrating good practice, but the two teachers discussing the video not only don't agree that this is exemplary practice, they want to say so to the person who wrote the commentary on the video that is also on the screen. So what do they do? First they compose a text message explaining where the teacher in the video needs to change his or her practice, but into that message they also paste a digitised clip from a video made that day in the classroom of one of the teachers, and include it as a video quotation, and then send the message, including the video quotation, over the Internet so that it pops up five minutes later as a new contribution in the discussion area of ICE in a form that can be accessed by other teachers from all over the country. For me, such a programme would be a valuable contribution to teacher development in the literacy field and beyond.

Coda

This chapter has aimed to reinforce the point that teacher development is crucial to literacy development, and to illustrate some of the ways in which that teacher development can and should proceed. I began this book by talking about reading and the reader. I want to end it by focusing on the teacher. I hope that this book will have encouraged those who read it to understand more about the reading process, and about how reading development takes place and can be improved. If the book does have any merit, I have no doubt that this will be largely attributable to the many teachers with whom I have worked and from whom I have learned. Some of them have generously permitted me to spend time in their classrooms, some have been my students, but to all of them I am, and shall remain, very grateful. Because of course reading development is not improved by books, but by teachers.

References

AEA (2003) *American Evaluation Association Position Statement on High Stakes Testing in PreK-12 Education.* Available at: http://www.eval.org/hst3.htm.

Alexander, P.A. and Jetton, T.L. (2000) 'Learning from text: a multidimensional and developmental perspective', in Kamil, M.L., Mosenthal, P.B., Pearson, P.D. and Barr, R. (eds), *Handbook of Reading Research: Volume III.* Mahwah, NJ: Erlbaum.

Armbruster, B.B. (1984) 'The problem of "inconsiderate texts"', in Duffy, G.G., Roehler, L.R. and Mason, J. (eds), *Theoretical Issues in Reading Comprehension.* White Plains, NY: Longman, pp. 202–17.

Armbruster, B.B. (1996) 'Schema theory and the design of content-area textbooks', *Educational Psychologist*, 21, 253–76.

Armitage, R. and Armitage, D. (1989) *The Lighthouse Keeper's Lunch*, Storytime Giants series. Edinburgh: Oliver & Boyd.

Bakhtin, M. (1973) *Problems of Dostoevsky's Poetics*, trans. R.W. Rotsel. Ann Arbor, MI: Ardis.

Bartlett, F.C. (1931) *Remembering: A Study in Experimental and Social Psychology.* Cambridge: Cambridge University Press.

BBC (2003) 'Tests "cause infants stress"', *BBC News online*, 25 April 2003. Source: http://news.bbc.co.uk/1/hi/education/2975529.stm.

Beard, R.F. (1999) *National Literacy Strategy: Review of Research and other Related Evidence.* London: Department for Education and Employment.

Beard, R.F. (2000) 'Long overdue? Another look at the National Literacy Strategy', *Journal of Research in Reading*, 23(3), 245–55.

Becta (2001) *ImpaCT2 – The Impact of Information and Communication Technologies on Pupil Learning and Attainment.* Coventry: Becta. Available: http://www.becta.org.uk/research/reports/impact2/index.cfm.

Bereiter, C. and Scardamalia, M. (1987) *The Psychology of Written Communication.* Hillsdale, NJ: Lawrence Erlbaum Associates.

Bettelheim, B. (1989) *The Uses of Enchantment: The Meaning and Importance of Fairy Tales.* New York: Vintage Books.

Bettleheim, B. and Zelan, K. (1981) *On Learning to Read.* London: Thames & Hudson.

Bransford, J.D. and Johnson, M.K. (1972) 'Contextual prerequisites for understanding: some investigators of comprehension and recall', *Journal of Verbal Learning and Verbal Behavior*, 11, 717–26.

Brooks, G. (1997) *Trends in Standards of Literacy in the United Kingdom, 1948–1996.* Paper presented at the Annual Conference of the British Educational Research Association, University of York, September.

Bruner, J. (2000) 'Reading for possible worlds', in Shanahan, T. and Rodriguez-Brown, F.V. (eds), *49th Yearbook of the National Reading Conference.* Chicago: National Reading Conference.

Bryant, P.E., Bradley, L., MacLean, M. and Crossland, J. (1989) 'Nursery rhymes, phonological skills and reading', *Journal of Child Language*, 16, 407–28.

Burkard, T. (1999) *The End of Illiteracy? The Discovery of the Holy Grail at Clackmannanshire.* London: Centre for Policy Studies.

Calasso, R. (1999) *Ka*, trans. T. Parks. London: Vintage

Cazden, C. (2000) 'Four innovative programmes: a postscript from Alice Springs', in Cope, W. and Kalantzis, M. (eds), *Multiliteracies: Literacy Learning and the Design of Social Futures.* London: Routledge, pp. 321–32.

Centre for Policy Studies (2002) *Mission Statement*. CPS homepage, at http://www.cps. org.uk/start.htm, accessed 30 October 2002.

Clark, M.M. (1976) *Young Fluent Readers*. London: Heinemann Educational.

Clay, M.M. (1979) *The Early Detection of Reading Difficulties*. Auckland, New Zealand: Heinemann Educational, for Octopus Publishing.

Cronbach, L.J., Linn, R.L., Brennan, R.L. and Haertel, E.H. (1997) 'Generalizability analysis for performance assessments of student achievement or school effectiveness', *Educational and Psychological Measurement*, 57(3), 373–99.

Daiute, C. (2000) 'Writing and communication technologies', in Indrisano, R. and Squire, J.R. (eds), *Perspectives on Writing: Research, Theory, and Practice*. Newark, DE: International Reading Association. Available: http://www.readingonline.org/past/ ast_index.asp?HREF=../research/daiute_excerpt/index.html.

Davidson, J., Elcock, J. and Noyes, P. (1996) 'A preliminary study of the effect of computer-assisted practice on reading attainment', *Journal of Research in Reading*, 19(2), 102–10.

Davies, F. and Greene, T. (1984) *Reading for Learning in the Sciences*. Edinburgh: Oliver & Boyd.

Davis, F.B. (1942) 'Two new measures of reading ability', *Journal of Educational Psychology*, 33, 365–72.

Derrida, J. (1976) *Of Grammatology*, trans. G.C. Spivac. Baltimore, MD: Johns Hopkins University Press.

DES (1975) *The Bullock Report*. London: HMSO.

Dole, J.A., Sloan, C. and Trathen, W. (1995) 'Teaching vocabulary within the context of literature', *Journal of Reading*, 38(6), 452–60.

Dostoyevsky, F. (1880/1958) *The Brothers Karamazov*, trans. David Magarshack. Harmondsworth: Penguin Books.

Dr Seuss (1957/1985) *The Cat in the Hat*. New York: Random House.

Dr Seuss (1962) *Green Eggs and Ham*. New York: Random House.

Duffy, G.G. and Roehler, L.R. (1989) 'Why strategy instruction is so difficult and what we need to do about it', in McCormick, C.B., Miller, G. and Pressley, M. (eds), *Cognitive Strategy Research: From Basic Research to Educational Applications*. New York: Springer-Verlag, pp. 133–54.

Duffy, G.G., Roehler, L.R. (and eight co-authors) (1987) 'Effects of explaining the reasoning associated with using reading strategies', *Reading Research Quarterly*, 22, 347–68.

Eagleton, T. (1983) *Literary Theory*. Oxford: Basil Blackwell.

EDinfo (2002) E-mail communication, subject line 'Scientifically Based Research: Seminar Transcript'. Source: Kirk Winters, EDinfo; US Department of Education, 4 March 2002.

Elmore, R. (2002) 'Testing trap: the single largest – and possibly most destructive – federal intrusion into America's public schools', *Harvard Magazine*, September–October 2002. Available: http://www.harvard-magazine.com/on-line/0902140.html.

Ericsson, K.A. and Simon, H.A. (1993) *Protocol Analysis: Verbal Reports as Data*. London: MIT Press.

Fairclough, N. (ed.) (1992) 'Introduction', in Fairclough, N. (ed.), *Critical Language Awareness*. Harlow, Essex: Longman, pp. 1–29.

Flaubert, G. (1857/1974) 'Letter to Mlle de Chantepie, June 1857', in *Oeuvres complètes de Gustave Flaubert, Tome 13: Correspondance 1850–1859*. Paris: Club de l'Honêtte Homme, p. 88.

Flower, L. (1994) 'Literate acts', in *The Construction of Negotiated Meaning*. Carbondale, IL: Southern Illinois University Press.

Foltz, P.W., Kintsch, W. and Landauer, T.K. (1998) 'The measurement of textual coherence with latent semantic analysis', *Discourse Processes*, 25, 285–307.

Foucault, M. (1977) *Power/knowledge: Selected Interviews and Other Writings (1972–1977)*. New York: Pantheon Books.

France Diplomatie (2000) 'The power of books', interview with Daniel Pennac. At: http://www.france.diplomatie.fr/label_france/ENGLISH/DOSSIER/2000bis/11pouvoir. html. Accessed 24 October 2002.

Freire, P. (1970) *Pedagogy of the Oppressed*. New York: Seabury.

Fullan, M. (2000) 'The return of large scale reform', *Journal of Educational Change*, 1, 15–27.

Goldman, S. and Rakestraw, J. (2000) 'Structural aspects of constructing meaning from text', in Kamil, M.L., Mosenthal, P.B., Pearson, P.D. and Barr, R. (eds), *Handbook of Reading Research: Volume III*. Mahwah, NJ: Lawrence Erlbaum Associates.

Goodman, K. (1970) 'Reading: a psycholinguistic guessing game', in Singer, H. and Ruddell, R.B. (eds), *Theoretical Models and Processes of Reading*. Newark, DE: International Reading Association.

Goswami, U. (1999) 'Causal connections in beginning reading: the importance of rhyme', *Journal of Research in Reading*, 22(3), 217–40.

Goswami, U. (2002) 'Rhymes, phonemes and learning to read: interpreting recent research', in Cook, M. (ed.), *Perspectives on the Teaching and Learning of Phonics*. Royston, Herts: United Kingdom Reading Association.

Goswami, U. and Bryant, P. (1990) *Phonological Skills and Learning to Read*. Hove: Lawrence Erlbaum Associates.

Hall, C. and Coles, M. (1999) *Children's Reading Choices*. London: Routledge.

Hardy, B. (1977) 'Narrative as a primary act of mind', in Barton, G., Meek, M. and Warlow, A. (eds), *The Cool Web: The Pattern of Children's Reading*. London: Bodley Head.

Harrison, C. (1995) 'The assessment of response to reading: developing a post-modern perspective', in Goodwyn, A. (ed.), *English and Ability*. London: David Fulton, pp. 66–89.

Harrison, C. (1996) 'Methods of teaching reading: key issues in research and implications for practice', *Interchange 39*. Edinburgh: Scottish Office Education and Industry Department.

Harrison, C. (1998) 'Improving literacy at Key Stage 3: policy, practice and evaluation', *Reading*, 33(1), 41–5.

Harrison, C. (1999) *Is it feasible to attempt to base a national literacy strategy on research evidence? A report on the implementation of the National Literacy Strategy in England*. Presentation given to the National Reading Conference, Orlando, Florida, 1 December.

Harrison, C. (2001) *What does research tell us about how to develop comprehension?* Presentation to ESRC Seminar, University of Nottingham, May.

Harrison, C. (2002a) *Key Stage 3 English: Roots and Research*. London: DfES.

Harrison, C. (2002b) *Key Stage 3 English: Roots and Research* [electronic version]. London, DfES. Retrieved 11 March 2003 from http://www.standards.dfes.gov.uk/midbins/keystage3/Roots%20and%20Research.PDF.

Harrison, C. (2003) 'Media analysis and the events of September 11th 2001', in Vogt, M.E. and Shearer, B.A. (eds), *Reading Specialists in the Real World: A Sociocultural View*. Boston: Allyn & Bacon.

Harrison, C. and Coles, M. (eds) (1992/2002) *The Reading for Real Handbook*. London: Routledge.

Harrison, C. and Gough, P. (1996) 'Compellingness in reading research', *Reading Research Quarterly*, 31(3), 334–41.

Harrison, C., Bailey, M. and Dewar, A. (1998) 'Responsive reading assessment: is postmodern assessment possible?', in Harrison, C. and Salinger, T. (eds), *Assessing Reading 1: Theory and Practice*. London: Routledge, pp. 1–20.

Harrison, C., Bailey, M. and Foster, C. (1998) 'Responsive assessment of reading', in Coles, M. and Jenkins, R. (eds), *Assessing Reading 2: Changing Practice in Classrooms*. London: Routledge, pp. 101–22.

Hayward, L. and Spenser, E. (1998) 'Taking a closer look: a Scottish perspective on reading assessment', in Harrison, C. and Salinger, T. (eds), *Assessing Reading 1: Theory and Practice*. London: Routledge, pp. 136–51.

Hellman, C. (1992) *Implicitness in Discourse*. Uppsala: International Tryck AB.

Hobsbaum, A. and Leon, A. (1999) *Catalyst for Change: The Impact of Reading Recovery in the United Kingdom*, Viewpoint 10, University of London Institute of Education.

Illich, I. (1988) *ABC: The Alphabetization of the Popular Mind*. New York: Vintage,

Illich, I. (1993) *In the Vineyard of the Text*. Chicago: University of Chicago Press.

Inkpen, M. (1995a) *Wibbly Pig is Upset*. London: Hodder Children's Books.

Inkpen, M. (1995b) *Wibbly Pig Likes Bananas*. London: Hodder Children's Books.

Iser, W. (1978) *The Act of Reading: A Theory of Aesthetic Response*. Baltimore, MD: Johns Hopkins University Press.

Jacob, B.A. and Levitt, S.D. (2001) *Rotten Apples: An Investigation of the Prevalence and Predictors of Teacher Cheating*. Available at: http://economics.uchicago.edu/download/teachercheat61.pdf.

Jensen, E. (1998) *Teaching with the Brain in Mind*. Alexandria, VA: Association for Supervision and Curriculum Development.

Johnson, K., Adamson, S. and Williams, G. (1994) *Spotlight Science 8*. Cheltenham: Stanley Thornes.

Just, M.A. and Carpenter, P.A. (1985) *The Psychology of Reading and Language Comprehension*. Newton, MA: Allyn & Bacon.

Kamil, M.L., Mosenthal, P.B., Pearson, P.D. and Barr, R. (2000) *Handbook of Reading Research: Volume III*. Mahwah, NJ: Lawrence Erlbaum Associates.

Kibby, M.W. and Scott, L. (2002) 'Using computer simulations to teach decision making in reading diagnostic assessment for re-mediation', *Reading Online*, 6(3). Available: http://www.readingonline.org/articles/art_index.asp?HREF=kibby/index.html.

Kintsch, W. (1988) 'The role of knowledge in discourse comprehension: a construction-integration model', *Psychological Review*, 95(2), 163–82.

Kintsch, W. (1998) *Comprehension: A Paradigm for Cognition*. Cambridge: Cambridge University Press.

Kintsch, E. and Kintsch, W. (1995) 'Strategies to promote active learning from text: individual differences in background knowledge', *Swiss Journal of Psychology*, 54(2), 141–51.

Kintsch, W., Patel, V. and Ericsson, K.A. (1999) 'The role of long-term working memory in text comprehension', *Psychologia*, 42(4), 186–98.

Kohlers, P. (1968) 'Reading is only incidentally visual', in Goodman, K.S. and Fleming, J.T. (eds), *Psycholinguistics and the Teaching of Reading*. Newark, DE: International Reading Association.

Kress, G. (2000) 'Design and transformation: new theories of meaning', in Cope, W. and Kalantzis, M. (eds), *Multiliteracies: Literacy Learning and the Design of Social Futures*. London: Routledge, pp. 153–61.

Landauer, T.K. (2002) 'On the computational basis of learning and cognition: arguments from LSA', in Ross, N. (ed.), *The Psychology of Learning and Motivation*, 41, 43–84: http://lsa.colorado.edu/papers/Ross-final-submit.pdf. Site constructed 1998; accessed 22 November 2002.

Landauer, T.K. and Dumais, S.T. (1997) 'A solution to Plato's problem: the latent semantic analysis theory of acquisition, induction and representation of knowledge', *Psychological Review*, 104, 211–40.

Langer, J.A. (1981) 'From theory to practice: a pre-reading plan', *Journal of Reading*, 25(2), 152–6.

Langer, J.A. and Nicolich, M. (1981) 'Prior knowledge and its effect on comprehension', *Journal of Reading Behavior*, 13(4), 373–81.

Latent Semantic Analysis (2002) http://lsa.colorado.edu/. Site constructed October 1998; accessed 1–10 April 2002.

Lewis, M., Fisher, R., Grainger, T., Harrison, C. and Hulme, P. (2000) *Curiosity Kits: The Impact of Non-fiction Book Bags on Children's Reading at Home*. Slough: NFER, Topic 25, Spring 2000, pp. 1–6.

Lord, A.B. (1982) 'Oral poetry in Yugoslavia', in Neisser, U. (ed.), *Memory Observed*. San Francisco: Freeman, pp. 243–57.

Lunzer, E.A. and Gardner, K. (1979) *The Effective Use of Reading*. London: Heinemann.

Lunzer, E.A. and Gardner, K. (1984) *Learning From the Written Word*. Edinburgh: Oliver & Boyd.

Lyotard, Jean-François (1984) *The Postmodern Condition: A Report on Knowledge*, trans. Geoff Bennington and Brian Massumi. Manchester: Manchester University Press.

McArthur, T. (ed.) (1992) *The Oxford Companion to the English Language*. Oxford: Oxford University Press.

McKee, D. (1980) *Not Now, Bernard*. London: Andersen Press.

Mandler, J.M. and Johnson, N.S. (1977) 'Remembrance of things parsed: story structure and recall', *Cognitive Psychology*, 9, 111–51.

Manguel, A. (1996) *A History of Reading*. New York: Viking.

Markman, E.M. (1978) 'Realizing that you don't understand: a preliminary investigation', *Child Development*, 48, 986–92.

Markman, E.M. (1979) 'Realizing that you don't understand: elementary school children's awareness of inconsistencies', *Child Development*, 50(3), 643–55.

Marshall, N. and Glock, M. (1978–79) 'Comprehension of connected discourse: a study into the relationships between structure of text and information recalled', *Reading Research Quarterly*, 14, 10–56.

Mayer, R.E. (1992) 'Cognition and instruction: their historic meeting within educational psychology', *Journal of Educational Psychology*, 84(4), 405–12.

Medvedev, P.N. and Bakhtin, M. (1978) *The Formal Method in Literary Scholarship*, trans. A.J. Wehrle. Baltimore, MD: Johns Hopkins University Press.

Medwell, J., Wray, D., Poulson, L. and Fox, R. (1998) *Effective Teachers of Literacy*. Exeter: University of Exeter School of Education.

Meek, M. (1988) *How Texts Teach What Readers Learn*. Stroud: Thimble Press.

Meyer, B.J.F. (1975) *The Organisation of Prose and its Effects on Memory*. Amsterdam: North-Holland.

Morrell, E. (2002) 'Toward a critical pedagogy of popular culture: literacy development among urban youth', *Journal of Adolescent and Adult Literacy*, 46(1). Available: http://www.readingonline.org/newliteracies/lit_index.asp?HREF=/newliteracies/jaal/9-02_column/index.html.

Morrison, C., Harris, A.J. and Auerbach, I.T. (1969) 'Staff after-effects of participation in a reading research project: a follow-up study of the craft project', *Reading Research Quarterly*, 4, 366–95.

Mulgan, G. (2001) *Analysis: Unreliable Evidence?* Transcript of a recorded BBC Radio 4 Current Affairs documentary. Broadcast date: 26 July 2001 Quotation from transcript downloaded on 5 August 2001 from: http://news.bbc.co.uk/hi/english/audiovideo/programmes/analysis/newsid_1470000/1470519.stm

National Reading Panel (2000a) *Report of the National Reading Panel: Reports of the Sub-groups*. Washington DC: National Development Clearinghouse.

National Reading Panel (2000b) *Teaching Children to Read: An Evidence-Based Assessment of the Scientific Research Literature on Reading and its Implications for Reading Instruction*. Washington, DC: National Institute for Child Health and Human Development, NIH Pub. No. 00-4769. Available at: http://www.nichd.nih.gov/publications/nrp/smallbook.htm.

Neisser, U. (ed.) (1982) *Memory Observed*. San Francisco: Freeman.

New London Group (1996) 'A pedagogy of multiliteracies: designing social futures', *Harvard Educational Review*, 66, 60–92.

Ogle, L., Sen, A., Pahlke, E., Jocelyn, L., Kastberg, D., Roey, S., and Williams, T. (2003) *International Comparisons in Fourth-Grade Reading Literacy: Findings from the Progress in International Reading Literacy Study (PIRLS) of 2001* (US Department of Education, NCES 2003–073). Washington, DC: US Government Printing Office.

Olson, L. (2002) 'Idaho to adopt "adaptive" online state testing', *Education Week*, 23 January, 21/19, pp. 6–7.

Palinscar, A.S. and Brown, A.L. (1984) 'Reciprocal teaching of comprehension – fostering and comprehension – monitoring activity', *Cognition and Instruction*, 1, 117–75.

Palmer, S. (2000) http://www.standards.dfee.gov.uk/literacy/prof_dev/?pd=ssm; site accessed 12 April 2002.

Pennac, D. (1992) *Reads Like a Novel*, trans. Daniel Gunn. London: Quartet Books.

Pichert, J.W. and Anderson, R.C. (1977) 'Taking different perspectives on story', *Journal of Educational Psychology*, 69, 309–15.

Pressley, M. (2000) 'What should comprehension instruction be the instruction of?', in Kamil, M.L., Mosenthal, P.B., Pearson, P.D. and Barr, R. (eds), *Handbook of Reading Research: Volume III*. Mahwah, NJ: Lawrence Erlbaum Associates, pp. 545–62.

Proust, M. (1905/1994) *On Reading*. New York: Penguin Books.

Rayner, K. (ed.) (1983) *Eye Movements in Reading: Perceptual and Language Processes*. New York: Academic Press.

Rayner, K. and Pollatsek, A. (1989) *The Psychology of Reading*. Englewood Cliffs, NJ: Prentice Hall International.

Reed, K. (1999) 'Reading strategies for "inconsiderate" texts'. Web-posted essay, University of Colorado at Denver (Summer, 1999). Accessed 21 October 2002: http://www.gollihar.com/cognition/critiques/reed99.htm.

Reinking, D. and Rickman, S.S. (1990) 'The effects of computer-mediated texts on the vocabulary learning and comprehension of intermediate-grade readers', *Journal of Reading Behavior*, 22(4), 395–411.

Reyna, V. (2002a) *What Is Scientifically Based Evidence? What Is Its Logic?* Transcript of presentation to US Department of Education seminar on Scientifically Based Research, 6 February 2002. Accessed 9 November 2002 at: http://www.ed.gov/nclb/research/reyna.html.

Reyna, V. (2002b) *What Is Scientifically Based Evidence? What Is Its Logic?* Contribution submitted to US Department of Education seminar on Scientifically Based Research, 6 February 2002. Accessed 9 November 2002 at: http://www.ed.gov/nclb/research/reyna-paper.html.

Rhodes, L.K. and Dudley-Marling, C. (1996) *Readers and Writers with a Difference*. Portsmouth, NH: Heinemann.

Robbins, C. and Ehri, L.C. (1994) 'Reading storybooks to kindergartners helps them learn new vocabulary words', *Journal of Educational Psychology*, 86(1), 54–64.

Ruddell, M.R. (1994) 'Vocabulary knowledge and comprehension: a comprehension-process view of complex literacy relationships', in Ruddell, R.B., Ruddell, M.R. and Singer, H. (eds), *Theoretical Models and Processes of Reading*, 4th edn. Newark, DE: International Reading Association, pp. 414–47.

Rumelhart, D.E. (1975) 'Notes on a schema for stories', in Bobrow, D.G. and Collins, A. (eds), *Representation and Understanding: Studies in Cognitive Science*. New York: Academic Press, pp. 211–36.

Salinger, T. (1998) 'Consequential validity of an early literacy portfolio: the "backwash" of reform', in Harrison, C. and Salinger, T. (eds), *Assessing Reading 1: Theory and Practice*. London: Routledge, pp. 182–203.

Schallert, D.L. (1982) 'The significance of knowledge: a synthesis of research related to schema theory', in Otto, W. and White, S. (eds), *Reading Expository Material*. New York: Academic.

Schank, R. (1982) *Dynamic Memory*. Cambridge: Cambridge University Press.

Smith, F. (1971) *Understanding Reading*. New York: Holt, Reinhart Winston.

Snow, C.E., Burns, M.S. and Griffin, P. (eds) (1998a) *Preventing Reading Difficulties in Young Children*. Washington, DC: National Academy Press.

Snow, C.E., Burns, S. and Griffin, P. (eds) (1998b) *Preventing Reading Difficulties in Young Children*. Washington, DC: National Academy Press. (Online version of Executive Summary accessed 23 October 2002 at: http://www.nap.edu/readingroom/books/prdyc/execsumm.html.)

Sparks, D. (2003) 'Interview with Michael Fullan: change agent', *Journal of Staff Development*, 24(1), Winter. Available at: http://www.nsdc.org/library/jsd/fullan241.html.

Spiro, R.J., Coulson, R.L., Feltovich, P.J. and Anderson, D.K. (1994) 'Cognitive flexibility theory: advanced knowledge acquisition in ill-structured domains', in Ruddell, R.B., Ruddell, M.R. and Singer, H. (eds), *Theoretical Models and Processes of Reading*, 4th edn. Newark, DE: International Reading Association, pp. 602–15.

Spiro, R.J., Feltovich, P.J., Jacobson, M.J. and Coulson, R.L. (1992) 'Cognitive flexibility, constructivism and hypertext: random access instruction for advanced knowledge acquisition in ill-structured domains', in Duffy, T. and Jonassen, D. (eds), *Constructivism and the Technology of Instruction*. Hillsdale, NJ: Erlbaum.

Stallings, J. and Krasavage, E.M. (1986) 'Program implementation and student achievement in a four-year Madeline Hunter follow-through project', *Elementary School Journal*, 87(2) 117–38.

Stanovich, K. (1980) 'Toward an interactive-compensatory model of individual differences in the development of reading fluency', *Reading Research Quarterly*, 16, 32–71.

Stanovich, K. (1986) 'Matthew effects in reading: some consequences of individual differences in the acquisition of literacy', *Reading Research Quarterly*, 21, 360–406.

Taylor, D. and Strickland, D. (1986) *Family Storybook Reading*. Portsmouth, NH: Heinemann Educational.

Taylor, B.M., Pearson, P.D., Clark, K.F. and Walpole, S. (1999) *Beating the Odds in Teaching All Children to Read*, CIERA Report No. 2–006. Ann Arbor, MI: Center for the Improvement of Early Reading Achievement, University of Michigan. (Based on a presentation to the International Reading Association Annual Convention, Orlando, 1998.)

Thorndyke, P.W. (1977) 'Cognitive structures in comprehension and memory of narrative discourse', *Cognitive Psychology*, 9, 77–110.

Tyrrell, J. (2001) *The Power of Fantasy in Early Learning*. London: Routledge-Falmer.

US Department of Education (2002) *Scientifically Based Research*. Transcript of seminar accessed 9 November 2002 at: http://www.ed.gov/nclb/research/.

Valencia, S. and Wixon, K. (2000) 'Policy-oriented research on literacy standards and assessment', in Kamil, M.L., Mosenthal, P.B., Pearson, P.D. and Barr, R. (eds), *Handbook of Reading Research: Volume III*. Mahwah, NJ: Lawrence Erlbaum Associates, pp. 909–35.

Vincent, D. and Harrison, C. (1998) 'Curriculum-based assessment of reading in England and Wales', in Harrison, C. and Salinger, T. (eds), *Assessing Reading 1: Theory and Practice*. London: Routledge, pp. 122–35.

Vygotsky, L.S. (1986) *Thought and Language*, revised edition. Cambridge, MA: MIT Press.

Waddell, M. and Benson, P. (illustrator) (1994) *Owl Babies*. London: Walker Books.

Wade, S. and Moje, E. (2000) 'The role of text in classroom learning', in Kamil, M.L., Mosenthal, P.B., Pearson, P.D. and Barr, R. (eds), *Handbook of Reading Research: Volume III*. Mahwah, NJ: Lawrence Erlbaum Associates.

Waterland, E. (1985) *Read With Me: An Apprenticeship Approach to Reading*. Stroud: Thimble Press.

Watson, J.E. and Johnston, R.S. (1998) *Interchange 5: Accelerating Reading Attainment – The Effectiveness of Synthetic Phonics*. Edinburgh: Scottish Executive. Accessed 30 October 2002 at: http://www.scotland.gov.uk/library/documents7/interchg.pdf.

Whitehead, F. (1975) *Children's Reading Interests*. London: Evans/Methuen Educational for the Schools Council.

Willis, P. (1997) *Learning to Labour: How Working Class Kids Get Working Class Jobs*. Westmead, England: Saxon House.

Wood, D. and Middleton, D. (1975) 'A study of assisted problem solving', *British Journal of Psychology*, 66, 181–91.

Wood, D., Bruner, J. and Ross, G. (1976) 'The role of tutoring in problem solving', *Journal of Child Psychology and Psychiatry*, 17, 89–100.

Wray, D. and Lewis, M. (eds) (2000) *Literacy in the Secondary School*. London: David Fulton.

Yin, R.K. (1994) *Case Study Research Design and Methods*. London: Sage, p. 1.

Young, M.F.D. (1971) *Knowledge and Control*. London: Macmillan.

Index